# THE EDWARDIANS AND AFTER

The Royal Academy
1900-1950

D1426034

**The exhibition has been organised by the
Royal Academy of Arts from its own collection**

IBM Gallery of Science and Art, New York
*27 September – 26 November 1988*

Meridian House International, Washington D.C.
*15 December 1988 – 1 February 1989*

Dixon Gallery and Gardens, Memphis, Tennessee
*25 February – 30 April 1989*

Newport Art Museum, Newport, Rhode Island
*8 July – 16 September 1989*

The preparation of this exhibition, and its showing in New York have been made possible by IBM.
The catalogue has received generous financial support from Christie's.
The subsequent tour in the United States of America has been organised by
The Trust for Museum Exhibitions, Washington D.C.

# THE EDWARDIANS AND AFTER

## The Royal Academy
## 1900-1950

*Edited by MaryAnne Stevens*

*Contributions by Lawrence Gowing and MaryAnne Stevens*
*with Helen Valentine, Elizabeth Waters and T. J. Barringer*

Royal Academy of Arts, London, 1988

Catalogue published in association with

Weidenfeld and Nicolson, London

Cover illustration: Sir Herbert James Gunn *Pauline Waiting*

© Royal Academy of Arts 1988

British Library Cataloguing in Publication Data

Stevens, MaryAnne
    The Edwardians and After: The Royal Academy 1900–1950
    1. British visual arts. Catalogues
    I. Title
    709'.41'074

House Editor: Luci Collings
Designer: Lindsey Rhodes

George Weidenfeld and Nicolson Limited
91 Clapham High Street, London sw4 7TA

Made in Great Britain by Butler & Tanner Ltd, Frome and London

# Contents

# Preface

*The Edwardians and After: The Royal Academy 1900–1950* has been initiated by the American Associates of the Royal Academy Trust and organised by the Royal Academy of Arts for exhibition in the United States. Between 27 September 1988 and 16 September 1989, it will be shown at the IBM Gallery of Science and Art, New York, Meridian House International, Washington D.C., the Dixon Gallery and Gardens, Memphis, Tennessee and at Newport Art Museum, Newport, Rhode Island.

Since 1983, the American Associates of the Royal Academy Trust has assisted the Royal Academy of Arts with its extensive efforts to renovate the historic home of the Royal Academy of Arts, Burlington House, to establish an endowment and to continue its outstanding international programme of exhibitions. The American Associates promote the exchange of exhibitions, students and scholars between the Royal Academy and the States, such as this special United States tour of *The Edwardians and After: The Royal Academy 1900–1950*. Activities of the American Associates include trips, exhibition previews, lectures, receptions and other special events.

# Foreword

The rise of Modernism in the early years of this century has tended to cloud our appreciation of those artists who, through deeply held convictions, sought alternative paths down which to explore the relevance of their art to our century. The Royal Academy of Arts, since its foundation in 1768, has played a central part in the debates that have formed British art over the past two hundred years. At no time during these years were the issues more acute or more hotly discussed than in the period covered by *The Edwardians and After: The Royal Academy 1900–1950.*

The permanent collection of the Royal Academy, from which this·exhibition is drawn, dates from its foundation. Although isolated masterpieces such as Michelangelo's *Taddei Tondo* have been acquired by other means, it is essentially a collection of works donated by the Academicians themselves. It includes major works by Gainsborough, Reynolds and Benjamin West, among the founder members, and by later Academicians of distinction such as Constable, Leighton, Millais and G. F. Watts. Indeed, it is a wise provision of the Instrument of Foundation which requires every member on election as an Academician to deposit with the Academy 'a specimen of his abilities', known as his Diploma Work. The collection thus serves as a visual record of the changing character of the institution across the years. And as one moves into the twentieth century so one finds, beside pieces donated by such renowned figures as John Singer Sargent, Walter Sickert and Stanley Spencer, the works given by artists who were admired in their day, but whose names prosperity has allowed, if only for a time, to decline into obscurity. It is the intention of this exhibition to bring to light the works of these artists for the enjoyment and illumination of our American public. While predominantly figurative in style, the works cover a rich and varied range of genres, from quintessentially English landscapes and quiet, domestic scenes to the highly polished portraits that record an age of privileges long since passed. In that they are representative of the work of artists deemed by their contemporaries to be masters of their art, the technical achievements of these paintings are often startling and always of a consistently high standard.

We have many people to whom we are grateful for having brought this important project to fruition. First, we owe our deepest debt of gratitude to Sir Lawrence Gowing, ARA, Honorary Curator and Chairman of the Exhibitions Committee of the Royal Academy and Curatorial Professor of the Phillips Collection, Washington D.C. It was Sir Lawrence who selected the works, and who has also contributed so sensitive and perceptive an appreciation of them in this catalogue. The main task for organising the exhibition has fallen to MaryAnne Stevens, Librarian and Head of Education at the Royal Academy, assisted by Kathleen Soriano, who has also been able to call upon the support of Helen Valentine and Ian Dejardin. All the works in the show have undergone conservation both of the paintings and of their frames, the latter always selected specifically by the artist prior to the work being deposited at the Royal Academy: we extend our thanks to our conservators, Isabel Horovitz, Helen Glanville, Amanda Paulley, Jenny Richenberg and Annie Ablett. This extensive conservation programme could not have taken place without a most generous grant from IBM. In the United States, therefore, our first and most sincere thanks must go to Richard Berglund of IBM, who initially accepted with such warmth the project of mounting this exhibition at the Corporation's prestigious Gallery of Science and Art in New York. We also extend our thanks to the Director and staff of the Gallery who have been of constant support to us in this venture. Christie's has most generously contributed towards the cost of the catalogue, as well as assisting this project in other material ways. The tour of the exhibition to Washington D.C., Memphis, Tennessee and Newport, Rhode Island has been arranged most competently by Ann Van Devanter Townsend of the Trust for Museum Exhibitions. Finally, without the encouragement and enthusiasm of the American Associates of the Royal Academy Trust, and in particular their Executive Director, Kathrine Ockenden, this magnificent project might never have been realised. Their support has permitted us all to experience the pleasure of rediscovering a rich and evocative period of British Art in the collections of the Royal Academy of Arts.

*Roger de Grey*
President
Royal Academy of Arts

# Organising Committee

Exhibition Selector:                Lawrence Gowing
Exhibition Organiser:            MaryAnne Stevens
Exhibition Assistant:             Kathleen Soriano
Exhibition Conservators: Paintings    Helen Glanville
                                     Isabel Horowitz
                                     Amanda Paulley
                                     Jennifer Richenberg
               Frames        Annie Ablett

# Acknowledgements

Ian Dejardin
Steve Eckleman
Peter Feroze
Jonathan D. Horwich
Nicolas Savage
Ally Scott
Peyton Skipwith
Marie Valsamidi

All photography has been undertaken by Photo Studios Ltd.
© Royal Academy of Arts

# Editorial Note

All works are oil on canvas unless otherwise stated.
Dimensions are given in centimetres and inches, height before width.

A.R.:          Annual Report
A.R.A.:        Associate of the Royal Academy
C.M.:          Council Minutes of the Royal Academy (held in the institution's Library)
Diploma Work:  Work of art submitted to the Council of the Royal Academy for deposit in the Permanent Collection by an artist on his or her election to full membership (R.A.).
G.A.:          Minutes of the General Assembly (held in the institution's Library)
R.A.:          Royal Academician

In 1896, the South Kensington Schools became the Royal College of Art. In the biographies of artists studying at the institution after 1896, the term Royal College of Art is always used.

All exhibitions in the catalogue entries are given in abbreviated form, city preceding name of institution, date and catalogue number (where known). A full exhibition list is given at the end of the catalogue. R.A. followed by a date refers to the Annual Summer Exhibition, held at the Royal Academy since 1769.

Biographies and the accompanying catalogue entries have been written by three members of the Royal Academy staff, Helen Valentine, Elizabeth Waters and Tim Barringer. Their initials H.C.V., E.C.W. and T.J.B. are given at the end of each relevant artist's biography.

Burlington House, Piccadilly, home of the Royal Academy of Arts since 1868

# Confidence Confirmed: The Unshaken Faith of the Royal Academy of Arts in London

*Lawrence Gowing*

In a changing world one of the most enduring things has been the constant testimony to their vocation that has been borne over some two hundred and twenty years by the members of the Royal Academy of Arts in London. Even during the early twentieth century their witness remained undisturbed and some of us find its products enlightening and refreshing. In the belief that there are some around the world who will be glad to share the experience, we have put together an anthology of the works which Academicians deposit on election and collect with their trust funds – a group of some sixty paintings gathered at Burlington House over about fifty years around the median date of 1925. There are one or two masterpieces among them and we at least find a respectable proportion of the number enjoyable. It may be that others will share with us the pleasure of the discovery that the confidence in which the Royal Academy worked at the beginning of this period remained unshaken to the end of it. There may even be a few surprises for those who thought they knew the august but usually unsurprising body well enough. Even when the works that belong essentially to the periods before and after – the Victorian age and the period of renewal in the mid-twentieth century – are separated from the deposits of those fifty years, there remains a remarkable variety. Britain was by no means as insular as we suppose.

It is well known that England had a seminal affinity with Impressionism and the earliest loyalty of the British Impressionists was of course to the New English Art Club. So the first surprise, and it is always good to be surprised by a great painter, is to be reminded that one of the best of them made his home at Burlington House. In the emergency of the 1940s, when the Royal Academy sheltered the United Artists, to which the present writer was probably the youngest contributor, I met Reginald Brundrit and the admiration which my friends and I felt for this remarkable artist has remained with me ever since. His pictures, never obtrusive, remain quite unique: there is more space across a field in his *English Landscape* (cat. 7) than most painters in this style dreamt of. The brusqueness with which he stated the tones of *Nightfall* (cat. 8), which was bought as his memorial after his death a quarter-century ago, belongs unequivocally with the noblest traditions of English painting.

Sir Donald Murray's prosaic field of *Swedes* (cat. 43) is lightened by quotations from livelier painters. The most famous of the English Impressionists, the expatriate American Mark Fisher, is represented by his concentrated little sketch of *An Orchard in Spring* (cat. 21). The man himself, painted in the first year of the century, was as bucolic as we could have imagined: he is recorded in the portrait by Clausen (cat. 11), whose shadowed *Interior of an Old Barn* (cat. 12) is a glimpse of the drama of the country scene, which we recognise in the novelists who were his contemporaries. In the years to come it will matter less and

less that British Impressionism was perennially marked by a sentiment that the continental variety avoided. When painting achieves its own kind of humanity, the quality is one that lasts.

The affinities with France were not limited to the virtues that we think of as progressive. Cézanne himself affected a respect for 'the salon of Bouguereau' and the qualities of Bouguereau are clearly reflected in *Startled* (cat. 16) by Sir Frank Dicksee, though only an English ironist would have contrived a disturbance in the shadows which may be either the splash of a satyric hoof or the flutter of wind in the willows. The figure pictures in this group show only an occasional and uncharacteristically decorative sparkle but Philip Connard's *Apollo and Daphne* (cat. 13) is innocent of paganism; it has only a twentyish dash of the Russian ballet. The ideal of English decoration is perhaps the herbaceous border, which can strike a vein of colour, like the welcome sight of a Worcestershire garden in Alfred Parsons's *Orange Lilies, Broadway* (cat. 50) which is hardly found elsewhere. The solemnity of Robert Anning Bell's *Women Going to the Sepulchre* (cat. 1), where the affinity was with Puvis de Chavannes, and the enchanting mystery with which Charles Sims imagined *Clio and the Children* (cat. 57) are both freshened by the purity of the downland air. Gardening does sometimes yield elusive patterns in English paintings. The model in George Henry's *Brambles* (cat. 31) appears to be fingering a lusty nettle; her attention is no doubt distracted by the charming twentyish dappling of the light. Earlier in the century the best colour in English painting was due to Whistler, as it no doubt was in J. J. Shannon's *Black and Silver* (cat. 55), but Whistler's own haughty detachment eluded imitation. Francis Dodd's portrait *In the Park* (cat. 17) could perhaps have been painted anywhere that a painter had the sense to look at Mary Cassatt but the concentrated patterns that enriched *art nouveau* and the New Sculpture of the *fin de siècle* were intensely romantic and English. F. C. Cowper's *Vanity* (cat. 14) has a softness that is not immune from the vice which is its subject but Maurice Greiffenhagen's *The Message* (cat. 26), like a latter-day nursery adaptation of the style, shows a fancy that is entirely his own.

Not only the poetry and the fantasy of Britain, but British weather and the scribble that passes for drawing have all left their marks on this collection. Ripples in water were the earliest subjects of modern art; one would hardly guess it from W. L. Wyllie's *The Portsmouth Fishing Fleet* (cat. 67) but the handwriting and the seamanship are nonetheless personal. One thinks of Farquharson, who called his Diploma work *When Snow the Pasture Sheets* (cat. 20), as essentially a Victorian painter, but it is the pleasure of the Academy to keep its acolytes waiting and Farquharson was elected a member at sixty-eight; he lived to enjoy the rank for twenty years. Arthur Hacker's *A Wet Night at Piccadilly Circus* (cat. 28) is notable for its clammy reminder of how much of the character of the place survives despite all that has happened in three quarters of a century.

The pictorial grandeur of British landscape descends straight from the Northern landscape tradition. The evening view in *Equihen, Pas de Calais* (cat. 32) by Sir Herbert Hughes-Stanton proclaims its affiliation to the painters of Barbizon. The rough-hewn cloudscape that Bertram Priestman saw *Near Wareham, Dorset* in 1923 (cat. 52) was even grander and more long-lasting. Priestman's trees against the broken clouds had a spacious nobility which originated in Holland in the seventeenth century.

The architectural subjects in the Diploma collection have a similar impressiveness. The theatrical magnificence of D. Y. Cameron's *Interior of Durham Cathedral* (cat. 10) is admittedly a little outclassed by *Santa Maria della Salute*, (cat. 56) which is a relatively modest sample of Walter Richard Sickert's output, but the sharp-eyed observation of Sydney Lee's *Red Tower* (cat. 39) and *House with the Closed Shutters* (cat. 40) bestow on it an undoubted pictorial presence. No native of a southern city ever drew the cobbles of a piazza so well. The picturesqueness of the paint-patch, exploited in pictures like Richard Jack's moorland portrait (cat. 33), rarely escapes a poster-like assertiveness, but again some of the purity of the air communicates itself to the painter's style. The atmospheric brilliance of Arnesby Brown's *Raincloud* (cat. 6), which was developed in his watercolours, reminds one of an aspect of British painting that is not represented in this group. One exponent of oil-paint was undeniably at home in the country, Sir Alfred Munnings. *Kilkenny Horse Fair* (cat. 42) is a deceptively casual display of the effortless mastery of a true horseman. The outline accented with a painting knife in Oliver Hall's *Spring* (cat. 29) has the appearance rather than the substance of Post-Impressionism but the observation remains evidently British.

There was a solidity in British painting before the First War whose originality remains undescribed. The solemn mosaic of deep tones in Alfred East's *Evening in the Cotswolds* (cat. 18) has an affinity with the good painters of the time who were never represented at Burlington House, at least until the advent of their descendants in whose leadership the Academy rejoices now. Few things in the history of early modern painting in Britain were more impressive than this remarkable picture, but 1913 — when Alfred East was elected and this picture deposited — was also the year of his death at sixty-four.

The realism that flourished in the wake of Impressionism has been one of the most elusive yet most durable of modern styles. Ethel Walker's portrait called *The Jade Necklace* (cat. 66) is defined with a simple, almost stumbling touch which has a most sympathetic candour. There is an iridescent delicacy in her style that few painters have commanded in any age. Harold Knight's portrayal of the pianist Ethel Bartlett (cat. 36) has a more dramatic timbre to it, while Augustus John's vision was more romantically idealised. His *Portrait of a Young Man* (cat. 34) has a dark intensity that is uncommon among figure paintings at Burlington House. In the story of figure painting the possibility of painting nudes from life out of doors has haunted modern painting, and it cannot be said that the Cornish artists who attempted such studies altogether put the problematic spectre to flight, although Tuke's *July Sun* (cat. 65) was as fluent and direct a record of vision as any Englishman achieved in the fruitful period that was cut short by the War. It was in the early

twentieth century that artists realised what the example of Turner might mean to modern painting and few understood it better than another Cornish painter, Julius Olsson, whose *Sunset: Cornish Coast* (cat. 47), painted in 1920, suggests a kind of expressionism which was not to take root at Burlington House until much later.

The recurrent intimism of English painting also touched the Cornish circle. The wholesomeness of plain living and modest betrothal in Stanhope Forbes's *Harbour Window* (cat. 22) is entirely delightful, although one might rather wish to share the evidently flirtatious *Confidences* that are being exchanged in Frank Bramley's more luxurious household (cat. 3). There are curious sidelights on manners to be gathered from the Diploma works. The pleasures of painting perhaps were understood to explain and excuse everything; they certainly account for the mystery and magic of a strange picture called *The Letter* (cat. 63), which was added to the collection on behalf of Annie Swynnerton who was elected A.R.A. in 1922 at the age of seventy-eight and remained in the rank until she died aged eighty-nine. Her subject seems to be under a medieval spell that is unexplained. The most truly enchanted image in this phase of the Academy's development was perhaps the chair-bound *Arabella* (cat. 64) painted before Leonard Campbell Taylor discovered the sublime but inimitable spaciousness of Vermeer.

The grandeur that Academy painting commands at its best is rendered with incomparable brilliance by John Singer Sargent's *An Interior in Venice* (cat. 54) which is apparently inhabited, most appropriately, by transplanted characters from Henry James. Very likely they are Daniel and Ariana Curtis from Boston who purchased the Palazzo Barbaro where Sargent visited them in 1882. Sargent's friend was their son, Ralph, who is surely the young man in the background. One would like to know more about the proposition that is being urged with casual yet convincing passion, to the discomfiture of the prosperous parents. This is one of the undoubted masterpieces of the collection, and *Fishing* (cat. 15) which was painted, evidently under Sargent's influence, by Wilfred De Glehn, is almost another. One imagines that the flashing brush is rendering the sparkle of a backwater in the Veneto. English life has no less grandeur, although the occupations pursued in *The Van Dyck Room, Wilton* (cat. 38) seem more settled and less passionate. But the surety of Lavery's touch is almost worthy of Sargent's example. When Sir William Orpen painted *Le Chef de l'Hôtel Chatham, Paris* (cat. 49) the certainty of tonal observation and the confident bearing of painter and model alike are as near as British painting ever came to Manet. The Academicians themselves inhabit a considerable palace and the lunches in the General Assembly Room that refresh the Selection and Hanging Committees each year are as well provided and attended as they were when Frederick Elwell painted them in 1938 (cat. 19).

Felicity of tonal observation was the essence of the style adopted by the later Impressionists in the Academy membership. Sir Walter Russell's picture of *Studland Beach* (cat. 53) establishes the bathing tents and perambulators of that delightful place with a dazzling economy of statement. Rodney Burn painted *Bracklesham Sands* (cat. 9) at low tide; the space rather than its scattered occupants was his subject. The Cornish painters had cosier tastes and the expanding ripples of Birch's *Our Little Stream, Lamorna* (cat. 2) eddied in a pattern which might in other countries have led to quite a different kind of picture. English painters persistently refused to develop the formal obsessions which led elsewhere to the abstractions that used to be thought the only characteristic modern art. *Lago Maggiore* (cat. 62), as painted by Adrian Stokes, reminds us that Segantini might have been painting not far away, but Stokes's standpoint remained obstinately British. When he died, an obituary recorded that nothing annoyed him more than to be confused with the young author of *The Quattrocento*.

A deeper appreciation of Italian places gives the sharply observed *Piediluco* (cat. 41) by Thomas Monnington (who became President at a turning point in the Academy's history) the visionary exactitude of a Dürer. The strangeness of the places that Charles Gere painted (cats 24, 25) is sometimes enhanced by a strangeness in the light. The exotic subjects beloved of travelled Academicians sometimes defy recognition. The barbaric wares sold at Brangwyn's *Market Stall* (cat. 4) are as chaotic as the mingled scents collected by the violet-gatherer, as painted by Henry La Thangue (cat. 37).

Portraits used to be the staple fare of the Academy's Summer Exhibitions. Some of them, such as Philpot's *Young Man* (cat. 51), had a quality that gave them the rank of independent pictures. An eerie smoothness of modelling was the common characteristic of the portraitists of Gerald Kelly's generation (cat. 35). Earlier practice allowed more various character and George Harcourt's violinist daughter (cat. 30) is a vivid reminder of the appalling recitals of one's childhood at which the lady soloist infallibly wore a hat. The neat fashions observed by James Gunn at the Ritz (cat. 27) were the elegant merchandise

of another generation; the hypnotic gaze of G. L. Brockhurst's *Ophelia* (cat. 5) is hard to forget.

The anthology that began with landscapes as atmospheric as any ends with the opposite quality, one that is no less precious. Sometimes the grace of bare trees is tragic. In the Diploma work (cat. 45) that John Nash deposited in 1951, one of three dead trees has already fallen. The forks of the two others, silvery in the cool sunlight and naked amid the heavy foliage around them, is thus quite apparently and sadly under threat. This grace is as appealing as anything in landscape but three years later the painter replaced it with a different picture, *The Barn, Wormingford* (cat. 44), a broader expanse of distance, as if he had come to prefer space to grace. *The Lake, Little Horkesley Hall* (cat. 46) which was bought four years later still reminds us that Nash was not only a botanist but a humorist. The straight stems of tall saplings are contrasted with the grappling limbs of a tree like a predatory insect. There is no limit to the meanings that are explored in drawing as responsive and economical as this. The winter woodland painted by Gilbert Spencer (cat. 58), in another of these Diploma works from the 1950s, is more complex and finely woven. Spencer painted himself in his unwarmed workroom (59); those who knew him will remember the shrewdness of his eye. The humour and fantasy of British painting are represented by two of his brother Stanley Spencer's paintings of the more grotesque incongruities of country life. Stanley himself is the elfin helper (cat. 60) who infallibly gets caught behind the opening gate. *The Dustbin, Cookham* (cat. 61), made out of a disused cold frame, is not a subject that would have occurred to any other painter or nation on earth.

Arthur Nowell (1862–1940), *Private View Day at the Royal Academy*, exhibited at the Royal Academy, 1933. The Arts Club, London.

# A Quiet Revolution: The Royal Academy 1900–1950

*Mary Anne Stevens*

*' . . . you did not speak of the Royal Academy if you pretended to be interested in modern art.'[1]*

It is generally assumed that Frank Rutter's dismissal of the Royal Academy's relevance to modern art, made in the decade preceding 1900, could equally well have applied half a century later to the art which that institution continued both to support through its membership and to enshrine in its annual Summer Exhibitions. To be sure, by 1950, the Royal Academy was still unwilling to elect as members such leading British modernists as Nicholson, Hepworth and Moore, and such representatives of the younger avant-garde as Francis Bacon. Indeed, it was only in the previous year, 1949, in his Annual Dinner speech, that the then President, Sir Alfred Munnings, issued a bitter attack on all art since Matisse. Yet Munnings had opened this assault with a specific reference to certain members of the Royal Academy itself: ' . . . I find myself a president of a body of men who are what I call shilly-shallying. They feel that there is something in this modern art.'[2] Such an admission suggests the existence of a greater liberalism within the institution than is perhaps generally recognised. Thus, while the Academy, during the period covered by the works included in this exhibition, was not the epitome of an enlightened, 'open' institution which fully welcomed all exponents of the most recent developments in contemporary art within its ranks, it would be over-simple to regard it as a passionately 'recalcitrant', determinedly conservative body whose main ambition was to uphold what had come to be seen by many as outmoded art.

In 1900, the Royal Academy of Arts was 142 years old. Founded by Royal Charter in 1768, with Sir Joshua Reynolds as its first President, it was charged in its Instruments of Foundation to fulfil three specific functions: to present an annual exhibition of works by living artists, to train young painters, sculptors and architects, and to support indigent artists and their families. An initial guarantee from King George III to underwrite all financial shortfalls secured the Royal Academy's finances and enabled it to fulfil all three functions without subsequent recourse to any state funds. In 1870, an additional responsibility was added to its brief: the mounting of the annual Winter loan exhibition of Old Masters which, between 1805 and 1867, had been organised by the British Institution. The first loan exhibition opened in January 1870 in the Academy's recently completed Main Galleries in its new home, Burlington House.

From its inception, authority was invested in the Members of the Royal Academy on major matters of national aesthetic and artistic concern. The Academy was invited to comment upon such questions as the purchase by the nation of the Elgin Marbles in 1816, the decoration of the new Houses of Parliament during the closing years of the 1830s, the proposals for major reforms in the postgraduate training of artists between 1914 and 1920,[3] and the establishment of a Fine Arts Commission in 1922.[4] Similarly, it was deemed wholly natural that the Academy, which could count two Directors of the National Gallery amongst its Presidents, would be a leading force in the discussions to establish a more scientifically based approach to the conservation of paintings in that institution.[5] On a more independent note, the Academy saw fit to pass comment upon plans to redevelop the Strand in London,[6] upon the protection of Dartmoor from flooding by new reservoirs[7] and, further afield, the threat to the Pyramids at Gizah posed by a scheme to erect buildings in too close proximity to these ancient monuments.[8]

The Academy's influential position was in large measure determined by the methods and practices of its membership. By 1900 membership was set at forty full Academicians and thirty Associates distributed between the three categories of practitioners: painters, sculptors and architects. Election to Associate status was by full members, and elevation from Associate to Royal Academician, the only method of attaining the higher status, was achieved through the same procedure. Members also dominated the annual Summer Exhibition of works by living artists in two specific ways. The Selection and Hanging Committees were drawn from the Academicians, thus ensuring that an 'Academy' aesthetic would be imposed upon the exhibition. Second, before the reforms of 1903, each member was entitled to submit, and to have hung, eight works. In so far as this privilege was linked to that of being given the prime exhibition position 'on the line', it was theoretically possible for up to one quarter of the hanging space in the galleries to be 'crowded' by Academicians' work, leaving relatively less space for an adequate representation of non-members' works.

Over the ensuing fifty years, there were several moments in the Royal Academy's history, as regards both its public acts and its membership and the character of its exhibitions, which might suggest that this apparent monopoly of aesthetic authority tended to reinforce the Academy's defence of tradition rather than to encourage aesthetic open-mindedness. Throughout much of its history, the Academy had been the subject of criticism. As early as the 1850s questions were being asked in Parliament concerning the quality of the teaching in the Schools, and the 1870s saw a series of discussions critical of the organisation and hence the quality of the Summer Exhibition. These were summarised in 1898 by W. J. Laidlay, in his book *The Royal Academy — its uses and abuses*, a blistering attack on the inadequacies of the Academy of his day. From a public standpoint, two major events post-1900 did little to improve the Academy's reputation: the Chantrey Bequest 'rumpus' and the Epstein Affair.

The Chantrey Bequest was financed by funds bequeathed to the Royal Academy by the sculptor Sir Francis Chantrey R.A. in 1841. On the death of his wife in 1875 the funds were used for 'the purchase of works of art of the highest merit in painting and sculpture, executed entirely within the shores of Great Britain, to form a public national collection of British Fine Art.'[9] In 1897 all works acquired through the Bequest were transferred to the Tate Gallery to be displayed as a separate collection. Yet the responsibility for selection and administration of the Bequest was inherently unsatisfactory. The Tate Gallery was charged with housing the works, but had no say in their selection, while the selection itself was made by the Academy, perhaps understandably, from the walls of its annual Summer Exhibition. By 1904, criticism of the narrowness of choice and the unwillingness of the Committee to consider any work by more avant-garde artists, especially those who had received training abroad, led to the appointing of a Select Committee of the House of Lords to inquire into its administration. Its recommendations were ill-received by the Royal Academy, which resented any suggestion that its members might be incapable of building up a representative collection of the best examples of contemporary British art.[10] As a gesture towards the Select Committee, however, it did offer to establish two sub-committees consisting of three painters and three sculptors who would advise on an initial selection, the final decision however still requiring the sanction of the President and Council of the Academy itself. In 1917, a more significant gesture was made in the direction of the newly appointed Director and Trustees of the Tate Gallery; the Royal Academy now agreed to consult them upon proposed purchases made for the Chantrey Bequest. Although conflict between the Tate and the Academy re-emerged at the end of Dicksee's presidency in 1927, this was resolved by the succeeding President of the Royal Academy, Sir William Llewellyn, to the satisfaction of both parties.

The Epstein Affair was possibly far more publicly damaging to the Royal Academy than the problems surrounding the handling of a bequest whose guidelines had been laid down in an earlier age. In 1935, the British Medical Association's headquarters in the Strand were acquired by the Rhodesian Government which subsequently proposed to take down the statues that Jacob Epstein had erected on the building in 1908. Controversial at the time of their unveiling, these statues never ceased to be the cause of bitter dispute. When a petition was presented to the then President of the Royal Academy, Sir William Llewellyn, he refused to sign it on the grounds that to do so would imply that he had the full backing of the Royal Academy, and he had not yet been able to convene a meeting of Council to discuss the affair. Such an apparent abrogation of the role of the Academy in the defence of art laid it open to major attack from outside and caused sufficient resentment to provoke on the one hand the decision of many 'modern artists' including Moore, to have nothing to with apparently so retrograde an institution, and on the other, the loss of its own member, Walter Sickert. In his letter of resignation, the artist declared: 'If the R A cannot throw its shield over a great sculptor, what is the Royal Academy for?'[11]

The Royal Academy's apparently persistent reluctance thoroughly to overhaul its Summer Exhibition also caused constant irritation to artists, critics and even to some members themselves. As Theo Cowdell has pointed out,[12] throughout the period 1900–30, the Academy was the constant butt of such sentiments. Roger Fry viewed the Academy's shows as the epitome of the dull and the conservative, sadly concluding that, 'as a nation we are incapable of the imaginative life, and therefore fit for nothing but a harsh and ungenerous puritanism.'[13] Criticism of the 'closed shop' character of the exhibitions came from conservative and liberal critics alike, Rutter going so far as to suggest in 1927 that recent Academy shows revealed few signs of change from those held thirty-five years before.[14]

Evidence of the existence of an inherent traditionalism within the Royal Academy during this period can be found in at least three other areas: the aesthetic leanings of its Presidents, the periodic disregard of the interests of its more progressive members, and the apparent public disenchantment with the annual Summer Exhibitions. When reviewing the artistic persuasions of its Presidents, the pattern emerges of 'safe' as opposed to 'adventurous' appointments. On the death of Sir John Everett Millais in 1896, the Presidency was invested in Sir Edward Poynter, past professor of the Slade School of Art and Director of the National Gallery. Already sixty when elected, he brought to the post an academicism acquired during his training in Paris, which he demonstrated in his own paintings and expounded in his *Lectures in Art*. Here, in phrases remarkably similar to those employed by Sir Joshua Reynolds a hundred years earlier, he exhorted his students to lay 'emphasis . . . upon discarding copying of minute details in nature' and called for a need to 'establish a comprehension of the beauty in nature, and [to avoid] its ugliness and deformity.'[15] From Poynter's retirement in 1919 to Sir Gerald Kelly's election thirty years later, the intervening Presidents reveal little concern to overturn these precepts. Neither of the two architect-presidents, Sir Aston Webb (1919–24) and Sir Edwin Lutyens (1938–44) could ever have been counted amongst the enthusiastic supporters of the Modern Movement in architecture, and the painter-presidents, Sir Frank Dicksee (1924–8) and Sir William Llewellyn (1928–38) merely echoed their position in respect of painting.

The Royal Academy's occasional insensitivity towards the views of some of its more progressive members surfaced at least twice during the 1930s. In 1935, the Selection Committee of the Summer Exhibition refused Stanley Spencer, recently elected an Associate member, permission to hang two large canvasses. Spencer promptly resigned from the Academy,[16] not to be lured back again until elected a full member in 1950. Three years after Spencer's resignation, the Selection Committee rejected Wyndham Lewis's *Portrait of T. S. Eliot*. Augustus John, by then a full Academician, was outraged, not so much out of admiration for Lewis's work, but rather because of the attitude towards modern art which the Committee's decision implied. John resigned amidst much public noise, issuing a statement to the Press in which he declared: 'I very much regret to make a sensation, but it cannot be helped. Nothing that Mr Wyndham Lewis paints is negligible or to be condemned lightly. I strongly disagree with this rejection. I think it is an inept act on the part of the Academy.'[17] John was re-instated two years later, but not before he had written to Laura Knight, a fellow Academician, stating that 'I wasn't thinking of doing anybody a kindness, . . . but I acted as a better R A than you who let the show go to

Members' Varnishing Day, April 1934; Dame Laura Knight shows fellow Academicians her portrait of Samuel John Lamorna Birch and his children.

pot from year to year.'[18]

Evidence of growing disenchantment with the annual Summer Exhibitions is revealed primarily in the attendance figures for the opening years of this century. In 1891, attendances stood at 385,988. Between 1900 and 1910, the average attendance dropped to 276,548, with a further more dramatic reduction recorded between 1911 and 1913 to an average of 191,750. Declining attendances meant a net fall in the Royal Academy's revenue from ticket and catalogue sales, and, when exacerbated by similar falling numbers of attendances at the Winter loan exhibitions, the Royal Academy moved into deficit in 1908.[19]

Beyond the walls of the Royal Academy, indirect criticism was expressed primarily through challenges to the institution's position as the leading exhibiting body for contemporary art, both British and foreign. Such disaffection had already been given its initial expression within the first few years of the Grosvenor Gallery, founded in 1876. It was reinforced by the establishment of such bodies as the New English Art Club in 1886 and the International Society in 1898, and, after 1900, the

proliferation of artists' exhibiting groups such as the Camden Town Group, the London Group and the Seven and Five. Outside London, the primacy of the Academy was also apparently at risk. The Glasgow Institute exhibition organised by D. S. MacColl in 1900 (Feb–May) intended, amongst other things, to 'explode the pretensions of the kind of paintings and sculpture seen in the annual exhibitions of the Royal Academy and to draw attention to the sterling work being done by (a) the painters of the Glasgow School, Joseph Crawhall, D. Y. Cameron, James Guthrie, Lawrey etc. and (b) some members of the New English Art Club, of whom the most distinguished was Philip Wilson Steer.'[20] An exhibition held two years later in Wolverhampton to coincide with an industrial exhibition, also gave prominence to members of the New English Art Club and 'dealt a very severe blow to the prestige of the Royal Academy'.[21]

In their role as supporters of contemporary foreign art, these alternative exhibition venues were reinforced by the annual Allied Artists Association exhibitions initiated in 1908 and the two Post-Impressionist exhibitions of 1910 and 1912 organised

Selection Committee, March 1939 (from left to right): W. R. Lamb (Secretary), Sir Edwin Cooper RA, Eric Gill ARA, R. G. Brundrit RA, Harold Knight RA, Oliver Hall RA, Sir Edwin Lutyens PRA, George Harcourt RA, T. C. Dugdale ARA, A. R. Lawrence RA. The President holds up the 'D' to indicate a 'Doubtful' submission.

by Clive Bell and Roger Fry at the Grafton Galleries. Whereas the International Society under the presidency of Whistler, had for its opening exhibition in 1898, been able to muster works by Degas, Manet, Monet, Renoir and Segantini, the Royal Academy's Winter loan exhibition of two years earlier devoted to 'Works by Deceased French Artists' could allow no more 'modern' a representation than works by Courbet, Corot, J. F. Millet, and members of the Barbizon School, Bastien-Lepage and Meisonnier. Similarly in the decade 1900–1910 that saw the opening exhibitions of the Allied Artists' Association which included works by Kandinsky, the Academy counted among its recently elected Honorary Academicians such pillars of nineteenth-century academicism as Jean-Léon Gérôme, Léon Bonnat and P. A. J. Dagnan-Bouveret.

Thus far, the history of the Royal Academy between 1900 and 1950 would appear fully to confirm Rutter's negative view. A closer examination of events within the Royal Academy and of its membership during the period, specifically as represented in this exhibition, *The Edwardians and After: The Royal Academy 1900–1950*, suggests that so harsh a view should be modified.

Although often slow to introduce change, the Academy embarked upon a number of organisational reforms. The teaching in the Schools was subjected to close scrutiny in 1918,[22] with the traditional method of providing instruction using two- or three-month Visitorships held by Academicians being replaced by a more permanent teaching establishment in 1927. The number of works submitted to the Summer Exhibition was reduced to six for members and three for non-members in 1903.[23] Laws governing the Membership of the Academy were also changed to permit both the admission of engravers to the ranks of the Associates and the full Academicians in 1928,[24] and the election of the first woman member since the Academy's foundation six years earlier. In addition, evidence suggests that its members were drawn from a broader artistic background. Of the fifty-eight artists represented in this exhibition, all born between 1840 and 1895, only ten had been trained through the Academy's own Schools, the remaining forty-eight having received their artistic formation at the leading provincial schools of art, at the South Kensington Schools (subsequently the Royal College of Art) or at the Slade School of Art. In addition, the

Hanging the Summer Exhibition, April 1938.

number of these Academicians who had completed their training abroad is impressive. Thirty-three of them attended ateliers in Paris, the most popular being the Académie Julian where eleven of them were enrolled; a further five painters – Cameron, Clausen, Dodd, Kelly and Sickert – all spent considerable time in that city, although they did not undertake any formal training there. Finally, the 1920s and 1930s saw a significant change in the pattern and quality of the Winter loan exhibitions. While the majority were primarily historical, for example *Dutch Art 1450–1900* and *Italian Art 1200–1900*, held in 1929 and 1930 respectively, and *Persian Art* in 1931, the Academy did offer to house such innovative shows as *British Art in Industry*, mounted in collaboration with the Royal Society of Arts in 1935. It was this exhibition which was largely responsible for the establishment of the Royal Society of Designers in Industry in 1936 and the Council for Industrial Design, two milestones in the development of the integration of art and industrial design.

These small but perceptible shifts in the constitution and the public persona of the Royal Academy were parallelled by a tolerance of and in many cases a cautious will to absorb certain elements of the avant-garde. As regards the character of its membership between 1900 and 1950, of the fifty-eight artists

represented in the current exhibition, thirty-six of them had exhibited at some stage in their careers with the 'alternative' exhibiting body, the New English Art Club, and twenty-four had actually become members. Since the New English Art Club had been set up as a specific gesture of revolt against the Royal Academy, the election to the Royal Academy of such founder members as Stanhope Forbes, Bramley and La Thangue suggests the presence of a more liberal spirit than is generally accorded the institution. Such rapprochement around 1900 between the more advanced groups of British artists and the Royal Academy was supported by a closer association between the traditionally more radical Slade School of Art and the Royal Academy and its Schools. This was achieved through the appointment of Walter Russell as an assistant teacher to Henry Tonks in 1897. A member of the New English Art Club from 1895, Russell chose to start exhibiting at the Royal Academy three years later, becoming an Associate in 1920 and a full member in 1926. The bridge between the two schools was finally secured when Russell moved from the Slade to become Keeper of the Royal Academy Schools in 1927, a post which he held until his retirement in 1942. Even outside the membership and teaching in the Schools, other signs of growing tolerance were apparent.

William Powell Frith, *The Private View at the Royal Academy*, 1887. Private collection.

When in 1918 the Council of the Royal Academy appointed a Special Committee to draw up guidelines on memorials to be raised to victims of the First World War, it is significant that in its report submitted to Council, the Committee Members avoided issuing any specific aesthetic directives. Rather, they displayed considerable open-mindedness on all matters relating to style, merely noting that in 'all memorials, simplicity, scale and proportion should be aimed at rather than profusion of detail or excessive costliness of material. It is the imaginative and intellectual quality of the work that gives it its final value.'[25] A similar lack of aesthetic proscription was displayed in the Academy's willingness to house two exhibitions in the Winters of 1919 and 1919–20, of works of art commissioned by the Canadian War Memorials Commission and the Imperial War Museum respectively. Both shows included works by artists deemed at that time to be in the vanguard of the British avant-garde: Nevinson, Wyndham Lewis, Epstein, Paul Nash and William Roberts. Furthermore, as the Annual Reports for these two years testify, no adverse comment was passed upon the presence of the work of these artists upon the walls of the Royal Academy. To be sure, no excessive enthusiasm was expressed at their inclusion, but, in so far as for both exhibitions the Royal Academy insisted upon approving the Hanging Committees, it also, if only passively, agreed to sanction these more progressive works.

Even outside the Royal Academy there were signs, as early as 1900, of a wish to see the institution reform itself and change its aesthetic attitudes, rather than to see it die. In 1900, a critic for the *Studio* enthusiastically welcomed the election of Tuke as an Associate member, declaring that he 'is perhaps the best painter of the open-air school which we have now with us'.[26] The following year, 1901, Henri Frantz, critic for the *Gazette des Beaux-Arts*, in his review of the Summer Exhibition of that year

also welcomed the presence of a small but significant number of artists including Sickert, East, Clausen, La Thangue and Wilfred De Glehn. He suggested that they were all worth watching since their work revealed important indications of new and interesting directions in British art.[27] By the 1920s it was possible to feel confident enough to recognise signs of considerable improvement in the Royal Academy shows, due in no small measure to the fact that by the end of that decade, the institution numbered amongst its recently elected members Orpen, John, Russell, Philpot, Connard and Sickert. The following decade saw the additions of John Nash, Meredith Frampton and Stanley Spencer, and in 1940, Pierre Bonnard was elected an Honorary Academician.

Stanley Spencer had resigned in 1935. He was re-elected as a full Academician in 1950, the year that ushered in the first months of Sir Gerald Kelly's presidency. Kelly came from a background responsive to the more advanced schools of art in Paris during the opening years of this century. He had known Degas, Monet, Renoir and Rodin. He was also knowledgeable about French Post-Impressionism, notably the work of Gauguin, an interest which he may have indirectly imparted to Clive Bell when the critic visited Paris in 1905. Unlike his more conservative predecessors, he determined to effect a permanent rapprochement between the Royal Academy and the rest of the art world. To this end, he initiated retrospective shows of two of the more 'modern' Academicians, Brangwyn (1952) and Augustus John (1954) and also persuaded the Academy to hold as its Winter loan exhibition of 1951 a major survey of the achievements of the Ecole de Paris.[28]

If progress towards a more modern taste was slow within the Royal Academy, it was none the less apparent by 1950. A careful study of the works included in this exhibition suggest that high technical standards were consistently demanded of its

The Royal Academy Dinner, 28 April 1949; Sir Winston Churchill giving his speech, with the President, Sir Alfred Munnings, in the President's chair to his right.

members, as was the subtle exploration of the accommodations possible between the traditions of English painting, notably in landscape and portraiture, and the innovations to be learnt from abroad. If abstract art figured not at all on the walls of the Royal Academy before 1950, then the consistent celebration of the figurative tradition combined with a quiet openness of mind established the parameters within which the Royal Academy has been able to retain its central position within the more recent history of British Art.

NOTES
1. F. Rutter, *Art in My Time*, London, 1933, p. 53.
2. A. Munnings, *The Finish*, 1952, p. 145.
3. A. R., 1914, pp. 6–7; A. R., 1920, pp. 6, 44–5, 91.
4. A. R., 1922, pp. 6–7.
5. A. R., 1923, pp. 6–7; A. R., 1924, pp. 8–9, 70–1; 1926, pp. 85–6.
6. A. R., 1903, pp. 7–8; A. R., 1906, pp. 8–9.
7. A. R., 1920, p. 10.
8. A. R., 1906, p. 8.
9. S. Hutchison, *The History of the Royal Academy 1768–1986*, London, 1986, p. 282.
10. A. R., 1904, pp. 65–6.
11. Letter from W. R. Sickert to Sir William Llewellyn, P. R. A., 19 May, 1935, R. A. Archives, RAC/1/517.
12. T. P. Cowdell, 'The Role of the Royal Academy in English Art 1918–1930', PhD Thesis, University of London, 1980.
13. V. Woolf, *Roger Fry, A Biography*, London, 1950, p. 108.
14. F. Rutter, *Since I Was Twenty-Five*, London, 1927, Chap. I.
15. E. Poynter, *Lectures in Art*, London, 1879, quoted in M. Holroyd, *Augustus John*, London, 1975, Vol. I, p. 39.
16. Letter from S. Spencer to W. R. M. Lamb, Secretary of the R. A., R. A. Archives, Stanley Spencer File.
17. Quoted, M. Holroyd, *Augustus John*, London, 1975, Vol. II, p. 106.
18. Letter from A. John to Laura Knight R. A. dated 9 April, 1939, quoted M. Holroyd, op. cit., Vol. II, p. 107.
19. For details of all attendance figures, see R. A. Annual Reports for the years 1891–1914.
20. F. Rutter, *Art in my Time*, London, 1933, p. 69.
21. ibid, p. 85.
22. A. R., 1918, pp. 53–60.
23. A. R., 1903, p. 11.
24. A. R., 1928, pp. 8–9.
25. A. R., 1918, p. 61.
26. 'F. K.', 'Studio Talk', *Studio*, XIX (1900), p. 121.
27. 'Le Salon Anglais en 1901', *Gazette des Beaux-Arts*, 3 pe'r, Vol. 26, August, p. 162.
28. R. A., Winter, 1951, *Ecole de Paris 1900–1950*.

# The Plates

14   Frank Cadogan Cowper *Vanity*

1   Robert Anning Bell *The Women Going to the Sepulchre*

26   Maurice Greiffenhagen *The Message*

16  Sir Frank Dicksee *Startled*

13   Philip Connard *Apollo and Daphne*

54   John Singer Sargent *An Interior in Venice*

38   Sir John Lavery *The Van Dyck Room, Wilton*

55   Sir James Jebusa Shannon *Black and Silver*

33   Richard Jack *On the Moors*

35  Sir Gerald Festus Kelly *Jane XXX*

27    Sir Herbert James Gunn *Pauline Waiting*

34   Augustus Edwin John *Portrait of A Young Man*

66   Dame Ethel Walker *The Jade Necklace*

3  Frank Bramley *Confidences*

22  Stanhope Alexander Forbes *The Harbour Window*

4 Sir Frank Brangwyn *The Market Stall*

50   Alfred Parsons *Orange Lilies, Broadway*

15   Wilfred Gabriel De Glehn *Fishing*

2   Samuel John Lamorna Birch *Our Little Stream, Lamorna*

43   Sir David Murray *Swedes*

6  Sir John Arnesby Brown *The Raincloud*

62   Adrian Stokes *Lago Maggiore*

25  Charles March Gere *The Mill Pool at Painswick*

53   Sir Walter Westley Russell *Studland Beach*

9   Rodney Joseph Burn *Bracklesham Sands*

40   Sydney Lee *The House with the Closed Shutters*

56   Walter Richard Sickert *Santa Maria della Salute, Venice*

44   John Northcote Nash *The Barn, Wormingford*

45   John Northcote Nash *The Fallen Tree*

58   Gilbert Spencer *From My Studio*

61   Sir Stanley Spencer *The Dustbin, Cookham*

60   Sir Stanley Spencer *The Farm Gate*

23 Meredith Frampton *Still Life*

# The Catalogue

# Robert Anning Bell
## 1863–1933

Robert Anning Bell was able to turn with great 'readiness and versatility' to any of the decorative arts as well as to oil, tempera and watercolour painting; in this, he reminded his contemporaries of 'the great artists of the Renaissance'.[1]

Born in London, Bell left school at fourteen because of family financial difficulties, and became articled to an architect, 'a preliminary groundwork and teaching for which he always expressed himself as grateful.'[2] He later decided, however, to follow a career as an artist, and studied at Westminster School of Art under Fred Brown before entering the Royal Academy Schools in 1881. He finally completed his studies in Paris, spending a year in the studio of Aimé Morot. On his return, he shared a studio with the sculptor Sir George Frampton for six months before leaving to travel around Italy: 'His real inspirations [and] his first true impulse to create came to him when he found himself for the first time in Italy.'[3] Bell's work had first been accepted by the Royal Academy in 1885, and in 1894 he exhibited a sculpture relief. Clearly influenced by the work of the Florentine della Robbia family, Bell's coloured and gilded reliefs were warmly praised as being 'full of graceful sentiment' and as manifesting the artist's 'good sense of colour'.[4]

In 1894 Bell became Professor of Art at University College in Liverpool, and carried out various commissions such as an altarpiece in low relief for the Church of St Clare in Liverpool. He returned to London in about 1897 and took a studio in Chelsea.

In the 1890s Bell illustrated many books and periodicals. In common with several other artists who were involved in the revival of fine book illustration, notably William Morris, Walter Crane, Ricketts and Shannon, he was much influenced in his black and white drawings by the woodcuts of the Venetian *Hypnerotomachia di Poliphilo* (1499). He was impressed by both the austere and graceful lines of these famous illustrations, and by the sensitive balance between image and text.

In 1911 Bell became Professor of Decorative Art at Glasgow School of Art, and later Professor of Design at the Royal College of Art from 1918 to 1924. An important member of the Arts and Crafts Movement he was elected Master of the Art Workers Guild in 1921, as well as being a member of the Arts and Crafts Society for which he organised many exhibitions in London, Brussels, Turin and Paris.

Bell's designs for stained glass and mosaics were greatly admired, and he received many important commissions. He exhibited designs for his completed mosaics at the Academy, including those for a tympanum over the west door of Westminster Cathedral in 1916, and designs for mosaics in the Houses of Parliament between 1924 and 1926. Whilst working on these commissions Bell made many visits to Venice, Ravenna and Sicily, and evolved a linear style characterised by simple, clear outlines and a minimum of modelling in his figures.

Despite the many demands on his time, Bell did not neglect painting. He was elected an Associate of the Academy in 1914, and in 1918 *Mary in the House of Elizabeth* (London, Tate Gallery)[5] was purchased for the Chantrey Bequest. The picture depicts the two women quietly sewing in a simple, but grand Italianate interior and the curved lines of the somewhat elongated figures provide a contrast to the plain background. He was elected a full member of the Academy in 1922. Bell's last major commission was for the Shakespeare window in Manchester Reference Library which he completed before his death in 1933 at the age of seventy. A memorial exhibition of his work was held at The Fine Art Society in 1934 with the intention of asserting 'how important a contribution this fine artist and craftsman made to the ecclesiastical and decorative art of this country.'[6]   H.C.V.

NOTES
1. Obituary, press cutting, R.A. Archives, R.A. Bell file.
2. idem.
3. *The Old Water-Colour Society's Club*, XII (1935), p. 51.
4. Obituary, press cutting, R.A. Archives, R.A. Bell file.
5. Repr., *Royal Academy Illustrated*, 1918, p. 90.
6. *Memorial exhibition of the works of Robert Anning Bell*, exhib. cat., London, Fine Art Society, 1934.

## 1   The Women Going to the Sepulchre

76 × 127 cm   30 × 50 in
Signed and dated br: *Robert Anning Bell 1912*
Diploma work, accepted 9 May 1922 (C.M. XXIV, p. 433)

Painted in 1912, ten years before Bell presented the picture to the Academy as his Diploma work, the scene depicts the procession of Holy women bearing myrrh and jars of ointment to anoint the body of Christ in the sepulchre. The Virgin Mary, wearing her traditional raiment of blue, is shown descending the steps to the sepulchre and Mary Magdalene is identifiable by the jar of ointment — rather than myrrh — which she carries, and by her long reddish hair.

Despite the solemnity of the figures, a contemporary reviewer complained that 'there is nothing to suggest that the women have just passed through one of the most awful times of tribulation' and that 'there is nothing to connect the scene with Jerusalem.'[1] However, Bell chose to depict the moment before the women had discovered the disappearance of Christ's body and he creates instead an atmosphere of simple piety by using subdued colours and a clear compositional arrangement reminiscent of fifteenth-century Italian frescoes. Bell's experience in mosaic and stained glass made him value simple clear outlines, which ensured that a work would have an impact from a distance. Here he places the women on a rampart overlooking a wide plain, which makes the procession appear as if part of a frieze. Critics were complimentary about the composition, finding that 'the colour and arrangement are good, and the general effect decorative.'[2]

NOTES
1. *Connoisseur*, 66 (1923), p. 111.
2. idem.

EXHIBITIONS: R.A., 1923 (cat. 96); Swansea, Glynn Vivian Art Gallery and Museum, 1985 (cat. 31); Japan, Tokyo Shimbun, touring exhibition, 1987 (cat. 52).

# Samuel John Lamorna Birch

## 1869–1955

1    *repr. in colour on p. 26*

Birch was torn throughout his life between his two great loves – painting and fishing: in 1923 the *Studio* lightheartedly recalled that 'he wanted to fish when he was painting and on fishing expeditions paintful yearnings tore his soul.'[1] He was fortunate in finding a place to live which provided a river landscape ideal for both activities, and with which he became so closely associated as to adopt its name, Lamorna, to distinguish him from a local painter, Lionel Birch.

Samuel Birch was born in Egremont, Cheshire, eldest son of a family of ten. His father died at an early age and the twelve-year-old Birch left school and began work as an office boy in Manchester. Ill health forced him to leave the city and to recuperate for a while at the home of a river bailiff, where he was introduced to fly fishing, and where he applied his early talent for drawing to the depiction of landscape. When he returned to work, as an industrial designer in a linoleum factory, Birch continued to sketch in his spare time and built up a local reputation for his paintings.

In 1889 Birch visited Newlyn, attracted by the group of distinguished artists, including Stanhope Forbes (q.v.) and Frank Bramley (q.v.), who had colonised this small Cornish fishing village. Birch did not immediately settle in Newlyn but, following Forbes's advice, left for Paris in 1895 to study in the *atelier* of Colorossi. Apart from this short period, Birch was entirely self-taught and even when in Paris he spent most of his time sketching on the banks of the Seine. On his return he exhibited and sold a collection of his Paris paintings at an exhibition held in Lancaster. Birch finally settled in Cornwall in about 1896 and the influence of the Newlyn painters became apparent in his use of a muted tonal range. In 1902 he moved to Flagstaff Cottage at Lamorna Cove, the area that provided him with his principal source of inspiration for the rest of his life. Birch's move to Lamorna was instrumental in bringing a second wave of artist settlers to Cornwall, including Laura and Harold Knight (q.v.) and Alfred Munnings (q.v.).

From 1906 several exhibitions of Birch's work were held at The Fine Art Society, and by this time his palette had brightened considerably, creating the bold juxtapositions of colours which were a hallmark of his style. Birch made numerous pencil sketches and in about 1911, as Laura Knight recalled, he began to paint watercolour washes over these pencil studies to obtain the 'fleeting effects over sea, stream, rock' of the 'sun chasing' shadows across a 'spread of landscape'.[2] His larger oils such as *Tregiffian Cliff, near Lamorna, c.*1922 (City of Bristol Museum and Art Gallery), painted at the same time as these delicate studies, show his concern with the formal and structural problems of landscape composition.

He was elected an Associate of the Academy in 1926, and became a full member eight years later. Birch was a prolific painter, sometimes travelling to other good fishing rivers in England, Scotland, and on the Continent, looking for new subject matter. In 1937 he visited New Zealand and Australia (where many museums purchased his work), and an exhibition of his Australian work was held at the Greatorex Galleries on his return. However, whether painting in Australia or at Lamorna, his 'favourite path would be beside the river and his chosen task to capture the gleam dancing on the ripples.'[3] Birch died in 1955 at the age of eighty-five, at his home in Lamorna.    H.C.V.

NOTES
1.  *Studio*, 85 (1923), p. 124.
2.  L. Knight, 'S. J. Lamorna Birch as I knew him', *Old Water-Colour Society's Club*, 32 (1957), p. 18.
3.  *Paintings and Watercolour Drawings of New Zealand by Lamorna Birch*, exhib. cat., London, Greatorex Galleries, 1937, foreword by A. Wimperis.

## 2  Our Little Stream, Lamorna

63.5 × 76 cm    25 × 30 in
Signed bl: *S. J. Lamorna Birch*.
Diploma work, accepted 23 April 1934 (C.M. XXVI, p. 311)

*Our Little Stream, Lamorna* depicts one of Birch's favourite and most frequently painted subjects. Laura Knight described Lamorna as a rural paradise, 'a densely wooded valley filled with lichen covered trees of greenish grey' where 'violet-tinted grey boulders bordered a stream that found its way to the sea.'[1] Birch not only responded to the beauty of the valley but 'with that knowledge which no one but a fisherman could have so fully', he managed to depict 'all the impetuosity of a rippling stream'.[2] Birch made this the subject of his Diploma work and clearly shows how the 'stream really runs' and creates 'its pattern around a bank or stone'[3] as it flows down to the sea. He concentrates on the stream, choosing a very high horizon with the main highlights deriving from reflections on the water and with the sky hardly visible. The restricted field of vision emphasises the intimacy of this quiet, secluded spot. Birch was attracted to moving water for the challenge it presented of painting the swirling patterns and the effects of dappled sunshine reflected on its surface; here he reserves the heaviest impasto for the highlights on the water and bank. The striking juxtapositions of bright yellows and greens with blue is typical of the tonal range of his work.

NOTES
1.  L. Knight, 'S. J. Lamorna Birch as I knew him', *Old Water-Colour Society's Club*, 32 (1957), p. 17.
2.  *Studio*, 64 (1915), p. 169.
3.  L. Knight, op. cit., p. 21.

EXHIBITIONS: R.A., 1934 (cat. 99); Bournemouth, Russell-Cotes Art Gallery & Museum, 1965 (cat. 4); R.A., Winter, 1968 (cat. 462); South London Art Gallery, 1973 (cat. 94); Leicestershire Museum and Art Gallery, 1982 (cat. 7).

2    *repr. in colour on p. 43*

# Frank Bramley
## 1857–1915

Frank Bramley's reputation was established by the success of his painting *A Hopeless Dawn* (London, Tate Gallery) which was purchased for the nation through the Chantrey Bequest in 1888. This gesture of recognition came at a crucial time for the Newlyn colony of painters (of which Bramley was a leading member) and, building on the acclaim accorded Stanhope Forbes's *A Fish Sale on a Cornish Beach* (Plymouth City Museum and Art Gallery), it affirmed the growing strength and vitality of the Newlyn School.[1]

Born in Sibsey in Lincolnshire, Bramley first studied at the Lincoln School of Art before leaving in 1879/80 for Antwerp, to complete his training at Verlat's Academy where his fellow students included Edwin Harris and W. J. Wainwright, both of whom later worked at Newlyn. After three years at the Academy, Bramley moved to Venice and in 1884 exhibited two Venetian subjects at the Royal Academy. However, his health later failed during a winter spent in Venice and he returned to England, settling in Newlyn during the winter of 1884–5. Forbes (q.v.) seemed surprised that so many artists were drawn to Newlyn, without knowing 'what lodestone of artistic metal the place contains ... but its effects were strongly felt in the studios of Paris and Antwerp particularly, by a number of young English painters studying there, who ... seemed drawn towards this corner of their native land.'[2] Although of a reserved disposition, Bramley's artistic talents soon made an impression on the Newlyn artists. In 1886 his *Domino!* (Cork Municipal Art Gallery) was the Newlyn School's first major interior subject to be exhibited at the Academy. In accordance with Newlyn principles this work placed equal emphasis on the domino players and their setting, reflecting a common concern 'to study humanity in relation to its surroundings.'[3] Bramley's particular contribution to the Newlyn group was to adapt the new style of realism to the painting of interior scenes.

*Domino!* received little notice in the press but two years later *A Hopeless Dawn* was eulogised by the critics. A contemporary reviewer thought the painting had 'a perfect blend of simple but profound human drama and of beautifully executed and very carefully observed effects of light and of colour and tone.'[4] Another felt that in avoiding 'melodrama or sentimentality ... it lacked artificiality and had instead "actuality"; it was about the problems of painting.'[5] Bramley continued to employ the technique of the Newlyn School painters in depicting dramatic narrative, but he never succeeded in recapturing the immediacy of this striking image; later works sacrifice their narrative impact to an ardent striving after realism. *For of Such is the Kingdom of Heaven* (New Zealand, Auckland City Art Gallery) exemplifies this tendency in its portrayal of a child's funeral, where neither the tiny coffin nor the figures of the mourners are emphasised; instead, as in Stanhope Forbes's work, country people are portrayed in their natural surroundings more as picturesque types than as characters in a drama.

Like his contemporaries Bramley used square brushes, and was described as one of the leading 'practitioners of this technique; ... indeed his strength and dexterity are marvellous.'[6]

3   *repr. in colour on p. 38*

Although he continued to use square brushes until 1893, the brushwork itself became softer, and his sombre tones were supplanted by brighter, decorative colour schemes.

In the 1890s the subjects of Bramley's paintings became more sentimental, with an emphasis on decorative effect. Figures were shown surrounded by a profusion of flowers, which he used as a symbolic device. In 1895, a year after his election as an Associate of the Academy, he left Newlyn, first moving to Droitwich in the Midlands and then to Grasmere in 1900. He continued to take subjects from village life, such as the *Grasmere Rushbearing* (Grasmere Village Hall) of 1905, which depicts a procession of young girls bedecked with flowers in a traditional spring ceremony.

In 1911 Bramley was elected an Academician, but soon after became seriously ill. Excusing himself from duties at the Academy in 1913,[7] he spent the last years of his life confined to his flat in London until his death in 1915.    H.C.V.

NOTES
1.  For a fuller discussion of the Newlyn School of painters see p. 92.
2.  'A Newlyn Retrospect', *The Cornish Magazine*, I (1898), p. 82; quoted C. Fox and F. Greenacre, *Artists of the Newlyn School 1880–1900*, exhib. cat., Newlyn Orion Galleries, 1979, p. 15.
3.  S. Forbes, 'Cornwall from a Painter's Point of View', reprinted from the *Annual Report of the Royal Cornwall Polytechnic Society* for 1900, Falmouth, 1901, p. 7; quoted C. Fox and F. Greenacre, op. cit., p. 16.
4.  *Art Journal*, 1889, p. 100; quoted C. Fox and F. Greenacre, op. cit., p. 163.
5.  *Magazine of Art*, 1903, p. 58; quoted C. Fox and F. Greenacre, op. cit., p. 163.
6.  R. Jope-Slade, 'The Outsiders', *Black and White Handbook to the Royal Academy and New Gallery*, 1893, p. 11; quoted C. Fox and F. Greenacre, op. cit., p. 165.
7.  C.M. XXIII, p. 2, 14 Jan 1913.

# 3 Confidences

89.5 × 75 cm    35¾ × 29½ in
Signed and dated br: *FRANK BRAMLEY 1911*
Diploma work, accepted 1912 (A.R., p. 62)

Bramley's artistic reputation derived from paintings depicting figures in an interior. His first submitted Diploma work, of unrecorded title, was rejected as the Academy wanted 'a picture more representative of his work as a figure painter'.[1] Its replacement, *Confidences*, was accepted as his Diploma work in 1912.

The subject of seated figures in conversation was one which occupied Bramley throughout his career. In his early pictures painted in Newlyn, such as *Old Memories*[2] and *Gossip*,[3] Bramley portrayed the everyday life of the villagers, depicting the interiors of their simple cottages in great detail. Here, however, Bramley chooses an opulent, middle-class interior as his subject: two young women, beautifully dressed, sit in their favourite parlour or drawing room chatting, one animated, one pensive. Revelling in the sensuous qualities of the surface textures, Bramley seems, by his choice of subject, to have reverted to a more conventional aesthetic than that of Forbes and the Newlyn painters, whose idea of beauty encapsulated a sense of locality and the everyday.

As early as 1893, Bramley had exhibited pictures featuring the symbolic use of flowers: in *Sleep*,[4] for instance, an abundance of poppies, traditionally an attribute of the God of Sleep, surround the form of a sleeping girl. In *Confidences*, the innocence of the two girls dressed in white, is emphasised by the lilies, a symbol of purity, seen behind the figures.

The contrast between the painting of light in *Confidences* and in Bramley's early works such as *A Hopeless Dawn* is marked. In the latter, the artist realistically captures the effects of the cool, grey light of dawn over the sea filtering through the window, underlining the tragedy of the central character, a young woman whose lover has been lost at sea. The lighting of *Confidences* complements the subject matter, appearing to emanate from a fire, although, as one reviewer noticed 'the artist apparently sees more blue in the shadows than would be visible to ordinary eyes.'[5] Firelight, however, is suggested by the long shadows, the glow on the girls' faces and the luxuriant stretching of the cat. The fall of light also emphasises the structure of the picture; the diagonal shadow on the wall mimics the arrangement of the figures and the highlights on the girls' dresses are painted in broad brushstrokes with great freedom of expression. Bramley achieves a feeling of intimacy by taking a low vantage point, limiting the spatial depth and bringing the figures closer to the spectator.

NOTES
1.  C.M. XXII, p. 451, 7 Nov 1911.
2.  Repr., *Royal Academy Pictures*, 1892, p. 108.
3.  Repr., ibid., 1899, p. 74.
4.  Repr., ibid., 1895, p. 106.
5.  *Connoisseur*, 33 (1912), p. 201.

EXHIBITION: R.A., 1912 (cat. 230).

# Sir Frank Brangwyn
## 1867–1956

During his lifetime Sir Frank Brangwyn was considered to be one of the greatest living artists, and received academic honours from over forty art institutions throughout the world. His creative energy was immense, and he produced at least twelve thousand works, including paintings, etchings, lithographs and monumental mural cycles in oil and tempera.

Brangwyn was born in 1867 in Bruges, of Welsh parents. His father, William Curtis, was an architect and ran a workshop which reproduced medieval embroideries and furnishings. Brangwyn received his early artistic training in his father's workshop, and this apprenticeship continued in London when the family moved there in 1875. Between 1882 and 1884 Brangwyn was employed in William Morris's studio in Oxford Street, where he copied tapestries and made working drawings for carpets and wallpapers.

Brangwyn first had his work accepted at the Academy in 1885, and he continued exhibiting annually until 1898. During this time he travelled extensively by sea, often working his passage on cargo boats. He travelled around Asia Minor in 1888, toured Spain in 1891, and visited Morocco in 1893. His travels also included Russia, South Africa and the West African Coast. During this period Brangwyn matured as an artist, with the development of a painterly style and the adoption of a richer palette. His work also began to gain a considerable reputation abroad.

In 1900 Brangwyn settled at Temple Lodge in Hammersmith, and four years later was elected an Associate of the Royal Academy. He began to undertake large-scale decorative schemes and his first such commission, for the Skinners' Hall in London, was for eleven panels, each over ten feet long, illustrating outstanding events in the history of the guild. This project occupied Brangwyn between 1902 and 1909. Many of his commissions for mural paintings came from America, including those for the Court House in Cleveland, Ohio (1913), the Missouri State Capitol (1915) and the Rockefeller Center in New York (1930–34).

During the First World War Brangwyn moved to Ditchling in Sussex where his studio could accommodate his largest works. Between 1913 and 1923 he painted sixteen panels depicting religious subjects in tempera for a chapel in Christ's Hospital in Horsham, Sussex, and his commissions also included decorative panels for the ship, the *Empress of Britain*, which was sunk in the Second World War. Brangwyn always regarded himself as a craftsman as well as an artist and he gave equal attention to his designs, whether they were for book illustrations or tapestries. In 1924 an exhibition of nearly five hundred of his paintings, drawings and etchings was held at 184 Queen's Gate, London, and was a tremendous success, being opened by the then Prime Minister, Ramsay MacDonald.

Brangwyn's greatest series of mural decorations was the sixteen British Empire panels, commissioned in 1926 by Lord Iveagh to form part of a War Memorial for the House of Lords. In these designs every conceivable flower, animal and race of people are depicted in strong, bright colours. However, when five of the panels were erected in 1930 the Royal Fine Arts Commission reported them unsuitable, and when the Lords debated the matter the majority voted against the scheme. Applications flooded in from around the world offering to house the panels, but they were finally presented to the City of Swansea, where they were placed in a specially constructed hall, subsequently named after the artist.

In 1936 Brangwyn donated his art collection and many of his works to the William Morris Gallery in Walthamstow and in the same year donated paintings and drawings to what became the Brangwyn Museum, in Bruges. At a later date a museum in Orange, France, was established which is also devoted entirely to Brangwyn's work. A knighthood followed in 1941. In 1952 the Royal Academy held a retrospective exhibition of Brangwyn's work which was the first ever to honour a living Academician. He died four years later at his home in Sussex, at the age of eighty-nine.    H.C.V.

## 4    The Market Stall

146 × 160 cm    $57\frac{1}{2}$ × 63 in
Signed bl: *F.B.* (monogram)
Diploma work, accepted 19 July 1921 (C.M. XXIV, p. 364)

Brangwyn was finally elected to full membership of the Academy in 1919 after having been an Associate for fifteen years. Feeling slighted by this somewhat tardy recognition he both chose not to exhibit at the Royal Academy between 1917 and 1922 and delayed in depositing his Diploma work until 1921. Finally, as he had no suitable painting available, Brangwyn bought back *The Market Stall* for £400 before presenting it to the Academy.

In his mural decorations Brangwyn often used still-life studies for decorative purposes or as a compositional device. Despite his increasing number of specific commissions Brangwyn enjoyed painting subjects such as *The Poulterer's Shop* (London, Tate Gallery) which was essentially a still life. Similarly, in *The Market Stall*, the human incident is secondary to the studies of the forms and colours of vegetables, fruit and poultry. Brangwyn's early training in copying and designing tapestries obviously influenced him throughout his life: in common with medieval Flemish tapestries, every corner of the canvas is filled. Brangwyn developed a very painterly technique, which is apparent particularly in the masterly handling of the foreground details. *The Market Stall* is a mature work, and Brangwyn imparts to this picture all 'the decorative spirit and flowing rhythm of his richest and most animated canvases.'[1]

NOTE

1.   R. Brangwyn, *Brangwyn*, 1978, p. 155.

EXHIBITIONS: R.A., 1922 (cat. 202); Worthing Museum & Art Gallery, 1951 (cat. 5); R.A., Winter, 1952 (cat. 403); Bournemouth, Russell-Cotes Art Gallery & Museum, 1957 (cat. 849); R.A., Winter, 1968 (cat. 426); London, Camden Arts Centre, 1969 (cat. 121); Swansea, Glynn Vivian Art Gallery & Museum, 1985 (cat. 26).

4    *repr. in colour on p. 40*

# Gerald Leslie Brockhurst
## 1890–1978

Brockhurst's austere and highly finished society portraits brought him much popular acclaim during the inter-war years. Born in Birmingham in 1890, he entered Birmingham School of Art in 1902 at the age of twelve where he benefited from the School's emphasis on drawing and design. When he was seventeen, Brockhurst enrolled at the Royal Academy Schools, winning many of the highest awards there, most notably the Gold Medal and the travelling Scholarship which he took up in 1914 after marriage to his first wife Anais Folin. The couple visited France and Italy where Brockhurst showed particular interest in the work of Botticelli, Piero della Francesca and Leonardo da Vinci. It was possibly around this time that he developed his interest in tempera painting. The outbreak of war curtailed his travels however, and by 1915 he and Anais had moved to Ireland where they were based for the next five years. Whilst in Ireland, Brockhurst produced a wide range of experimental work which showed the influence of contemporaries such as Ambrose McEvoy, Augustus John (q.v.) and W. R. Sickert (q.v.) as well as the Italian masters. In 1919, however, an exhibition of his work at the Chenil Galleries in Chelsea established his distinctive style, described by one critic as that which 'is not nervously responsive and gives an edge to forms which vision does not experience.'[1]

On his return to London, Brockhurst's career as a printmaker also flourished in the 1920s and the relationship between the etched and painted image continued to interest him throughout his life. Furthermore, he began to enjoy increasing material success and standing in artistic circles. In the early years of the decade, for example, he became a member of the Royal Society of Painter-Etchers and Engravers, and in 1928 was both elected A. R. A. and served on the jury of the Venice International Exhibition.

Anais inspired much of his art during these years acting as the model for his numerous allegorical and symbolic portraits until the early 1930s when he met the sixteen-year-old model, Kathleen Woodward who changed the course of his life and art. Rechristened 'Dorette' by Brockhurst, her compelling features became the hallmark of some of his most popular and famous portraits, although the contemporary press was scandalised by the relationship.

At the same time Brockhurst was painting rich and famous sitters such as Marlene Dietrich (1938) and the Duchess of Windsor (1939) as well as several influential Americans, notably, J. Paul Getty (1938) and Mrs Paul Mellon (1939). In 1939, at the height of his popularity (he was charging 1,000 guineas a canvas and undertaking a maximum of 20 commissions a year), Brockhurst left England for the east coast of America where he found much patronage and support for his prints and his paintings. He took out citizenship in 1949 and lived there with Dorette until his death in 1978.    E. C. W.

NOTE
1. *Vogue*, 15 April 1919; quoted in *Gerald Leslie Brockhurst R.A. (1890–1978)*, exhib. cat., Sheffield City Art Gallery, 1986, p. 16.

## 5  Ophelia

102 × 81 cm    40 × 32 in
Signed br: *BROCKHURST*
Diploma work, accepted 25 Nov 1938 (C.M. XXVII, p. 159)

Portraits of Dorette by Brockhurst appeared annually at the Royal Academy between 1933 and 1939. Sometimes the model was given a guise, as in this painting where she is cast as Ophelia, the tragic heroine of Shakespeare's play, *Hamlet*. Two distinct features of this portrait, the dramatic lighting and the almost hypnotic gaze of the sitter, are characteristic of Brockhurst's other paintings of Dorette in the 1930s. Referring to another portrait of her entitled *Jeunesse Dorée* which was exhibited at the Academy in 1934, a contemporary critic wrote that, 'again and again I saw people ... standing before the picture, vainly trying to fathom the secret of those curiously haunting, deep ... eyes.'[1] Unlike most of the other portraits of Dorette and many of the commissioned pieces, Ophelia is not set against an Italianate landscape but is elegantly posed in a stage-like setting. The theatrical theme is further emphasised by the fact that the model is wearing historical dress rather than the fashionable garments featured in most of the other portraits executed around this time.

In comparison with the more classical portraits of his first wife Anais, Brockhurst's portraits of Dorette represented a very particular feminine ideal. Her distinctive, sharply defined features were perfectly suited to Brockhurst's perfectionist technique and mastery in rendering surface realism. The resultant images were photographic, glossy and highly finished, yet they were also remote and lacking in emotion, emphasising the fashionable veneer of the sitter's appearance rather than her personality.

NOTE
1. *Daily Mail*, 8 May 1934; quoted in *Gerald Leslie Brockhurst R.A. (1890–1978)*, exhib. cat., Sheffield City Art Gallery, 1986, p. 18.

EXHIBITIONS: R.A., 1939 (cat. 438); Bournemouth, Russell-Cotes Art Gallery & Museum, 1965 (cat. 6); R. A., Winter, 1968 (cat. 58); Leicestershire Museum and Art Gallery, 1982 (cat. 12); Swansea, Glynn Vivian Art Gallery, 1985 (cat. 42); Cheltenham Art Gallery and Museums, 1985 (cat. II); Sheffield City Art Gallery, 1986 (cat. 3).

5

# Sir John Arnesby Brown
## 1866–1955

An article in the *Studio* in 1917 attributed Sir Arnesby Brown's great popularity to the 'broadly bucolic interest' of the subject matter of his pictures, and said that 'without sentimentality' or 'special reference to sport ... they combine two of the most fundamental interests of the great majority of English people: love of the country and love of animals.'[1]

Born in Nottingham, Brown received all his artistic training in England. He had worked for a year in an office until 'commerce was once and for all abandoned',[2] and had then enrolled at Nottingham School of Art before entering the studio of the Nottingham painter Andrew McCallum (1821–1902). Here he painted 'in the open air' and 'learned the importance of seeing clearly and correctly.'[3] Between 1889 and 1892 he studied at the Herkhomer School in Bushey where he gained greater technical expertise.

Brown began exhibiting at the Royal Academy in 1890, returning briefly to Nottingham after completing his studies at Bushey. Painting portraits to supplement his income – as he did until about 1925 – Brown saved enough to move to St Ives: there he met artists such as Adrian Stokes (q.v.) and Julius Olsson (q.v.) who had been similarly attracted by the mild climate. Brown, however, was not interested in depicting the sea, but instead concentrated on rural scenes, usually featuring cattle. The purchase of *The Drinking Pool*[4] by the Corporation of Manchester in 1895 seemed to confirm to Brown that he had chosen the right direction in his art.

Brown first visited Norfolk in 1896 and spent the summer at Haddiscoe where he made many studies of the moon rising over the marshes. These culminated in the *Herald of the Night*,[5] which was exhibited at the Academy in the following year and was bought by Worcester Art Gallery. Soon after his marriage in 1896 to Mia Edwards, a painter of children's portraits, Brown bought a house in Norfolk (first at Ludham and then at Haddiscoe) and his life took on a regular pattern. He spent the summer and autumn painting in Norfolk, then, late in the year, he would go to St Ives, and, in a studio by the sea, he would work on his pictures for the spring exhibitions.

Although Brown worked out of doors, the final composition was painted in his studio, as he felt this should be treated 'in an entirely different manner' and should 'contain all I have to say on that subject ... I know the effect in nature I am working for, and I can remember my first impression of the scene vividly for a long time, which is a decided asset.'[6]

In the 1900s Brown's reputation became firmly established. A work entitled *Morning* (London, Tate Gallery) was purchased for the Chantrey Bequest and in 1903 he was elected an Associate of the Royal Academy. Following a successful one-man exhibition at the Leicester Galleries, Brown bought a house in Chelsea in 1910 and ceased visiting Cornwall, preferring to spend the winters in London. He was elected a full member of the Academy in 1915.

After the death of his wife in 1931 he retired to Norfolk, making only occasional sketching tours to Scotland, Cumbria and Nottinghamshire. In his later paintings his favourite cattle subjects tended to be treated in twilight conditions, rather than under the midday sun. His work continued to be highly regarded: he was one of the artists represented in the British section at the Venice Biennale exhibition in 1934, and that same year a retrospective exhibition of his work was held at Norwich Castle Museum. In 1938 Brown received a knighthood, and at about the same time his eyesight began to fail; he became totally blind at the age of eighty-two. When he died in 1955, a friend, the parish priest, wrote that although 'a little lonely ... he knew no bitterness or resentment in his enforced retirement.'[7]

H.C.V.

NOTES
1. *Studio*, 71 (1917), p. 129.
2. *Art Journal*, 1903, p. 86.
3. ibid., p. 86.
4. Repr., *Royal Academy Pictures*, 1895, p. 151.
5. Repr., ibid., 1897, p. 54.
6. *The Artist*, August 1933, p. 187.
7. *Sir Arnesby Brown*, exhib. cat., Norwich Castle Museum, 1959, p. 5.

*repr. in colour on p. 45*

## 6  The Raincloud

63.5 × 76.5 cm    25 × 30½ in
Signed bl: *Arnesby Brown*
Diploma work, accepted 11 May 1915 (C.M. XXIII, p. 291)

Cattle (presumably in a Norfolk landscape), the subject matter of *The Raincloud*, is typical of Brown's work. In 1917 the *Studio* commented that 'Eastern Counties, with their tall thundery skies, rolling woods, lush meadows', and 'broad-flanked bullocks' inspired the highest qualities in Brown's paintings.[1] The title of the work is also characteristic. Brown never used a line of poetry to help evoke an atmosphere, but instead chose a title 'as short and simple' as he could find, thinking that 'if an artist has felt a scene sharply, he ought to be able to pass on that feeling to the spectator' without the use of literary quotations.[2]

Although Brown worked out of doors he felt that for the final composition 'the artist must re-arrange, must eliminate and add, and must design to suit his ideas.'[3] Thus in *The Raincloud*

the cows, the trees, and the sky were all designed to fit his final composition. Trees, for instance, interested him as 'cliffy masses rather than individual organisms' and he showed no inclination 'to dwell on the tracery of the boughs.'[4] Likewise his cows 'are felt as parts of the whole, so that his profound knowledge of their anatomy is concealed rather than exposed.'[5] Brown often made the sky the main motif of a painting; here it creates an oppressive atmosphere suggesting an impending storm, which pervades the entire picture. To Brown, skies were never 'mere backgrounds' but were 'always of vital importance in his general scheme' as they have 'a dramatic quality which is immensely valuable.'[6] Contemporary critics admired Brown's efforts to capture the realities of nature in broad, decisive terms, and found *The Raincloud* 'vigorous'[7] and 'most convincing in its power'.[8] They also respected his 'boldly architectural conception' of a scene and in particular its representation of space, finding 'its weighty foundations below and its lofty vaults above'[9] most satisfying.

The broad effects which Brown achieved in his landscapes were due largely to his bold brushwork and occasional use of a palette knife. Even the brushstrokes 'in both scale and direction' bore 'the strictest organic relation to the general design'.[10] In *The Raincloud*, for instance, the movement of the cows walking towards the spectator is partly suggested by the strong vertical brushstrokes in the foreground of the picture.

NOTES
1. *Studio*, 71 (1917), p. 135.
2. *The Changing Hours*, exhib. cat., London, Leicester Galleries, 1909, p. 7; *The Artist*, August 1933, p. 187.
3. *The Artist*, August 1933, p. 187.
4. *Studio*, 71 (1917), p. 130.
5. idem.
6. *Studio, Modern Painting III: The Work of Arnesby Brown*, 1921, p. 4.
7. *Connoisseur*, 42 (1915), p. 122.
8. *Studio*, 65 (1915), p. 25.
9. *Studio*, 71 (1917), p. 130.
10. ibid., p. 134.

EXHIBITIONS: R.A., 1915 (cat. 182); Bournemouth, Russell-Cotes Art Gallery & Museum, 1957 (cat. 882); Norwich Castle Museum, 1959 (cat. 5); Bournemouth, Russell-Cotes Art Gallery & Museum, 1965 (cat. 7); R.A., Winter, 1968 (cat. 481); London, Royal Society of British Artists, 1971 (cat. 97).

# Reginald Grange Brundrit
## 1883–1960

Although born in Toxteth, Liverpool, Reginald Brundrit was associated most closely with the landscape of Yorkshire. For many years his north-country landscapes were a mainstay of the Royal Academy's Summer Exhibitions.

Brundrit's connection with Yorkshire began when, after the death of his father in 1886, he moved with his family to Skipton, a small market town bordering on the Yorkshire Dales. After a grammar school education, he attended Bradford School of Art, and in 1903 the Slade School of Art in London where the teaching staff included the landscape painter Philip Wilson Steer. Brundrit claimed, however, that his greatest debt was to John M. Swan, the esteemed animal painter and teacher at a private art school in Stratford Road, Kensington, where Brundrit's art education was completed. In 1906, Brundrit took a flat in Skipton and a studio in the nearby village of Grassington. He exhibited at the Cartwright Hall Spring Exhibitions in Bradford, and his work was first shown at the Royal Academy in the Summer Exhibition in 1906.

The First World War interrupted his career and he served as a volunteer driver for the British Red Cross, seeing action in the Battle of Isnozo in Trentino. Five of his wartime drawings were subsequently purchased by the Imperial War Museum.

During the 1920s, Brundrit's paintings acquired a technical assurance and a solidity of statement which distinguished them in the Academy's exhibitions. Acutely aware of surface texture, he seems to have built up his dour colour schemes with layers of oil rubbed off with a rag, before adding the final layer with brushes. Bright highlights were also a feature of landscapes such as The Last of the Snow (private collection)[1] and Ribblesdale (Blackpool, Grundy Art Gallery),[2] in which he captured the dramatic chiaroscuro of cloud shadow on a valley landscape.

During the 1930s Brundrit rose to quiet eminence in the established art world, being elected an A.R.A. in 1931 and in R.A. in 1938. He was deeply committed to the Academy and during his long career exhibited a total of 201 paintings in the Summer Exhibitions, his main point of contact with the public. He involved himself closely in the workings of the Royal Academy as a member of the Council and in 1938 wrote to the Secretary, Sir Walter Lamb, proposing 'drastic reform' of the candidature system for the election of members.[3] Brundrit's brief moment of glory in the Academy came in 1949 when, after the resignation of the President, Sir Alfred Munnings (q.v.), Brundrit received the greatest number of votes in the first ballot to decide a successor. However, in the later rounds Sir Gerald Kelly (q.v.) won the day, holding the post until 1954.[4] Munnings had attacked modern art in his notorious speech at the 1949 Annual Dinner,[5] but it seems that Brundrit's attitudes were more conciliatory. He is reported to have appealed for painters of the 'advanced schools' to submit their works for selection, promising them 'careful and impartial consideration'.[6]

In 1934, he scored a success with his painting 'Fresh-Air' Stubbs (London, Tate Gallery),[7] a half-length profile portrait which captured the bluff character and ruddy colouring of a Yorkshire publican known for his love of hunting and fishing.

More conventional portraits became an important part of Brundrit's output and he found a niche as the favourite portraitist of northern aristocrats, wool barons and civic dignitaries. His late work was considered by The Times to have acquired a 'greater variety of colouring and more reliance upon the constructive play of light and atmosphere',[8] and he abandoned the thick impasto characteristic of his earlier paintings. By the time of his death in 1960, he was a forgotten figure. However, an exhibition of his work organised by Bradford Museums and Art Galleries in 1980 has helped to re-establish him among the foremost landscape Academicians of the century.    T.J.B.

NOTES
1. Repr., H. M. Smith, Reginald Brundrit R.A. 1883–1960, Bradford Museums, 1980 (cat. 2).
2. Repr., Royal Academy Illustrated, 1929, p. 109; H. M. Smith, op. cit. (cat. 6).
3. Reginald Brundrit to Sir Walter Lamb, 20 July 1938, R.A. Archives, R. G. Brundrit File.
4. S. Hutchison, The History of the Royal Academy, 1768–1986, London, 1986, p. 171.
5. Sir Alfred Munnings, The Finish, London, 1952, pp. 144–7.
6. The Yorkshire Post, 29 April 1948, quoted H. M. Smith, op. cit.
7. Repr., Royal Academy Illustrated, 1936, p. 67; H. M. Smith, op. cit. (cat. 19).
8. The Times, 28 Nov 1960.

## 7  English Landscape

54 × 74 cm    $21\frac{1}{4}$ × $29\frac{1}{8}$ in
Signed br: Brundrit
Diploma work, accepted 15 March 1938 (C.M. XXVII, p. 95)

Brundrit's choice of Diploma work reflects his wish to be remembered as a painter of the English countryside. Eschewing a topographical title, he painted a stretch of lowland England, a gently undulating country with a ploughed field in the foreground, crowned by a dramatic, cloudy sky. Despite evidence of a knowledge of Impressionism, there is nonetheless something uniquely English in his application of many colours of paint to depict sunlight shining through a layer of cloud. In this picture, Brundrit employs a characteristic technique, applying two distinct layers of paintwork; the lower layer, unthinned, provides a tonal background over which, using a greatly thinned upper layer, he depicts details of the ruts and furrows, trees and clouds. The Connoisseur considered the 'slumberous atmosphere' of An English Landscape to 'proclaim Mr Brundrit as one of the foremost interpreters of the British scene'.[1]

NOTE
1. Connoisseur, June 1937, p. 351.

EXHIBITIONS: R.A., 1937 (cat. 106); R.A., 1938 (cat. 160); Bournemouth, Russell-Cotes Art Gallery & Museum (cat. 8); R.A., Winter, 1968 (cat. 478); Bradford Art Galleries and Museums, 1980 (cat. 23).

## 8  Nightfall

51.5 × 61 cm    $20\frac{1}{4}$ × 24 in
Signed br: Brundrit
Purchased by the Royal Academy (Stott Fund) 1 August 1961 (C.M. XXIX, p. 455)

EXHIBITIONS: R.A., 1940 (cat. 519); R.A., 1961 (cat. 237); Bradford Art Galleries and Museums, 1980 (cat. 25).

7

8

# Rodney Joseph Burn
## 1899–1984

Noted for his seascapes and landscapes, Burn also executed portraits and figure drawings as well as several paintings of mothers and children, one of which he deposited as his Diploma work on being elected an Academician in 1963. Burn was born in London in 1899, one of three sons of Sir Joseph Burn KBE, General Manager of the Prudential Assurance Company. After attending Harrow School, Burn went to the Slade School of Art in 1918 where he was a student of Henry Tonks. Following a successful career at the Slade, during which time he won the Summer Composition Prize of 1921, he gained the support of leading figures in the art world such as Charles Aitken, then Director of the Tate Gallery, and D. S. MacColl, Keeper of the Wallace Collection. In 1922, he was one of eight students from leading London Art Schools to be chosen to paint lunettes for the new County Hall, home of the London County Council, although the commission was never actually completed.

In 1923 Burn married the sculptress Margaret Sherwood Smith, the same year that he began exhibiting regularly at the New English Art Club. Three years later he was elected a member and also showed at the Goupil Gallery. He later became the Honorary Secretary of the Club. His works were first hung at the Royal Academy in 1945, to which he was elected an Associate in 1954 and a full Academician in 1962. Burn had a distinguished teaching career, working at the Royal College of Art from 1929 to 1931 and for some years after the Second World War. He later taught at the City and Guilds School of Art and in the early 1930s spent three years in the United States as joint Director of the Boston Museum School of Fine Arts. He also taught briefly at Edinburgh College of Art. Burn was awarded an Honorary Fellowship by the Royal College of Art and by University College, London and was President of the St Ives School of Artists for a while.

Burn's favourite subject was the sea. Working in oil and watercolour, he frequently chose to depict coastal scenes near Chichester in Sussex, especially East and West Wittering and Bracklesham Bay, and the Isle of Wight. A seascape featuring Bembridge on the Isle of Wight was purchased for the Chantrey Bequest in 1953. Burn also painted several views of the River Thames near Strand-on-the-Green, Chiswick, his home for twenty-eight years. Although much of his work is characterised by its sketchy and impressionistic technique it nevertheless reveals Burn's strength as a draughtsman and his underlying interest in carefully structured compositions. Examples of his work can be found in the collections of the Tate Gallery, the Victoria & Albert Museum and many provincial galleries. E.C.W.

*repr. in colour on p. 49*

## 9  Bracklesham Sands

51 × 61 cm    20 × 24 in
Signed br: *R J B*
Purchased by the Royal Academy (Harrison Weir Fund) 29 April 1965

This is one of four paintings of the beach at Bracklesham that Burn exhibited at the Royal Academy between 1965 and 1967. Throughout his career he painted many seascapes of this area near Chichester in Sussex. In this painting his principle interest is the broad expanse of sand and sky revealed at low tide. The figures are almost incidental and positioned so as to enhance the overall sensation of space. Together with the tide mark, breakwater and surf they also serve to structure the composition, and to lead the spectator's eye to the horizon. As in many of his paintings the artist has taken a low viewpoint for greater involvement in the scene. Burn's impressionistic handling of the paint contributes to the sense of light and atmosphere in the picture.

EXHIBITIONS: R.A., 1965 (cat. 79); Stour Music Festival, 1967.

# Sir David Young Cameron
## 1865–1945

A distinguished painter, etcher and watercolourist of landscape and architectural subjects, Cameron was born in Glasgow in 1865, the son of the Rev. Robert Cameron. He began his studies at the Glasgow School of Art around 1881 before enrolling at Edinburgh School of Art in 1885. Encouraged by the amateur artist George Stevenson, Cameron took up etching and achieved early success in this medium. In 1889, he was elected an associate of the Royal Society of Painter-Etchers, where he exhibited regularly between 1889 and 1902. Inspired by a variety of locations both in his native Scotland and abroad in Holland, Belgium, France and Italy, his etchings showed the influence of Rembrandt, Whistler and Meryon. A master of line and tone, he often romanticised his subjects and there was always a ready market for his work. He began exhibiting at the Royal Academy in 1903 and was elected an Associate member in the engraver class in 1911.

Cameron's early paintings and watercolours were eclectic and demonstrated his interest in artists such as Velazquez, Whistler and the Barbizon School painters. A visit to Holland around 1892 familiarised him with the work of the Hague School of Artists, particularly the Maris brothers whose evocative landscapes, genre scenes and church interiors also had an effect on his work. By the time he was elected an Associate member of the Royal Academy, this time as a painter in 1916, Cameron was well known for his atmospheric highland landscapes and poetic architectural scenes. Writing about some of his Scottish and Egyptian landscapes in 1912, the critic from the *Studio* praised the order and simplicity of his compositions as well as the 'regard for tonal relationship ... and for breadth of unity and effect',[1] before going on to remark: 'In Mr. Cameron's work every line seems selected and final. So determined, so selective is Mr. Cameron's design that one feels on studying one of his canvases that each note, each line, each passage possesses an individuality of its own.'[2]

Characterised by spare drawing and thin but powerful washes of colour, Cameron's watercolours received similar acclaim. Elected a member of the Royal Society of Painters in Watercolour in 1906, Cameron was a regular exhibitor at the annual exhibitions. In 1929 a critic from *Apollo* praised one of his watercolours of the Scottish highlands for 'the constructive masses formally balanced, like those of light and shade, so much indicated, so little elaborated, the hint of a deer sufficient to suggest wild solitudes'.[3] Cameron also exhibited at the International Society of Artists and at the Goupil Gallery and sent in work to the Royal Scottish Academy of which he was elected an Associate in 1904 and a full member in 1918. He was knighted in 1924 and appointed King's Painter and Limner in Scotland in 1933. A Trustee of the Tate Gallery between 1921 and 1927, he died in Perth in 1945. E.C.W.

NOTES
1. *Studio*, 55 (1912), p. 263.
2. idem.
3. *Apollo*, Vol. 10 (1929), p. 221.

## 10 Interior of Durham Cathedral

91 × 73 cm    35 × 28 in
Signed bl: *D. Y. Cameron*
Diploma work, accepted 23 March 1920 (C.M. XXIV, pp. 205–08)

This interior view along an aisle of Durham Cathedral is a typical example of the series of architectural subjects which Cameron had started painting around 1916. The critic from the *Connoisseur* found it more naturalistic than most of the artist's work to date. He also remarked that 'it shows great restraint in its colouration. An impressive effect is produced by the arrangement of a deep framework of shadow around the high lights of the picture, but the darks are almost too massed together, and consequently appear heavy and monotonous.'[1] Like his landscapes, the painting is characterised by its simple design and atmospheric tone. The dramatic play of light which divides the painting into solid blocks of colour is reminiscent of Dutch prototypes, whilst the precisely recorded, linear detail on the pillars is indicative of Cameron's work as an etcher.

NOTE
1. *Connoisseur*, June 1921, p. 116.

EXHIBITIONS: R.A., 1920 (cat. 325); Bournemouth, Russell-Cotes Art Gallery & Museum, 1957 (cat. 11); Glasgow Art Gallery and Museum, 1965, (cat. 36); R.A., Winter, 1968 (cat. 482).

*(Illustrated overleaf)*

10   Sir David Young Cameron *Interior of Durham Cathedral*

# Sir George Clausen
## 1852–1944

Although he studied abroad, Clausen's work was quintessentially English, depicting Hardyesque characters 'of uncouth manner and aspect, stolid understanding and snail like movement'.[1] As in Hardy's novels, Clausen's canvasses tended to idealise rural life rather than to comment on social conditions.

Clausen was born in London in 1852, son of a decorative painter of Danish descent. By the age of fifteen, he was working for Messrs. Trollope, a firm of decorators, and studying perspective in the evenings at the South Kensington Schools. After a fortuitous meeting with the painter Edwin Long, Clausen began to pursue his career as a painter more seriously. He attended the South Kensington Schools for two years, during which time he researched details in the British Museum for the subjects of Long's classical and biblical paintings. He concluded his studies by travelling to the Low Countries and France. As a contemporary critic wrote: 'although he cannot be said to have received any academic training Mr. Clausen was thrown into the society of men who had, and through their influences he may be said to have lost his timidity in Antwerp, and, later on, to have acquired the refinements of contour and modelling of the French school.'[2]

Influenced particularly by the Hague School, Clausen exhibited Dutch subjects until 1883. *High Mass at a Fishing Village on the Zuyder Zee* (Nottingham Castle Museum), his first work to be exhibited at the Royal Academy, was favourably received. At the Grosvenor Gallery in 1880, he was impressed by the work of his fellow exhibitor Jules Bastien-Lepage. Like other British painters, Clausen was particularly drawn to Bastien-Lepage's brand of realism: the French artist depicted his subjects, wrote Clausen, 'without the appearance of artifice, but as they live; and without comment, as far as is possible on the author's part.'[3] Clausen moved into the Hertfordshire countryside, to Childwick Green, and, using the square brush technique of Bastien-Lepage, began to paint farm labourers 'doing simple things under good conditions of lighting'.[4]

In 1882 Clausen was painting at Quimperlé in Brittany with Stanhope Forbes (q.v.), also an admirer of Bastien-Lepage. Remaining in France the following year, he briefly attended the Académie Julian under Bouguereau. The prevalent mood among the many British artists whom Clausen met in France was one of disenchantment with the quality of the teaching and of the exhibited paintings in England. In 1886 some of these discontented artists grouped together to form the New English Art Club. Although Clausen was a founding member, he ceased to exhibit there once elected an A.R.A. in 1895, and transferred his allegiance to the Academy exhibitions.

*The Girl at the Gate*, 1889 (London, Tate Gallery), marks the height of Bastien-Lepage's influence on Clausen's work. The painting was bought for the Chantrey Bequest, but in spite of this accolade Clausen began to question his reliance on the French artist's example. He came to value Courbet, in whose work 'everything was cleared away but the essentials; and at a little distance Courbet showed in full power and completeness', whereas Lepage's 'delicate and beautiful work ... was lost and the picture flat and unintelligible. No doubt Bastien-Lepage worked for truth of impression and of detail too, but it is apparently impossible to get both.'[5] Whilst Clausen continued to produce rustic subjects on an intimate scale, he also began to work on mural-like paintings of monumental proportions, suitable for exhibition at the Royal Academy. This grand manner is exemplified in *The Boy and the Man* (Bradford Art Galleries & Museums), exhibited in 1908, the year he was elected a full Academician. His work in pastels from the early 1890s had invigorated his oils with a sense of movement and richer colours.

Clausen's reaction to the First World War found expression in two major canvasses. *In the Gun Factory at Woolwich Arsenal 1918* (London, Imperial War Museum), a work commissioned by the Ministry of Information, represents his grand public manner. In *Youth Mourning* (London, Imperial War Museum), however, Clausen betrayed a more personal response to a war in which his daughter's fiancé had been killed.

At seventy-five he undertook an important mural commission in the House of Commons to paint *The English People reading Wycliffe's Bible*, the success of which resulted in a knighthood in 1927. After the completion of the Westminster mural he increasingly concentrated on small landscapes in oil and watercolour, many of which dwell on morning mists in the Essex countryside near his country retreat at Duton Hill. In his eighties and nineties, fêted as the 'grand old man' of British art, Clausen increasingly turned to watercolour, feeling that it had 'something of the spontaneity and effortless rightness that one finds in Nature itself.'[6] Throughout Clausen's experimentation with various styles and subjects he believed that a 'fine painting like a fine piece of literature, gives more than it professes and in the guise of simple representation conveys to us the experience, perceptions and emotions of a peculiarly sensitive nature.'[7]
H.C.V.

NOTES
1.  T. Hardy, 'The Dorsetshire Labourer', *Longmans Magazine*, July 1883, p. 252, quoted K. McConkey, *Sir George Clausen, R.A. 1852–1944*, exhib. cat., Bradford Art Galleries and Museums and Tyne and Wear County Council Museums, 1980, p. 11.
2.  D. Bates, 'George Clausen, A.R.A.', *Studio*, 5 (1895), p. 4.
3.  Sir G. Clausen, 'Autobiographical Notes', *Artwork*, 25 (Spring 1931), p. 19; K. McConkey, op. cit., p. 29.
4.  G. Clausen, 'Bastien-Lepage and Modern Realism', *Scottish Art Review*, I (1888), p. 114; K. McConkey, op. cit., p. 31.
5.  G. Clausen, 'Jules Bastien-Lepage as artist' in A. Theuriet, *Jules Bastien-Lepage and his Art*, 1892, p. 115; K. McConkey, op. cit., p. 33.
6.  J. Littlejohns, *British Watercolour Painting and Painters of Today*, 1931, p. 31; K. McConkey, op. cit., p. 97.
7.  G. Clausen, *Royal Academy Lectures on Painting*, 1913, p. 325.

## 11  Mark Fisher R. A.

61.5 × 51.5 cm    24¼ × 20¼ in
Signed and dated bl: *G. CLAUSEN 1900*
Purchased by the Royal Academy (Stott Fund) 18 Jan 1938 (C.M. XXVII, p. 78)

George Clausen and Mark Fisher (q.v.) were close friends, both living at Widdington in Essex during the 1890s. In his appreciation written for the catalogue of Fisher's memorial exhibition of 1924, Clausen recalled that '[Fisher's] friends will remember not only the fine artist, but the attractive personality of the man, full of light and shade of "accents" like his paintings, his shrewd simplicity, his worldly wisdom and his kindness.'[1]

NOTE
1. *Memorial exhibition of works by Mark Fisher*, exhib. cat., London, Leicester Galleries, 1924; quoted V. Lines, *Mark Fisher and Margaret Fisher Prout*, 1966, p. 27.

EXHIBITION: London, Arts Club, 1957–64, long term loan.

## 12  Interior of an Old Barn

91.5 × 76.5 cm    36 × 30 in
Signed and dated br: *G. CLAUSEN, 1908.*
Diploma work, accepted 3 Nov 1908 (C.M. XXII, p. 173)

Acknowledging his election as an Associate in 1895 Clausen wrote to the Academy: 'I am very proud to be thought worthy [of] this distinction: may I say from my heart that I will do my utmost to prove myself so.'[1] In spite of his earlier involvement with the rival New English Art Club, Clausen's commitment to the Academy was confirmed by his appointment in 1903 as

Professor of Painting at the Royal Academy Schools. His first series of lectures given in 1904 ran to three editions, and his election to full membership of the Academy in 1908 came as no surprise. He considered this a great honour and was anxious to produce a worthy Diploma work. In July 1908 he wrote to Council 'apologising for not having sent in his Diploma work within the prescribed time, but hoping to have it ready by October.'[2] It was finally sent in November.

As early as 1884, barn and stable interiors appear in Clausen's sketchbooks, but it was not until 1897 that the first in a long series of such subjects was exhibited at the Royal Academy. Entitled *The Old Barn* (untraced),[3] it similarly contrasted a farmer resting on a stick in the middle distance with a man working in the background. In a painting such as *The Golden Barn* (Rochdale Art Gallery) he suffused the interior with warm yellow light, but in many of his other representations his main concern was the strong contrast of light and shade. His Diploma work was particularly admired for being 'full of knowledge and skill'[4] and for its 'true treatment of the cross lights.'[5] The chiaroscuro is pronounced, with the nearest figure seen only in silhouette. Perhaps influenced by his work in pastels, the painting is unusually highly coloured, with light entering the barn from both the side and rear, and blue highlights showing on the man and the ground. The brushwork, liberated from Bastien-Lepage's influence, is free and uninhibited.

By 1908 Clausen was no longer living in the country, but, having bought himself a bicycle in 1906, would regularly spend several weeks sketching around Clavering in Essex. Often, as here, the importance of the figurative element in his work lessened, perhaps because he no longer had the opportunities to observe labourers at work all the year round. A sketch in the Academy's collection shows that Clausen was particularly concerned with the pose of the man leaning on a stick. In the final version, the man leans more heavily on his support and the figure has greater animation. Contemporary reviewers felt that Clausen's Diploma work was a very satisfactory variation on one of his favourite themes. The *Art Journal* noted that 'Mr Clausen is no stranger to studies of this kind: but he introduces a deeper note ... a really excellent Clausen year.'[6]

NOTES
1. Letter from G. Clausen to the Secretary of the R.A., 27 Jan 1895, R.A. Archives, RAC/1/CL 1.
2. C.M. XXII, p. 165, 28 July 1908.
3. Repr., *Royal Academy Pictures*, 1897, p. 27.
4. *The Saturday Review*, 8 May 1909, p. 590.
5. *The Academy*, 8 May 1909, p. 82.
6. *Art Journal*, 1909, p. 168.

EXHIBITIONS: R.A., 1909 (cat. 25); Bournemouth, Russell-Cotes Art Gallery & Museum, 1957 (cat. 865); Bournemouth, Russell-Cotes Art Gallery & Museum, 1965 (cat. 13); R.A., Winter, 1968 (cat. 423); Bradford Art Gallery, 1980 (cat. 103); Swansea, Glynn Vivian Art Gallery & Museum, 1985 (cat. 22).

12

# Philip Connard
## 1875–1958

Born in 1875 at Southport in Lancashire, Connard first went into the building trade as a house painter and attended evening classes in art. His career as a fine artist began in earnest in 1896, when he won a National Scholarship to attend the Royal College of Art at South Kensington. In 1898 he went to Paris to continue his studies under Benjamin Constant and Jean-Paul Laurens assisted by a British Institute travelling scholarship which lasted for six months. At the end of this time, he worked for a short while as a designer in a carpet factory at Liège.

Back in London, Connard was employed as an illustrator before taking up a teaching position at the Lambeth School of Art. Meanwhile he gained a reputation as a painter of decorative compositions, *plein-air* landscapes and interior scenes executed in a fresh and spontaneous manner. From 1901 he began exhibiting work at the New English Art Club and, with the support of Philip Wilson Steer and Henry Tonks, was elected a member in 1909. In addition he also painted portraits and became a founder member of the National Portrait Society in 1911. Following the success of his first one-man show at the Leicester Galleries in 1912, Connard gave up his teaching post and took up painting full-time. Until the outbreak of the First World War, under the influence of Steer, he concentrated on painting portrait groups of his family, and river scenes in London, Suffolk and Norfolk in varying weather conditions. During the War he saw active service in France until he was invalided out in 1916 and became an Official War Artist attached to the Royal Navy.

Connard first exhibited at the Royal Academy in 1918 and was elected an Associate member in the same year. Although best-known for his stylised pastoral landscapes with figures and decorative bird paintings which he exhibited there throughout the 1920s, Connard continued to paint naturalistic *plein-air* seascapes and bathing scenes, leading the critic of the *Studio* to remark that, 'in spite of his academic honours, he is not academic in the generally accepted sense, and the honours are, for that reason, a credit to the Academy. He belongs, if anywhere, to the middle school of modern art: he would be "New English" if he were not so much himself, having some of that school's whimsical lightness of touch, and freedom from the improper propriety of drawing and attitude associated with the diehard Academician.'[1] Elected an R.A. in 1925, Connard became Keeper of the Schools twenty years later from 1945 to 1949. His major commissions included murals on the theme of Royal Residences for the Queen's Doll's House at Windsor in 1924 and a decorative panel on the subject of England for the dining room of the liner *Queen Mary*. He was awarded a C.V.O. in 1950.

Apart from oils, Connard also worked in watercolour. He exhibited regularly at the Royal Society of Painters in Watercolour and, from 1932 made many studies in both media of scenery around Richmond, Surrey where he lived until his death in 1958. The brilliant colour key of the early landscapes gave way to more subtle silvery-grey tones through which the artist captured the effects of light and atmosphere.   E.C.W.

NOTE
1.  *Studio*, 85 (1923), p. 305.

*repr. in colour on p. 29*

## 13   Apollo and Daphne

76.5 × 63 cm    30¼ × 25 in
Signed br: *Connard*
Diploma work, accepted 30 April 1925 (C.M. XXV, p. 131)

It is perhaps significant that, despite his continuing interest in *plein-air* landscapes and seascapes, Connard chose to deposit a painting with a classical theme as his Diploma work. The subject is drawn from the Greek myth of Apollo's attempt to seduce Daphne, the daughter of the river god Peneus. When she refused to submit, Apollo attempted to ravish her but she fled. Like the pastoral scenes he exhibited at the Royal Academy in the early 1920s, *Apollo and Daphne* is poetic in mood and decoratively painted. There is an emphasis on movement and both the figures and the landscape are spontaneously and freely painted. The speckled brushstrokes underline the fleeting nature of the theme and the drama is heightened by the use of artificially bright colours.

EXHIBITIONS: R.A., 1925 (cat. 3); Bournemouth, Russell-Cotes Art Gallery & Museum, 1965 (cat. 14); R.A., Winter, 1968 (cat. 457); Folkestone Arts Centre, 1974 (cat. 10); South London Art Gallery, 1973 (cat. 44).

# Frank Cadogan Cowper
## 1877–1958

*The Times* obituary recalled that there had been 'little of the traditional artist in Cowper's appearance and he is said to have worn higher collars than any other man in the country.'[1] Cowper's work was in many ways similarly outdated, in that he was influenced throughout his artistic career by Pre-Raphaelite painters, notably Burne-Jones.

Frank Cadogan Cowper was born in 1877, at Wicken in Northamptonshire, the son of an author. He entered St John's Wood Art School in 1896 and enrolled at the Royal Academy Schools in 1897. He was greatly influenced during this time by exhibitions of the work of Ford Madox Brown (1896), Rossetti (1898) and Millais (1898). Cowper's work was first accepted at the Academy in 1899, and his first notable success was *An Aristocrat Answering the Summons to Execution, Paris, 1793*,[2] exhibited in 1901. In 1902, after completing his training, Cowper travelled in Italy before working for six months in the studio of E. A. Abbey R.A., a painter of historical subjects. In common with the earlier Pre-Raphaelite painters, minute detail and rich colours predominated in Cowper's work, and his output in early years appears to have been small (he only exhibited one or two pictures each year at the Academy until 1913). Following the example of the Pre-Raphaelite, Holman Hunt, Cowper took immense trouble researching his subjects, travelling to Assisi before painting *St Francis of Assisi and the Heavenly Melody*,[3] and having a grave dug for his depiction of *Hamlet – the churchyard scene*, exhibited in 1902.

Cowper usually chose historical, literary or religious subjects for his pictures in which it was thought that he 'showed a good deal of invention'.[4] In 1905 *St. Agnes in Prison receiving from Heaven the 'Shining White Garment'* (London, Tate Gallery)[5] was bought for the Chantrey Bequest: the minutely observed straw on the floor of the prison cell is reminiscent of that in Millais's *The Return of the Dove to the Arc* (Oxford, Ashmolean Museum). His reputation, however, was firmly established with *The Devil, disguised as a vagrant troubadour, having been entertained by some charitable nuns, sang to them a song of love*.[6] The scene was set against a backdrop of the fifteenth-century stained glass windows of Fairford Church in Gloucester, and the picture was highly praised for its 'splendid painting of the great flaming window ... the very clever grouping of the figures' and for the 'accurate and expressive chiaroscuro of the whole scene.'[7] After the success of this picture, Cowper was elected A.R.A. in 1907, while still only thirty years old. However, he had to wait another twenty-seven years before being made R.A., in 1934.

In 1910 Cowper was commissioned to paint a mural for the House of Commons depicting a Tudor scene, and in 1912 completed further decorative panels there. By this time he had begun to exhibit portraits at the Academy which, in the 1910s, were often painted in historicist guises derived from earlier painters. For example, in his portrait of *Sir Eyre Coote*,[8] Cowper adopted the manner of Holbein, depicting his sitter in sixteenth-century costume. In the 1920s he began painting numerous portraits of women, with softer effects and a 'cloying sweetness'. Critics thought them unsuccessful, finding them failing 'less from a lack of ability than from a confusion of aim; a mixture of the decorative and the realistic that spoiled both.'[9]

During the Second World War Cowper moved to Jersey, but later returned to England, and settled in Gloucestershire in 1944. There was some controversy over certain of his pictures in the 1950s, such as *The Jealous Husband*, exhibited in 1952, depicting a man disguised as a priest hearing his wife's confession, a subject which some felt inappropriate for exhibition at the Academy. Cowper continued to exhibit until 1957. He died in Cirencester the following year, aged eighty-one.   H.C.V.

NOTES
1. *The Times*, 20 Nov 1958.
2. Repr., *Royal Academy Pictures*, 1901, p. 185.
3. Repr., ibid., 1904, p. 162.
4. *The Times*, 20 Nov 1958.
5. Repr., *Royal Academy Pictures*, 1905, p. 23.
6. London, Christie's catalogue, 27 Nov 1987, lot. 136.
7. *Daily Telegraph*, 17 May 1907.
8. Repr., *Royal Academy Pictures*, 1912, p. 80.
9. *The Times*, 20 Nov 1958.

14   *repr. in colour on p. 25*

## 14 Vanity

57 × 38 cm  22½ × 15 in
Signed and dated br: *F C COWPER 1907*
Diploma work, accepted 23 June 1936 (C.M. XXVI, p. 502)

Cowper initially offered the Academy his painting *Yseult the Fair, Queen of Cornwall* for his Diploma work (presumably the picture exhibited at the Academy in 1928, no. 467). The Council, however, asked Cowper to offer, if possible, several smaller works from which a Diploma work could be selected.[1] A similar request had been made to Mark Fisher (q.v.) in 1920, so presumably lack of space was still a problem in the Diploma Galleries where the works were destined to hang. Cowper therefore offered *Vanity*, a picture he regarded highly, which he had bought back at Christie's in 1921 for £125, and which he 'really wanted to keep'.[2] Cowper wrote to the Council that he was sending 'one of my best known works'[3] which 'was beautifully placed' when exhibited in 1907 and that it 'probably had more to do with my election [as Associate] than my larger picture "The Devil and the Nuns".'[4]

Cowper's signature appears on a small cartellino, painted to appear as if pinned to the cloth. An article in the *Studio* in 1903 had singled out Cowper as 'rapidly coming to the front as the leader of the group of young painters known as the "Label School"'[5] because of the way in which they signed their work. Other members of this 'School', probably no more than a group of loosely-associated artists, included John Byam Liston Shaw and Eleanor Fortesque Brickdale, both also strongly influenced by Pre-Raphaelite painters.

The subject matter and format here are derived from Italian Renaissance painting. In the traditional manner, Cowper has bedecked the figure with jewels and given her the usual attribute of a mirror to convey the idea of vanity. The pose of the figure leaning on the parapet, covered by a cloth, was a common compositional device used in many depictions of the Virgin and Child during the Renaissance. The serpentine design on the dress of the figure was either directly or indirectly inspired by a portrait of *Isabella d'Este* attributed to Giulio Romano (London, Hampton Court Palace). Edward Burne-Jones, in his watercolour depicting *Sidonia von Bork*, 1860 (London, Tate Gallery), also used this design. Cowper was probably influenced by Burne-Jones's composition, although it is possible that he went to Hampton Court Palace to study the original.

Cowper would not have known the Pre-Raphaelite painters he so admired, as most of them had died before he reached artistic maturity. Nonetheless in *Vanity* he consciously revived many of the distinctive decorative elements so characteristic of Pre-Raphaelitism; the use of rich colours, minutely observed details of luxurious fabrics, and the adoption of a style strongly reminiscent of Florentine Renaissance painters.

NOTES
1. C.M. XXVI, p. 499, 3 June 1936.
2. Letter from F. C. Cowper to the Secretary of the R.A., 21 June 1936, R.A. Archives, RAC/1/CO 16.
3. ibid.
4. Letter from F. C. Cowper to the Secretary of the R.A., 22 June 1936, R.A. Archives, RAC/1/CO 17.
5. *Studio*, 27 (1903), pp. 58–9.

EXHIBITIONS: R.A., 1907 (cat. 122); R.A., Winter, 1937 (cat. 93); Bournemouth, Russell-Cotes Art Gallery & Museum, 1965 (cat. 15); Cheltenham Art Gallery and Museums, 1985 (cat. 9); Japan, Tokyo Shimbun, touring exhibition, 1987 (cat. 60).

# Wilfred Gabriel De Glehn
## 1870–1951

De Glehn was primarily renowned for his portraits, landscapes and figure paintings in an Impressionist manner although he also designed some stained glass. He was born in London in 1870, the son of a merchant, Alexander von Glehn, and nephew of the painter Oswald von Glehn (Wilfred's surname was changed from 'von' to 'De' at the time of the First World War). After a general schooling at Brighton College, he studied at the South Kensington Schools for a short time. In 1890 he went to Paris, where he became a student at the Ecole des Beaux-Arts, studying initially under Elie Delaunay and then with Gustave Moreau. He stayed in Paris for six years during which time he developed his characteristic style under the influence of Impressionism. He began exhibiting at the Salon in 1891, and at the Galerie Durand-Ruel.

After his return to London, De Glehn began showing at the New English Art Club, of which he became a member in 1900, and at the Royal Academy where his works were hung regularly from 1896 until his death in 1951 (with the exception of the years during the First World War when he saw active service on the Italian Front). His first one-man show was held at the Carfax Gallery in 1908 and he also had exhibitions at the Goupil Gallery and Knoedler's. In 1904 he married Jane Emmett, a New Yorker and an associate of Henry James. She was an artist in her own right who also exhibited at the Academy and was known mainly for her portrait drawings. Elected an A.R.A. in 1923 and a R.A. in 1932, De Glehn was also a member of the Royal Society of Portrait Painters.

De Glehn painted a range of subjects throughout his career including formal and informal portraits of women, *plein-air* landscapes, mythological and decorative panels and sensuous nudes lying in interior or outdoor settings. Technically his work reflects the influence of his friend and colleague John Singer Sargent (q.v.) in terms of its loosely handled paint, thick impasto and interest in recording the play of light across the surface of rich materials such as silk and satin. De Glehn first came into contact with Sargent during the 1890s when he assisted him with the latter's mural commission for the Boston Public Library. They formed a lasting friendship and the De Glehns frequently accompanied Sargent on his sketching tours abroad. De Glehn travelled extensively during his lifetime, visiting Italy, France and North America on several occasions.   E.C.W.

*repr. in colour on p. 42*

## 15   Fishing

55.9 × 69.9 cm   22 × 27½ in
Signed bl: *De Glehn*
Diploma work, accepted 8 March 1932 (C.M. XXVI, p. 140)

De Glehn painted several subject-pictures such as *Fishing* which showed decorative young ladies in an idyllic outdoor setting. Stylistically and thematically, this summery scene shows the artist's affinity with the work of the Impressionists as well as his friend John Singer Sargent's later figure pictures (q.v.). His primary interest is in the effects of light on the figures, water and river bank, all of which are painted in the same high-keyed colours with directness and ease. Although loosely defined, De Glehn does not allow the forms to dissolve into light. Instead their underlying structure is maintained and some areas are highlighted with thick impasto.

EXHIBITIONS: R.A., 1932 (cat. 23); Bournemouth, Russell-Cotes Art Gallery & Museum, 1965 (cat. 17); Cheltenham Art Gallery and Museums, 1985 (cat. 7).

# Sir Frank Dicksee
## 1853–1928

Frank Dicksee was born in London in 1853 into an artistic family, and 'could not remember when he did not draw'.[1] His father, Thomas Francis Dicksee, taught him the rudiments of draughtsmanship before Dicksee entered the Royal Academy Schools in 1871.

In 1875 Dicksee won a gold medal for *Elijah confronting Ahab and Jezebel in Naboth's Vineyard*, which was subsequently exhibited at the Royal Academy in 1876. In the following year he exhibited *Harmony* (London, Tate Gallery) which was a great popular success and was purchased for the Chantrey Bequest. A medieval costume-piece, the picture depicts a youth listening raptly to a girl playing music. Dicksee had previously worked in the studio of Henry Holiday, a history painter and notable designer of stained glass, and this influence is evident in *Harmony* where Dicksee illuminates the scene by golden light flooding through a large stained glass window behind the young couple. The painting's subject was originally suggested by an evening at the Langham Sketching Club during which members were invited to make sketches on the theme of 'music'.

During the 1870s Dicksee worked extensively as an illustrator, contributing work to periodicals such as *Cornhill Magazine* and the *Graphic*. In the 1880s he received an important commission from Cassell and Co. to illustrate Longfellow's *Evangeline* (1882) and two plays from their Royal Shakespeare series, *Romeo and Juliet* and *Othello*. Partly stimulated by this work, and in common with Pre-Raphaelite painters, literary quotations from Shakespeare, Dante, Tennyson and Keats provided the subjects for many of Dicksee's works.

In 1881 at only twenty years of age, Dicksee was elected an Associate of the Academy. In the following year he toured Italy, where he developed a particular admiration for Giorgione, Titian and Veronese. In later years he also visited Holland, Switzerland, Germany and Tangiers.

In the 1890s Dicksee began painting portraits more frequently and, from the later 1910s, most of his exhibits at the Academy were portraits. In works such as *The Duchess of Buckingham and Chandos*[2] Dicksee delighted in depicting his subject's elaborate dress of brocade and lace. He did not, however, neglect subject painting and in 1891 exhibited *The Mountain of the Winds*.[3] This vigorous composition, following the work of G. F. Watts, bore a subtitle taken from a Greek quotation describing a mountain top 'where the four winds prepare to take breath for their courses on the earth'. Having achieved such success in the 1870s, Dicksee, unlike some of his fellow students, was not influenced by the more advanced ideas and techniques from the Paris *ateliers*; instead he continued to strive after an ideal of beauty derived from an academic tradition common to both the Royal Academy and the Paris Salon.

In 1891 Dicksee was elected a full Academician and his continuing popularity was confirmed with *The Two Crowns* (London, Tate Gallery). When exhibited in 1900 it was voted the 'Picture of the Year' by *Daily News* readers and was purchased for the Chantrey Bequest. The picture depicted the return of a medieval king, whose attention, in the midst of a triumphal procession, is caught by the sight of a crucifix. In 1924 Dicksee was elected President of the Royal Academy, and a knighthood followed in 1925. In the two discourses he gave to the students of the Royal Academy shortly before his death, he expounded his theory of art. He told students to 'get all the help you can from literature',[4] but said that their 'art should be guided by reference to nature and upheld by an ideal of beauty.'[5] Yet it must also be able 'to stir us to the depths of our being.'[6]

Dicksee died in London in 1928.   H.C.V.

NOTES
1. *Magazine of Art*, 1887, p. 217.
2. Repr., *Royal Academy Pictures*, 1901, p. 183.
3. Repr., ibid., 1891, p. 110.
4. F. Dicksee, *Discourse delivered to . . . on the Distribution of the Prizes*, 1925, p. 9.
5. ibid.; quoted *Country Life*, Jan 1985, p. 242.
6. F. Dicksee, *Discourse delivered to . . . on the Distribution of the Prizes*, 1927, p. 10.

## 16  Startled

99.5 × 69 cm   39½ × 27¼ in
Signed and dated br: *FRANK DICKSEE 1892*
Diploma work, accepted 28 March 1892 (C.M. XIX, p. 389)

Dicksee must have painted *Startled* in the winter of 1891–2, as he wrote to the Council in November 1891 informing them that he was still working on his Diploma painting.[1] It depicts two naked girls who have been surprised while bathing by what appears to be a Viking longship. *The Academy* found the subject matter confusing, saying that it 'does not appertain exactly either to idealistic or realistic art, and halts, indeed, somewhat unsatisfactorily between the two.'[2] Unlike most of Dicksee's previous work there is no quotation appended to the title, and the scene does not appear to illustrate a subject from literature. Instead, like *Harmony* (London, Tate Gallery), it is a purely imaginary subject, similarly resulting possibly from an evening spent at the Langham Sketching Club.

The figures here are lit by the setting sun and Dicksee, using a favourite compositional device, has the main light source emanating from behind them (in *Harmony* the figures are also illuminated from the back of the picture). The *Art Journal* questioned 'whether the rays of the sun, striking on the naked body through a canopy of green leaves, would not show greenish as well as the ruddy tones given.'[3] However, the luminous effect that Dicksee has achieved, through the suffusion of a warm, golden light, sets the mood of the picture.

Dicksee felt that Greek sculpture 'demonstrated ... the perfection of human form'[4] and his study of female nudes in *Startled* reflects his indebtedness to the academic tradition. Designing his pictures carefully, Dicksee made many preliminary studies; the Royal Academy collection includes a detailed study of the younger girl, in which he was primarily investigating the effect of light falling from behind. The strong white chalk highlights in this study are translated into golden highlights in the final picture. A contemporary critic wrote that the composition lacked the 'harmony which arrives from cunning balance and contrast', and that in addition it showed 'too great a monotony of line in the chief figures'.[5] However, another felt that in *Startled* Dicksee 'showed his mastery of the nude, simply studied in the open air' and that it was a 'spontaneous, unaffected and delightfully painted picture'.[6]

NOTES
1. Letter from Frank Dicksee to the Secretary of the R.A., 23 Nov 1891, R.A. Archives, RAC/1/DI 5.
2. *The Academy*, 7 May 1892, p.450.
3. *Art Journal*, 1892, p. 217.
4. F. Dicksee, *Discourse delivered to ... on the Distribution of the Prizes*, 1925, p. 6.
5. *The Academy*, 7 May 1892, p. 450.
6. *The Christmas Art Annual*, 1905, p. 12.

EXHIBITIONS: R.A., 1892 (cat. 150); R.A., Winter, 1933 (cat. 168); Harrogate City Art Gallery, 1966 (cat. 76).

16   *repr. in colour on p. 28*

# Francis Dodd
## 1874–1949

Francis Dodd was born in Holyhead in Anglesey in 1874, the son of a Wesleyian minister. He studied at Glasgow School of Art (under Archibald Kay and Francis H. Newbery) where he was a contemporary of the etcher Muirhead Bone, who later married his sister. In 1893 he won the Haldane travelling scholarship which enabled him to visit Paris, Italy and Spain. On his return to England in 1895, he initially settled in Manchester and became closely involved with the intellectual and artistic life of the city. In 1904 he moved to London and lived at Blackheath, where he painted many local scenes in oil and watercolour.

Dodd was a regular exhibitor at the New English Art Club from 1894, becoming a member in 1904 and Honorary Secretary from 1919 to 1922. Like a fellow N.E.A.C. artist, Ambrose McEvoy, Dodd was a friend and patron of the sculptor Jacob Epstein, and in 1911 he commissioned him to make a bronze head of his first wife, Mary.[1] He first began exhibiting at the Royal Academy in 1923, and was elected A.R.A. in 1927 and R.A. in 1933. Dodd was an etcher as well as a painter in oils and watercolour although according to his obituary in *The Times*, he 'had not the extreme virtuosity of his brother-in-law Sir Muirhead Bone, but was master of his craft and produced many plates, notably a series of portraits of fellow artists, of an incisive economy.'[2] In oil, he was best known for his commissioned portraits, realistically painted townscapes and suburban scenes, together with his paintings of women with thematic titles such as *Traveller's Joy*,[3] *In The Parlour*,[4] and *Suburban Wits*.[5] Elected an associate member of the Royal Society of Painters in Watercolour in 1923, Dodd's small watercolours of Dulwich, Brixton, Streatham and Blackheath were always popular.

During the First World War, Dodd was an Official War Artist and was commissioned to do a series of portraits of British Army Generals which were praised for their careful study of facial expression and their 'unfailing veracity.'[6] Also greatly praised when it was painted in 1910 was Dodd's portrait of a lady entitled *Signora Lotto* (Manchester City Art Gallery). He is represented in the Tate Gallery by the paintings *A Smiling Woman* (purchased 1924) and *Miss Dacre*, as well as by the portrait drawing in charcoal of *Edward Garnett*. Dodd was a Trustee of the Tate Gallery between 1928 and 1935, and in 1938 he stood for election as President of the Royal Academy together with Harcourt (q.v.), Knight (q.v.), Kelly (q.v.), Munnings (q.v.), Lee (q.v.) and Connard (q.v.), but was defeated by Sir Edwin Landseer Lutyens. In 1944, a major retrospective of his work was held at Cheltenham Art Gallery. He committed suicide in 1949.    E.C.W.

NOTES
1. E. Silber, *The Sculpture of Epstein*, cat. 32, p. 128.
2. *The Times*, 10 March 1949.
3. Repr., *Royal Academy Illustrated*, 1931, p. 20.
4. Repr., ibid., 1938, p. 53.
5. Repr., ibid., 1940, p. 23.
6. *The Times*, 10 March 1949.

## 17   In the Park

Oil on canvas on panel
81.5 × 66 cm    32 × 26 in
Signed and dated br: *FRANCIS-DODD 1916*
Diploma work, accepted 19 Nov 1935 (C.M. XXVI, p. 436)

*In the Park* is one of a series of female portraits with thematic titles which Dodd executed in the 1930s and 1940s. The same model, possibly his wife Mary, was used in several of his paintings. Like most of his portraits it is fresh and naturalistic and involves a direct encounter with the sitter. Light and decorative, the same high-keyed colours are used for the park and the figure. Although the handling of the background is quite schematic, the sitter and the objects in the foreground of the painting are described very literally, with an emphasis on linear detail.

EXHIBITIONS: R.A., 1936 (cat. 27); Bournemouth, Russell-Cotes Art Gallery & Museum, 1965 (cat. 18); Folkestone, Arts Centre, 1974 (cat. 12); South London Art Gallery, 1973 (cat. 105); Cheltenham Art Gallery & Museums, 1985 (cat. 10).

# Sir Alfred East
## 1849–1913

John Ruskin's theory that landscape paintings should be assembled from studies of minutely-observed details in nature such as leaves or blades of grass was anathema to East. Rather such paintings should 'express ... something of the living soul of nature, gaining the harmony and broad effect which follow on a spiritual comprehension' of the natural world.[1]

Alfred East was born in Kettering, Northamptonshire in 1849. Although he showed a talent for drawing from an early age, his parents felt that to earn a living as a painter was too precarious, so he went instead to work in his brother's shoe factory. Sent to Glasgow on business in 1874, he began evening classes at the Government School of Art. In 1880 East decided to abandon his commercial career and left for Paris, initially to study at the Ecole des Beaux-Arts, and then at the Académie Julian where he was taught by Fleury and Bouguereau. Whilst in France, he sketched in the forests around Barbizon and at Grès-sur-Loing, and was strongly influenced by many of the Barbizon School painters of the mid-nineteenth century, in particular Corot and Rousseau. On completing his studies, East initially returned to Glasgow, but later settled in London in 1884. In the previous year the Royal Academy had accepted a work painted at Barbizon, and from this date East exhibited at the Academy every year until his death. His subject matter usually derived from the Cotswolds, Cornwall or the Lake District.

As well as painting in oil and watercolour, East produced many fine etchings, and in 1885 became one of the early members of the Royal Society of Painter-Etchers and Engravers. He developed a straightforward technique, drawing his main outlines onto the waxed plate in watercolour, before taking it out of doors to work on the plate directly.

The current taste for Japanese art led to East being commissioned by The Fine Art Society to execute a series of watercolours and drawings of the Japanese landscape. He travelled via Egypt and Ceylon to Japan, where he spent about six months visiting celebrated beauty spots. East concentrated on capturing general effects rather than topographical details, but was aware that while Japanese artists 'selected what suited their purpose from a decorative point of view' he 'unconsciously, had expressed nature from the European point of view.'[2] The Fine Art Society held an exhibition of these works in 1890, which proved a great critical success.

At the Royal Academy, East annually exhibited pastoral landscapes such as The Golden Valley,[3] a carefully composed scene of sheep grazing in the meadows surrounding a shepherd's cottage. Always concerned with the effects of light on a landscape, he held an exhibition at The Fine Art Society in 1895 which included pictures of the same scene, painted at varying times from dawn until moonrise.

East was elected an Associate of the Academy in 1899, and President of the Royal Society of British Artists in 1906. In that year he also published The Art of Landscape Painting in Oil Colour, a manual for the use of students and amateur painters which conveyed his sensitive approach to the art of landscape painting.

His second book on technique, Brush and Pencil Notes in Landscape, was published posthumously in 1914.

During the last ten years of his life East made frequent visits to the United States, exhibiting his work and arranging other exhibitions. His landscapes were very favourably received there and were purchased by many important art institutions, to the extent that he 'grew to be almost the recognised ambassador of English Art abroad.'[4] East was knighted in 1910 and in the following year offered a collection of his oils and watercolours to his home town, Kettering, which built a special gallery to house the collection. In 1913, two months before his death, East was elected an Academician shortly before the gallery was opened in Kettering. His body was placed in the gallery for three days and nearly eight thousand people witnessed his lying in state. H.C.V.

NOTES
1. Memorial Exhibition of the late Sir Alfred East, intro. by E. Gosse, exhib. cat., London, Leicester Galleries, 1914, p. 15.
2. Studio, 37 (1906), p. 97.
3. Repr., Royal Academy Pictures, 1893, p. 27.
4. Memorial Exhibition, 1914, p. 13.

## 18   Evening in the Cotswolds

104.1 × 149.9 cm   41 × 59 in
Signed bl: ALFRED EAST
Diploma work, accepted 5 Dec 1913 (G.A. X, p. 17)

Unusually, because of his untimely death shortly after his election to full membership of the Academy, East did not present his own Diploma work. Initially the Council was not prepared to accept Evening in the Cotswolds when it was offered by his widow.[1] However, through the persistence of Lady East, the matter was put to the General Assembly of Academicians where it was unanimously agreed that East's name should be entered on the Roll of Academicians and his Diploma work be accepted.

East believed that in painting a landscape an artist should 'never fall in love with any pretty detail'[2] but that he should build up the picture 'from broad masses' and not 'particularise his blades of grass'.[3] In comparison with earlier works such as An Evening Song,[4] in which he depicted the tracery of boughs quite clearly, East's style by the time of Evening in the Cotswolds had acquired greater breadth, and here it is the contours of the landscape that appear most important. East felt that these natural rhythms, as well as expressing the underlying form of the landscape, 'must be big in feeling and noble in design.'[5] Trees always feature prominently in his landscapes and were described by him as 'those peers of the nobility of nature'.[6] Edmund Gosse explained how East would 'treat a particular tree as a living model, and sketch it from the front, from the back, from either side, until there was no fact about its physical conformity which was not clearly known to him.'[7] In this way he strove towards capturing 'the living impression of a tree as a whole' rather than as 'a colossal repository of detail'.[8] Thus the mass of the trees here, although very broadly painted, is thoroughly convincing.

Typically, the title of East's work refers to no specific place, reflecting his aim 'to seize the passing mood of Nature and portray the evanescent impression of beauty.'[9] East's intention in *Evening in the Cotswolds* was to evoke the peaceful atmosphere of the dusky evening in a secluded valley, an effect which he achieves through long shadows stretching across the meadows and the distant scene of a shepherd driving his flock homewards.

NOTES

1. C.M. XXIII, p. 99, 18 Nov 1913.
2. *Studio*, 37 (1906), p. 97.
3. A. East, *The Art of Landscape Painting in Oil Colour*, 1906, p. 20.
4. Repr., *Royal Academy Pictures*, 1898, p. 176.
5. A. East, op. cit., p. 37.
6. *Sir Alfred East*, exhib. cat., Kettering, Alfred East Art Gallery, 1949–50.
7. *Memorial Exhibition of the late Sir Alfred East*, intro. by E. Gosse, exhib. cat., London, Leicester Galleries, 1914, p. 15.
8. A. East, op. cit., p. 20.
9. *Illustrating the Effects from Dawn to Moonrise*, exhib. cat., London, Fine Art Society, 1895.

EXHIBITIONS: R.A., 1914 (cat. 320); London, Royal Society of Portrait Painters, 1971 (cat. 32).

# Frederick William Elwell
## 1870–1958

A tribute to Elwell in *The Yorkshire Post* in 1958 referred to their local son as 'one of Britain's most accomplished painters of interiors and still life'.[1] Born in Beverley, Yorkshire, in 1870, Elwell was the son of James Elwell, a woodcarver of international standing and Mayor of the town. He began his career at Lincoln School of Art, winning the Gibney Scholarship in 1887 and subsequently attending the Antwerp Academy for four years. He returned to England, working in London and Beverley before continuing his studies at the Académie Julian in Paris. He exhibited at the Paris Salon from 1894 and at the Royal Academy from 1895. In 1931 he was elected both A.R.A. and a member of the Royal Society of Portrait Painters. He became a full member of the Royal Academy in 1938.

Elwell returned to Beverley around 1903 and married his pupil Mary Dawson Bishop (1874–1952) in 1914. Settling there, he celebrated the ordinary life of Beverley in his work, painting local landscapes and townscapes such as *Beverley Minster*, and *The County Court, Beverley*, although he was occasionally represented at the Academy by foreign landscapes. It was as a painter of commemorative portraits that he was best known, although in most of his works the interior setting was as important as the subject. His almost Pre-Raphaelite attention to detail was in keeping with the realist tradition of the Antwerp Academy and is well demonstrated in works such as *The Earl and Countess of Strathmore and Kinghorne in their Drawing room at Glamis*,[2] *The Lying-in-State, Westminster Hall*, *Lord and Lady Blackford on their Golden Wedding at Compton Castle*[3] and *The Royal Academy Selection and Hanging Committee, 1938*, his Diploma work. During the Second World War he was commissioned by the Sheriff of Hull to record the scene at the Guildhall, Hull when Winston Churchill visited the city in 1942. He was later made a freeman of his home town.

After his death in 1958, his achievements were assessed in *The Times* thus: 'Suavity of manner was the distinguishing character of his work. He was a persuasive rather than an arresting artist, in some danger of declining into prettiness, particularly in colour, but generally saved by the modesty of attitude to his subjects and his excellent craftsmanship.'[4]  E.C.W.

NOTES
1. *The Yorkshire Post*, 4 Jan 1958.
2. Repr., *Royal Academy Illustrated*, 1932, p. 34.
3. Repr., ibid., 1936, p. 67.
4. *The Times*, Jan 1958.

## 19  The Royal Academy Selection and Hanging Committee 1938

118 × 144.5 cm 46½ × 56⅞ in
Signed and dated br: *Fred Elwell. 1938*
Diploma work, accepted 11 April 1939 (C.M. XXVII, pp. 200–1)

This commemorative group portrait shows the Royal Academicians who served on the Selection and Hanging Committee for the 1938 annual Summer Exhibition at the traditional lunch in the General Assembly Room at the Royal Academy. From left to right the sitters are: the painter himself (standing), Sir Edwin Cooper, Sir William Russell Flint, Sydney Lee (q.v.), Sir William Llewellyn (President), Sir Walter Lamb (Secretary), Oliver Hall (q.v.), George Harcourt (q.v.), Sir Walter Russell (Keeper, at the end of the table) (q.v.), James Woodford, Stephen Gooden, Gilbert Ledward, S.J. Lamorna Birch (q.v.) and Harold Knight (q.v.).

The General Assembly Room is one of the fine rooms on the first floor of Burlington House in Piccadilly, home of the Royal Academy since 1869. It dates from the early eighteenth century and forms part of Lord Burlington's Neo-Palladian mansion. Here it has provided Elwell with an appropriately rich, classical setting for this official painting. It is particularly significant that Elwell emphasises the dignity and authority of the committee in 1938, the year in which they rejected Wyndham Lewis's portrait of T.S. Eliot. In the ensuing furore, Augustus John (q.v.) referred to the decision as an 'inept act on the part of the Academy'[1] and resigned his membership forthwith proclaiming, 'the Academy is stagnant—dead'.[2] Explaining his action further John said 'I know I haven't done anything directly to affect the policy of the Institution. It seemed pretty hopeless to oppose the predominant junta of deadly conservatism which rules. If by my beastly action I shall have brought some fresh air into Burlington House I shall feel justified.'[3]

The supposed conservatism of the Royal Academicians is supported in the painting. Executed in a highly realistic, almost photographic manner, the group portrait is as much concerned with still life, with the Academy's collection of crystal and silver prominently displayed on the vast dinner table. The General Assembly Room is naturally quite dark, just as Elwell has painted it here, the main light source coming from the windows behind the painter. The sharp contrasts between light and shade have been used to advantage in order to highlight the details of the room and the objects on the table in an almost Pre-Raphaelite style, which reflects Elwell's training at the Antwerp Academy.

NOTES
1. M. Holroyd, *Augustus John*, Vol. II, 1975, p. 106.
2. M. Holroyd, op. cit., p. 107.
3. idem.

EXHIBITIONS: R.A., 1939 (cat. 163); London, Camden Arts Centre, 1969 (cat. 123); Cheltenham Art Gallery and Museums, 1985 (cat. 14); Swansea, Glynn Vivian Art Gallery, 1985 (cat. 43).

19

# Joseph Farquharson
## 1846–1935

In *The Times* obituary it was said that Farquharson's pictures 'conveyed to many people the romance of the Highlands'.[1] The majority of his paintings depict the beautiful countryside around his home at Finzean in North-East Scotland and from his frequent representations of sheep in snow-covered landscapes he acquired the nickname 'Frozen Mutton Farquharson'.

The Farquharsons were an old Highland clan who had lived at Finzean since 1579. Joseph's father Francis, 10th Laird of Finzean, was a doctor practising in Edinburgh, and a keen amateur artist. Joseph was allowed to use his father's studio at weekends, but his real training began at the Trustees Academy, Edinburgh and at the life class run by the Royal Scottish Academy where, at the age of 15 he had his first picture exhibited.

Peter Graham, a family friend and an established Scottish landscape painter who specialised in scenes of Highland cattle in misty glens, proved a strong influence in the 1860s. Sir George Reid thought Farquharson's paintings in 1867 had 'much of Peter Graham's feeling and touch over them, but good and full of promise'.[2] His first work was accepted in the Royal Academy in 1873, although he continued to exhibit at the Royal Scottish Academy until the early 1880s. His early work included sentimental subjects such as children lost in woodlands as well as misty landscapes reminiscent of Graham.

In 1874, a visit to Holland with the Scottish artist George Paul Chalmers enabled Farquharson to meet the distinguished Hague School painter Jozef Israels. Israels's work was much admired in Scotland and the Dutch tour inspired Farquharson to paint several domestic interiors. Crucial to his artistic development, however, were the three or four winters, from 1880, spent in the Paris *atelier* of the successful society portraitist Carolus-Duran. Here he worked in oils directly from the life model, concentrating more on colour and form than on drawing.

In the mid-1880s and early 1890s he made several trips to Egypt. He exhibited the resulting works at the Royal Academy from 1886. The experience gained in Paris is apparent in these Egyptian pictures which often depict figures in architectural settings.

Although landscape painting was not taught in Carolus-Duran's *atelier* many students visited the Forest of Fontainebleau, made famous by the Barbizon School, to practise *plein-air* painting. It is probable that Farquharson, interested in landscape painting from early on, accompanied these students. He certainly continued to paint directly from nature on his return to Scotland, and to cope with the climate he had a painting hut built equipped with wheels and a stove, enabling him to paint in all weathers. By the 1920s he had several of these huts situated in the Finzean woodlands, allowing him to work on a number of canvasses at once, depending on the atmospheric conditions.

Through his repeated depictions of the Scottish winter landscape, Farquharson developed an instantly recognisable idiom. Publication of large editions of prints testified to his success in capturing the popular imagination. His steady rise within the art establishment culminated in his election as a Royal Aca-demician in 1915. In 1918, in succession to his brother, he became 12th Laird of Finzean, and managed the estate with the businesslike spirit which he had always brought to his artistic career: four ledgers, still in the possession of the artist's family, record each of his paintings, with details of prices and buyers. Farquharson continued to paint until his death in 1935 though in later years his subjects were increasingly restricted to the beautiful gardens of Finzean and small pictures of rose pergolas and herbaceous borders.    H.C.V.

NOTES
1.  *The Times*, 16 April 1935, p.21.
2.  *Joseph Farquharson of Finzean*, exhib. cat., Aberdeen Art Gallery and Museums, 1985, p.6.

## 20  When Snow the Pasture Sheets

57 × 91.5 cm    22½ × 36 in
Signed bl: *J. Farquharson*
Diploma work, accepted 7 April 1915 (C.M. XXIII, p.281)

Farquharson's genuine feeling for nature found its fullest expression in the representation of the bleakness of winter. Sickert (q.v.), when comparing Farquharson's work with that of Courbet, appreciated this gift, realising that 'Farquharson has painted subjects that interest him in the familiar traditional style that a succession of good painters have taught the world to read currently. There is no jolt. The painter immerses his audience in the subject, partly because he does not distract their attention by archaisms or neologisms of technique.'[1] Sickert felt that his 'extraordinary virtuosity had been developed by experience' and 'arises certainly from the fact that he is thinking of telling his story.'[2]

The title Farquharson chose for his Diploma work is taken from Shakespeare's *Anthony and Cleopatra*:

> Yea, like the stag, when snow the pasture sheets
> The barks of trees thou browsed'st ... [3]

The use of literary quotations by landscape painters was common. Farquharson had twice before exhibited works at the Royal Academy with this same title, the first in 1877.[4] A quotation such as this elevated the status of the landscape painting as well as setting a mood and underlining the particular characteristics of the painting. In contrast to the leafy opulence of favoured Victorian landscapes Farquharson here depicts the severest winter conditions; the windswept and desolate qualities of the frozen landscape where food is scarce are emphasised by the lines from Shakespeare. Unusually for Farquharson, the landscape is bathed in moonlight, causing the trees to cast ghostly shadows and creating an eerie atmosphere.

When Farquharson first submitted this and another picture to the Royal Academy on 23 March 1915, the Academy's Council Minutes recorded the paintings as 'unfinished' and noted that the artist should be informed 'of the law that, once finally accepted, a Diploma work may not be removed from the Academy.'[5] Presumably this was to make it clear to Farquharson

that he could not have one of the paintings back to finish later. *When Snow the Pasture Sheets* was accepted on 7 April 1915⁶ so was probably never completely finished. Two strange streaks of paint in the middle foreground lend credence to this theory. However, 'unfinished' in this instance could mean that the painting, rather than being a sketch, was less highly finished than was generally deemed acceptable at that date. The painting was hung in Gallery I at the Royal Academy Summer Exhibition of 1915 where one reviewer considered that it 'shows [Farquharson] in his typical vein' and 'though mannered, it shows much delicate observation.'⁷ Sickert similarly appreciated his work, although if 'he enjoyed a Farquharson it would be with a slight sense of playing truant from Bloomsbury, and a hope

that his treat would remain a secret from his more highbrow friends.'⁸

NOTES
1. *Daily Telegraph*, 7 April 1926; reprinted W.R. Sickert, *A Free House!*, ed. O. Sitwell, 1947, p. 205.
2. ibid., p. 206.
3. *Anthony and Cleopatra*, Act I, scene 4, line 65.
4. R.A. Summer Exhibition, 1877 (cat. 1017), 1895 (cat. 450).
5. C.M. XXIII, p. 277, 23 March 1915.
6. C.M. XXIII, p. 281, 7 April 1915.
7. *Connoisseur*, 42 (1915), p. 122.
8. Sickert, op. cit., p. 205.

EXHIBITIONS: R.A., 1915 (cat. 20); Bournemouth, Russell-Cotes Art Gallery & Museum, 1957 (cat. 831); Aberdeen Art Gallery, 1985 (cat. 73).

# Mark Fisher
## 1841–1923

In his contribution to the catalogue of Mark Fisher's memorial exhibition, Sir George Clausen (q.v.) recalled that the quality which 'Fisher loved best in a picture' was 'that it should have breadth of life'. The subjects of his paintings, 'the sky, the trees, the beasts of the field' Clausen tells us, were treated not as 'a record of facts, but as expressing his own sense of their vitality and beauty under the conditions of light and air.'[1]

Born in Boston, Massachussetts, in 1841 'of poor but honest parents as the story goes',[2] Fisher was apprenticed at fourteen years of age to a sign and house painter. In the winter months he attended drawing classes at the Lowell Institute, and in about 1859 became a pupil of the American landscape painter George Inness, who lived near Boston. Encouraged by Inness, Fisher decided to concentrate his efforts on landscape, rather than on figure subjects or portraits. In 1863 he sailed to Paris and entered Gleyre's *atelier*, where, as Clausen explained, 'new ideas were in the air, and the younger school of French painters, Manet and those associated with him, were gaining ground.'[3] Initially Fisher was greatly impressed by Corot and the Barbizon School of painters, and after a visit to Honfleur, he became enthusiastic about the work of Boudin. However, his work gradually became closer to that of Alfred Sisley, the English-born Impressionist, whom he knew personally. Both artists were concerned with rendering the effects of sunlight and shadow on a landscape. Fisher returned to Boston, but, unable to make a living as an artist, sailed for France in 1871 and finally settled in England in 1872. He set up home in London, where he lived for a few years, but subsequently moved to Steyning in Sussex, the first of several moves around the country. Although Fisher occasionally visited Normandy and made trips to Holland, Algiers and Morocco, his subject matter was unadventurous, consisting principally of the landscapes and rural scenes in the countryside surrounding his various homes.

Fisher exhibited at the Royal Academy from his arrival in England, and his Academy paintings of 1883 were praised by Lucien Pissarro, who wrote to his father, Camille, explaining that he had found 'only two painters who did not make me regret the money I had paid for admission.' One of these was Mark Fisher 'who draws trees in a very knowledgeable way and paints freely'.[4] The younger Pissarro's enthusiasm for these paintings signifies the extent to which Fisher had assimilated Impressionism within the limits considered to be acceptable by the Selection Committee of the Royal Academy.

The Dutch Gallery, a cosmopolitan art dealership in London which specialised in the work of Corot, Daubigny and Monet, became an important patron of Fisher's work. An exhibition of his paintings held at the gallery in 1895 was very favourably received, and the highly regarded critic R.A.M. Stevenson described him as 'the foremost of the English "vibrists" or "iridescents".'[5] These obscure terms do not refer to organised groups or even to identifiable tendencies, but rather acknowledge the impressionistic freedom of Fisher's brushwork and colouring in comparison with the orthodoxies of contemporary academic painting.

In 1901 Fisher moved to Hatfield Heath in Essex, and by this time his reputation was firmly established; his election as an Associate of the Royal Academy followed in 1911. At about this time, attracted by the strong light of the region, he began to make regular trips to the south of France. Elected a full Academician in 1919, at the age of seventy-eight, Fisher voiced some concern about his advancing years: 'old age seems so much out of fashion', he wrote, and joked about 'dying my hair and putting my age back'.[6] Following his death in 1923 there was a memorial exhibition at the Leicester Galleries. Clausen, in his appreciation of Fisher's work, recalled that in his later years Fisher found many subjects to paint in his own garden, and that 'he was not greatly interested in views, or in places picturesque in themselves but could find beauty anywhere.'[7] H.C.V.

NOTES
1. *Memorial exhibition of works by Mark Fisher*, exhib. cat., London, Leicester Galleries, 1924, with an appreciation by G. Clausen, p. 9.
2. Letter from Mark Fisher to the Secretary of the R.A., 16 April 1919, R.A. Archives, RAC/1/FI 11.
3. *Memorial exhibition of works by Mark Fisher*, p. 7.
4. Quoted V. Lines, *Mark Fisher and Margaret Fisher Prout*, 1966, p. 9.
5. ibid., p. 20.
6. Letter from Mark Fisher to the Secretary of the R.A., 16 April 1919, R.A. Archives, RAC/1/FI 11.
7. Quoted V. Lines, op. cit., p. 27.

## 21 An Orchard in Spring

46 × 61 cm    18¼ × 24 in
Signed bl: *Mark Fisher*
Diploma work, accepted 30 March 1920 (C.M. XXIV, p. 209)

On his election to full membership of the Royal Academy in 1919, Mark Fisher offered a large canvas, *Almond Blossom and Artichokes*, as his Diploma work.[1] However, due perhaps to the lack of space in the Diploma Galleries of the Academy, where the picture was destined to hang, the Council asked for a smaller work. Accordingly, the artist presented *An Orchard in Spring*. Although this work is not dated, a letter written by Fisher's wife to the Academy in March 1920, states that he could not send the work in 'till the end of the month',[2] implying that he was still working on the painting.

This painting was probably executed entirely in the open air; the *Art Journal* records that Fisher worked on larger compositions in his studio, 'pulling pictures together, making changes',[3] but painted smaller works on the spot, ensuring their 'qualities of freshness, brightness and movement'.[4] Fisher's main concern in *An Orchard in Spring* was to render sunlight on the blossom and the grass; the 'open-air' feeling of the painting was his specific contribution, owing something to the English landscape tradition as well as to the Impressionists. *The Times* critic in 1928 felt that 'in his small landscapes [Fisher] forms a most interesting link between Constable and Monet',[5] presumably because the atmospheric conditions of the sunny,

windy day give the whole picture its character, dabs of bright colour investing the canvas with sparkling light.

Fisher deliberately limited the vistas in his landscapes: his intention was to discover beauty in the everyday landscape, rather than to restate the sublime and picturesque categories of subject matter typical of English landscape painting. As the *Art Journal* noted, 'the panorama does not tempt him',[6] and here, typically, the field of vision is limited by houses and a hedge in the middle distance. These set the boundaries of the composition, which is built up around the strong central motif of a fruit tree in full blossom. While a contemporary critic found the work 'good, of course, but without any sense of surprise or adventure in it',[7] the painting does epitomise 'the brilliance, the glitter, and the freshness of the world'[8] which the critic of the *Art Journal* had identified in his work ten years earlier.

NOTES
1. C.M. XXIV, p. 206, 23 March 1920.
2. Letter from Mrs Mark Fisher to the Secretary of the R.A., 9 March 1920, R.A. Archives, RAC/1/FI 12.
3. *Art Journal*, 1910, p. 17.
4. ibid., p. 18.
5. Quoted V. Lines, *Mark Fisher and Margaret Fisher Prout*, 1966, p. 7.
6. *Art Journal*, 1910, p. 10.
7. *The Times*, 13 May 1920, p. 10.
8. *Art Journal*, 1910, p. 10.

EXHIBITIONS: R.A., 1920 (cat. 119); Bournemouth, Russell-Cotes Art Gallery & Museum, 1957 (cat. 845); R.A., Winter, 1968 (cat. 493).

# Stanhope Alexander Forbes
## 1857–1947

A critic writing in 1901 recalled the impression that Stanhope Forbes's *A Fish Sale on a Cornish Beach* (Plymouth City Museum and Gallery) had made when it was exhibited in 1885: '. . . the fresh vitality of it seemed like a wholesome breeze from the sea breathed in a studio reeking with oil and turpentine, while its brilliant new technique fell upon the younger painters as a revelation.'[1] The picture focused attention on what became known as the Newlyn School of painters, an artists' colony of which Forbes was seen as 'the centre and rallying point'.[2]

Stanhope Alexander Forbes was born in Dublin in 1857, the son of a railway manager. He attended Dulwich College and Lambeth School of Art before entering the Royal Academy Schools in 1874. Whilst studying he accepted portrait commissions as a reliable source of income, and continued to do so throughout his life. In 1880 he went to Paris to complete his training at the *atelier* of Bonnat. Influenced by the *plein-air* painters of the Barbizon School and contemporaries such as the naturalist painter Jules Bastien-Lepage, Forbes recounted that 'most of us young students were . . . forsaking the studios with their unvarying north light, to set up our easels in country districts, where we could pose our models and attack our work, in sunshine or in shadow, under the open sky.'[3] In pursuit of this ideal, he spent the summer of 1881 in Brittany with H. H. La Thangue (q.v.), a fellow student from the Academy Schools. Despite their common aims, Forbes described 'a want of sympathy between us' but wished to emulate La Thangue's 'industry which is his strongest point'.[4] Adopting square brushes, and with careful observation of detail, Forbes painted subjects in the new style of British *plein-air* realism. Official recognition came with the purchase of *A Street in Brittany* by the Walker Art Gallery, Liverpool, which vindicated Forbes's choice of direction in his art. Having returned to London in 1883 he decided to abandon Brittany, and instead went to Falmouth. Whilst exploring the area in 1884 he discovered the Cornish fishing village of Newlyn. Attracted by 'a mild climate suitable for out of doors work, a grey roofed village overhanging a lovely bay',[5] Forbes was not the first painter to work there, but he was instrumental in encouraging other artists to form a colony in the area (although many treated the village merely as a summer retreat). In 1889, after his marriage to the painter Elizabeth Armstrong, Forbes decided to settle permanently in Newlyn and remained there until his death.

The Newlyn School painters, rigorous in their commitment to *plein-air* painting, also felt that the artist 'must live amongst the scenes he sought to render, and become thoroughly familiarised with every aspect of nature' and in particular to 'study humanity in relation to its surroundings'.[6] The subject matter of Forbes's early work at Newlyn was almost exclusively the lives of the fishing community, but after 1894 he broadened his range to include the agricultural life of the countryside around Newlyn.

The establishment of the New English Art Club in 1886 grew from a need felt by the more progressive artists to hold exhibitions outside the stifling régime of the Royal Academy. Despite being a founder member, Forbes never fully transferred his allegiance to the New English Art Club. He refused to support La Thangue's scheme for more radical reforms and he continued to send his important exhibition pictures to the Academy. Many of these, such as *The Health of the Bride*, 1889 (London, Tate Gallery) met with critical acclaim and Forbes's success at the Academy was acknowledged by his election as an Associate in 1892.

In 1899 Forbes and his wife opened the Newlyn School of Painting 'for the student who wishes to learn how seriously to study painting and drawing according to the recent development in English Art.'[7] The School continued until 1938 and helped to foster a new generation of artists working in and around Newlyn. The training they received there included drawing from plaster casts, and classes in *plein-air* painting.

Around the time of his election as a full member of the Academy, Forbes abandoned the sombre tones of his early work and adopted a lighter, more highly coloured palette. He continued painting subjects from Newlyn and its environs, although figures play a more incidental role in his later works, and the realisation that the world he depicted was fast disappearing lends a nostalgic atmosphere to some of his later paintings. Forbes died in 1947 having lived and painted in Newlyn for sixty-three years. H.C.V.

NOTES
1. *Studio*, 23 (1901), p. 84.
2. *Art Journal*, 1896, p. 58.
3. S. Forbes, 'Cornwall from a Painter's Point of View', reprinted from the *Annual Report of the Royal Cornwall Polytechnic Society for 1900*, Falmouth, 1901, pp. 4–5; quoted C. Fox and F. Greenacre, *Artists of the Newlyn School 1880–1900*, exhib. cat., Newlyn Orion Galleries, 1979, p. 16.
4. Letter to Forbes's mother, 31 July 1881; quoted C. Fox and F. Greenacre, op. cit., p. 55.
5. *Studio*, 23 (1901), p. 88.
6. S. Forbes, op. cit., pp. 4–5; quoted C. Fox and F. Greenacre, op. cit., p. 16.
7. *Art Journal*, 1889, p. 320; quoted C. Fox and F. Greenacre, op. cit., p. 62.

## 22 The Harbour Window

114 × 89 cm   45 × 35 in
Signed and dated bl: *Stanhope A. Forbes. 1910.*
Diploma work, accepted 22 Nov 1910 (C.M. XXII, p. 360)

Forbes declared that he had always 'carried large pictures right through to the last touch in smithies, stablesheds and amid all sorts of queer surroundings under conditions which when starting seemed absolutely hopeless and prohibitive.'[1] Despite this commitment to scenes of outdoor life, paintings of interiors represent some of Forbes's finest work, manifesting the same uncompromising attitude towards truthful tonal values and keenly observed detail.

In his early days at Newlyn, Forbes found that one of 'the great drawbacks to this place is the girls will not pose'.[2] However, he soon persuaded the people of Newlyn to sit for him and only used professional models from London for nude studies. *The Harbour Window*, depicting village people in their everyday environment, is typical of Forbes's work. Painted in the family's upstairs sitting room of the Ship Inn, at Mousehole, it portrays Annie Blewett, who lived next door.[3]

The everyday subject matter chosen by Forbes and other Newlyn painters offended the tastes of highbrow critics such as George Moore, who considered it to be vulgar and thus inappropriate. Forbes's defence was trenchant: 'that which might seem awkward and rough, suited as it is to the conditions of its life, and in harmony with its surroundings may be most beautiful.'[4] He felt that 'the many signs which tell of the hardships of poverty ... should be faithfully recorded; for without them the study is half told and its value lost.'[5] Forbes chose these subjects, however, more for their pictorial qualities than for their social import.

The image of a single needlewoman was central to a tradition of Victorian genre painting stemming from Richard Redgrave's *The Sempstress* (1844). These often sentimental studies, popular with Victorian audiences, had drawn attention to the plight of needlewomen, whose pitiful circumstances in the industrial cities were the cause of much philanthropic concern. Although Forbes's image is similar, his intentions in treating the figure of a woman sewing were quite different, as the relatively affluent interior and the quality of the fabric testify. *The Harbour Window* depicts a needlewoman — perhaps a housewife or domestic servant — in her everyday surroundings and locates the scene in a specific place. Indeed, by taking his title from Mousehole Harbour, seen through the window, Forbes diverts the viewer's attention from the narrative content to the landscape context.

This work was painted at a time when Forbes was experimenting with a brighter palette. The effects of using a square brush were also less pronounced and the strong impasto highlights were laid on with softer brushmarks. However, in rendering this subject, his intentions were, as always, 'strength — strength of impression, strength of illumination, of contrasts'.[6]

22   *repr. in colour on p. 39*

NOTES
1. *Art Journal Christmas Number*, 1911, p. 23.
2. Letter from Forbes, 10 Feb 1884; quoted C. Fox and F. Greenacre, *Artists of the Newlyn School 1880–1900*, exhib. cat., Newlyn Orion Galleries, 1979, p. 64.
3. Letter from Sylvia Johns, 24 June 1981, R.A. Archives, Forbes file.
4. Galley proof of *The Treatment of Modern Life in Art*, (c. 1891/2), by Stanhope Forbes; quoted C. Fox and F. Greenacre, op. cit., p. 66.
5. idem.
6. L. Birch, *Stanhope A. Forbes and Elizabeth S. Forbes*, 1906, p. 88.

EXHIBITIONS: R.A., 1911 (cat. 264); Bournemouth, Russell-Cotes Art Gallery & Museum, 1957 (cat. 817); Plymouth Art Gallery, 1964 (cat. 31); South London Art Gallery, 1981 (cat. 41); Swansea, Glynn Vivian Art Gallery & Museum, 1985 (cat. 24).

# Meredith Frampton
## 1894–1984

Frampton's impeccable portraits and precisely articulated still-life paintings were a regular feature of Royal Academy Summer Exhibitions during the inter-war years. Like those of his contemporaries Kelly (q.v.), Gunn (q.v.), Brockhurst (q.v.) and Harold Knight (q.v.), Frampton's paintings were characterised by a careful, measured technique and a sharp-edged, almost photographic realism. Although he did paint some landscapes, the static, airless quality of his work was more appropriate to portraiture and still life. Sometimes these two genres were combined in paintings which focused as much attention on the attributes surrounding the sitter as on the subject himself. As a result of his painstaking craftsmanship and obsession with detail, Frampton's paintings often took up to a year to complete. The majority of his work was executed on commission, and tended to represent sitters who were connected with either the arts or public service.

Meredith Frampton was born in London in 1894, son of the sculptor Sir George Frampton R.A. (1860–1928) and the painter Christabel Annie Cockerell (1863–1951). After leaving Westminster School in 1910, he enrolled at St John's Wood Art School before going on to the Royal Academy Schools in 1912. During his three years at the Royal Academy he benefitted from the sound technical training offered by the Schools and won first prize and silver medal for a decorative design for a public building entitled *A Harvest Procession*. Frampton's interest in the practical side of art was also strengthened by his election in 1915 as a member of the Art Workers Guild, for which he was proposed by his father and the painter George Clausen (q.v.).

During the First World War, Frampton joined the Artists' Rifles before working with a field survey company making aerial sketches of enemy trenches on the Western Front. On being demobilised he worked in a studio adjoining his father's in St John's Wood, London, where he painted almost all his pictures until it was bombed in the Second World War. He then moved to Wiltshire to a house he had designed for himself. Towards the end of the Second World War Frampton's eyesight deteriorated and, since he was no longer able to achieve the same degree of precision in his work, he stopped painting in 1945. He was elected A.R.A. in 1934 and R.A. in 1942. A major retrospective of his work was held at the Tate Gallery in 1982. He died in 1984. E.C.W.

*repr. in colour on p. 56*

## 23 Still Life

102 × 81.5 cm   40 × 32 cm
Signed and dated tr: *MF 32*
Diploma work, accepted 3 Nov 1942 (C.M. XXVII, p. 438)

This clinically cool *Still Life* exemplifies Frampton's precise and ordered vision. Each object has been carefully chosen and meticulously observed. There is an emphasis on geometrical shapes, all of which are strongly defined, expressing Frampton's interest in outline, relief and recession. The calm, even surfaces and the restrained use of colour underline the disquieting mood of the composition, which is heightened by the strange, almost surreal juxtaposition between natural and man-made forms. The funerary masonry, the anguished head and the axed trees are cold and lifeless, their eeriness only relieved by the apparently fresh flowers and the calm landscape. Like many of Frampton's later paintings there is a reference to the artist's interest in planning and architecture in the form of the disc-shaped tape measure in the foreground. Although Frampton's paintings are highly realistic, he did not make preliminary drawings or use photographs, preferring to draw directly with the brush onto the canvas.

EXHIBITIONS: R.A., 1943 (cat. 319); Bournemouth, Russell-Cotes Art Gallery & Museum, 1965 (cat. 24); Hull, Ferens Art Gallery, 1982 (cat. 16); London, Tate Gallery, 1982 (cat. 16); Cheltenham Art Gallery and Museums, 1985 (cat. 17); Swansea, Glynn Vivian Art Gallery, 1985 (cat. 45).

# Charles March Gere
## 1869–1957

The work of Charles March Gere unites two aesthetic traditions which are often considered to be mutually exclusive: English landscape painting and the decorative work of the Arts and Crafts Movement.

Gere was born in Birmingham in 1869 and, during his early training under E.R. Taylor at the Birmingham School of Art, assimilated the techniques and aesthetics of the Arts and Crafts Movement. In Gere's art the decorative element was first to make its mark and, as a young teacher at the Birmingham School of Art, he was noticed and adopted by William Morris. His frontispiece to Morris's *News from Nowhere* showed his talents as an illustrator, but more elaborate designs for the bloodthirsty Norse legend *Sigurd the Volsung* — ill-suited to Gere's placid temperament — disappointed his mentor.

Gere only began to excel as an artist when he turned to landscape painting, although some of his early panels such as *The Game of Tennis*,[1] betrayed a sophisticated decorative style derived from Gere's elder fellow members of the Birmingham Group of Painters and Craftsmen, such as Joseph Southall (1861–1945).[2] Among the unifying features of this group was its members' use of tempera as a medium; 'tempera' simply implies the use of egg or size rather than oil to mix with pigment, a technique used by Italian Renaissance painters and suggested to Gere during a visit to Northern Italy with the painter J. D. Batten. As early as 1901, when he was thirty-two years of age, Gere was mentioned in a seminal article, 'The Revival of Tempera Paintings', as 'another Birmingham artist whose small tempera painting ... is aglow with the sunlight of the South, [who] was drawn into the tempera movement five or six years ago.'[3]

In 1904, Gere and his half-sister Margaret, also a painter, settled in Painswick in the hills between Stroud and Gloucester. Here, the 'upland country of sudden prospects and narrow, steeply wooded valleys ... inspired him to find his true vocation as a landscape painter.'[4] Gere's vision of rural England was never one of fresh, outdoor observation, tempera being essentially 'a studio medium [which] leads him to the habit of making pencil notes and training the memory to make the most of these.'[5] Many of Gere's works were painted on silk which accounts in part for the refinement of texture he was able to achieve.

His paintings became celebrated at the exhibitions of the New English Art Club in the 1900s, and there he 'established a reputation as a landscape painter of great individuality.'[6] From 1924, Gere became a regular exhibitor at the Royal Academy and gained an increasingly large public. The refined treatment of his subjects reflected Gere's contentment in his Gloucestershire home. A critic wrote that 'of this neighbourhood in a mood of nature most characteristic of its principal charm, Mr Gere has been the poet in a series of delicate panels.'[7] Gere led an uneventful life, 'the even tenor of which was broken only by a few weeks painting holiday every year, either at home or abroad.'[8]

Gere was elected an Associate of the Royal Academy in 1934 and a full member in 1939. Although *The Times*[9] obituary suggested that 'his limitations as an artist were seen when, after he was elected to the Academy, he enlarged the size of his pictures', Gere's work remained consistent in quality and workmanship until his retirement in 1957,[10] two months before his death at the age of eighty-eight.    T. J. B.

NOTES
1. *The Arts and Crafts Movement*, exhib. cat., London, Fine Art Society, 1973, p. 73.
2. For the Birmingham Group of Painters and Craftsmen, see *The Earthly Paradise*, London, Fine Art Society, 1969.
3. Vallance, 'The Revival in Tempera Painting', *Studio*, 23 (1901), p. 155.
4. Foreword, *Charles Gere Memorial Exhibition*, Gloucester, Wheatstone Hall, 1963.
5. O. Hurst, 'The Landscape Paintings of Charles M. Gere', *Studio*, LIX (1913), p. 90.
6. idem.
7. ibid, p. 87.
8. *Charles Gere Memorial Exhibition*, op. cit.
9. *The Times*, 6 August 1957.
10. Charles March Gere to the Secretary, Royal Academy, 17 July 1957, R.A. Archives, Charles March Gere File.

## 24   The Blue Lake at Sierre

Tempera on silk laid on canvas
61 × 76 cm    24 × 30 in
Signed and dated bl: *CHARLES GERE 1938*
Diploma work, accepted 31 Oct 1939 (C.M. XXVII, p. 241)

Probably painted from sketches made on a tour of Switzerland in the summer of 1938, *The Blue Lake at Sierre* is a fine example of Gere's use of tempera on silk. Gere was not alone in using silk rather than canvas as a material for his pictures. Unlike other more flamboyant artists, for example, Conder, who used silk, his work is particularly delicate, but does not lose its naturalism. Indeed, a critic noted this quality in his oeuvre, remarking that 'hitherto we have associated delicate use of colour, upon a material so marvellously responsive to touch as silk, with an art like Conder's, artificial in its intention and result. We had not thought of the method as the very one for an expression of the spring fragrance of a wooded hill-side....'[1]

Tempera dries very much faster than oil paint and must be applied swiftly, particularly on to so absorbent a material as silk. Gere's brushwork here utilises this effect to great effect, creating patterns with rhythmic hatching strokes.

When exhibited at the Royal Academy in 1939, the critic H. Glanville Fell of the *Connoisseur* identified in 'the delightful work by C. M. Gere ARA', this quality peculiar to Gere's landscapes: 'a fine designer is Mr Gere, with a strong sense of rhythmic lay-out in all his landscapes.'[2]

NOTES
1. O. Hurst, 'The Landscape Paintings of Charles M. Gere', *Studio*, 59. (1913), p. 90.
2. H. Glanville Fell, 'Some topics of the moment', *Connoisseur*, 1939, pp. 347–8.

EXHIBITIONS: R.A., 1940 (cat. 106); Bournemouth, Russell-Cotes Art Gallery and Museum, 1965 (cat. 25); Cheltenham Art Gallery and Museums, 1985 (cat. 15); Swansea, Glynn Vivian Art Gallery and Museum, 1985 (cat. 44).

*(Illustrated overleaf)*

24

25   repr. in colour on p. 47

## 25   The Mill Pool at Painswick

77.5 × 63.5 cm    30½ × 25 in
Signed and dated bl: *Gere 1945*
Purchased by the Royal Academy (Stott Fund) 24 July 1947 (C.M. XXVIII, p. 193)

*The Mill Pool at Painswick* depicts the Cotswolds landscape which Charles Gere made his own. He had settled in Painswick in 1904, 'then an unspoiled village in the hills between Stroud and Gloucester'[1] where he lived for over fifty years. Early in his career a critic had noted that 'the characteristic of the English scenes in his art is a lyrical spirit'[2] and it is precisely this vein of lyricism, richly worked over the years, in which Gere here depicts the mill pool. Although he occasionally strayed to Italy and Switzerland, Gere's most characteristic work is saturated in the knowledge and memory of a locality gained through years of observation. 'He is constantly attracted to one neighbourhood', wrote Oakley Hurst in 1913, 'through his affection for a certain class of scenery and thus it is that his art is almost sentimental in feeling and full of the fascination of local associations.'[3] The painting was not exhibited at the Royal Academy, but was purchased through funds from the Edward Stott Bequest.

NOTES
1.   Foreword, *Charles Gere Memorial Exhibition*, Gloucester, Wheatstone Hall, 1963.
2.   O. Hurst, 'The Landscape Paintings of Charles M. Gere', *Studio*, 59 (1913), p. 90.
3.   idem.

# Maurice Greiffenhagen
1862–1931

Maurice Greiffenhagen was born in London in 1862, his parents having emigrated from the Baltic coast to England. He demonstrated a talent for art at an early age, drawing sculpture in the British Museum when he was only fourteen, and entering the Royal Academy Schools at sixteen, in 1878. He remained a student in the Schools for seven years, but began earning his living by drawing black and white illustrations for periodicals such as *Judy* and *The Lady's Pictorial*. His work as an illustrator became well known and he was described as a 'powerful delineator of modern life'.[1]

Greiffenhagen's work, first exhibited at the Royal Academy in 1884, included portraits as well as mythological subjects such as *The Mermaid*,[2] in which the mermaid with 'long auburn hair floating upward'[3] creates a spiralling pattern suggestive of art nouveau designs. At this time Greiffenhagen aspired to create works 'graceful in form' and 'superb in colour'.[4] He continued his black and white work – characterised by great economy of line and freedom of expression – illustrating many of Rider Haggard's books.

Greiffenhagen was greatly encouraged when one of his most popular paintings, *The Idyll* (exhibited at the Academy in 1891), was bought by the Walker Art Gallery, Liverpool. He had painted 'a picture of a young man and a maiden embracing in the fields with all the sentiment of youth and nature about it.'[5] The intensity of their embrace brought to his work an overt emotionalism lacking in *The Mermaid*, in which he had concentrated on purely decorative effects.

By 1900 Greiffenhagen was painting an increasing number of portraits, and was particularly successful in treating male subjects. These portraits were praised for their 'skilful use of black, providing a strong framework in which brighter colours as of official robes could be inset without any garish effect' and that although 'generally rather flat in treatment' they were firm in outline.[6]

In 1906 he became Master in Charge of the Life Department of Glasgow School of Art, where he was remembered for his 'trenchant criticism and fine example, for he taught rather by demonstration than by precept.'[7] He remained in this post for twenty-three years, although he put himself forward as a candidate for Keeper of the Royal Academy Schools after the resignation of Charles Sims (q.v.) in 1926. Greiffenhagen explained that he found it 'increasingly difficult to spend so much of my time going up to Glasgow' and would be grateful of the opportunity 'to remain in London without giving up my very real interest in students and teaching.'[8] He was unsuccessful, however, and in 1928 the Keepership passed, after a brief interregnum, to Sir W.W. Russell (q.v.). He retired from teaching in Glasgow in 1929.

Greiffenhagen's reputation was greatly enhanced after 1910. *Women by a Lake* (London, Tate Gallery) was purchased for the Chantrey Bequest in 1914, and he was elected an Associate of the Academy in 1916. He received commissions for decorative work, such as a panel for the Langside Library in Glasgow School of Art, which commemorated the Battle of Langside, and which was exhibited at the Royal Academy in 1919.[9] Greiffenhagen's acute sense of the relation of picture to architectural setting, resulted in a commission to decorate the British Pavilions for the International Exhibitions in Paris in 1926, and in Antwerp in 1930.

Greiffenhagen was elected an Academician in 1922 and, throughout the 1920s, continued to paint idyllic subjects, including another Chantrey picture, *Dawn* (London, Tate Gallery), exhibited at the Academy in 1926. In this work three naked figures, set against a simple landscape in a frieze-like arrangement, are shown awakening. He was also sought after as a decorative artist; his commissions included one particularly successful travel poster advertising the London, Midland and Scottish Railway Company: *The Gateway to the North*. Greiffenhagen died in St John's Wood, London in 1931 at the age of sixty-nine.   H.C.V.

NOTES
1. *Studio*, 9 (1897), p. 236.
2. Repr., *Art Journal*, 1894, p. 226.
3. *Art Journal*, 1894, p. 226.
4. ibid., p. 228.
5. *Studio*, 9 (1897), p. 242.
6. Obituary, press cutting, R.A. Archives, M. Greiffenhagen file.
7. idem.
8. Letter from M. Greiffenhagen to the Secretary of the Royal Academy, 18 June 1927, R.A. Archives, RAC/1/GR 10.
9. Repr., *Royal Academy Illustrated*, 1919, p. 103.

## 26 The Message

95.2 × 85.1 cm    37½ × 33½ in
Signed and dated bl: *MAURICE GREIFFENHAGEN 1923*
Diploma work, accepted 17 April 1923 (C.M. XXIV, p.520)

In 1921 Greiffenhagen began exhibiting religious paintings at
the Royal Academy. His decision to present such a picture as
his Diploma work was evidence that 'he considers it typical of
his present methods and artistic aims.'[1] Greiffenhagen refined
his style in these works, removing 'all the extraneous qualities'.[2]
A contemporary critic wrote that from 'the emotional and
romantic atmosphere of his earlier work', such as *The Idyll*
(Liverpool, Walker Art Gallery), Greiffenhagen had moved 'into
the loftier regions of pure decoration'.[3] To Greiffenhagen,
beauty of design was fundamentally important, although the
subject surely had more meaning for him than one critic suggested: that 'the beautiful *The Message* has a title is merely a
concession to the makers of catalogues; it is as decoration that
the work appeals.'[4]

The subject of *The Message* is clearly the Annunciation. In
treating this subject Greiffenhagen was directly influenced by
Italian Renaissance painters, both in iconography and in style.
The angel holds a lily, symbolising purity, and the Virgin Mary
is clothed in the traditional blue cloak, symbolic of heaven.
Greiffenhagen also includes an Italianate landscape.

By eliminating all shadow and using bright colours and clear
outlines, Greiffenhagen concentrates on the linear qualities of
the design, delighting in the folds of the drapery. No contact
is made between the figures, and he carefully prevents the stem
of the lily from cutting across the landscape. The figures are
linked by their gestures and by the movement of the angel as
he descends to the ground.

NOTES
1.  *Studio*, 88 (1924), p.129.
2.  ibid., p.124.
3.  idem.
4.  ibid., p.129.

EXHIBITIONS: R.A., 1923 (cat. 454); R.A., Winter, 1933 (cat. 310); Leicestershire Museum
and Art Gallery, 1982 (cat. 37); Japan, Tokyo Shimbun, touring exhibition, 1987 (cat. 51).

26    *repr. in colour on p. 27*

# Sir Herbert James Gunn
## 1893–1964

Gunn was born in Glasgow in 1893, the son of a prosperous tailor. After a general education at Glasgow High School he went on to Glasgow School of Art at the age of fourteen. He subsequently attended Edinburgh College of Art for three years before going to the Académie Julian in Paris where he studied under Jean-Paul Laurens. A trip to Spain soon after enabled him to see the work of Velasquez which was to have a significant influence on his later portraits. Although he went on to achieve a reputation as a portrait painter and rarely exhibited any other subjects, Gunn painted a number of landscapes around this time which were characterised by their broad tonal design and boldly applied paint.

Gunn's career was interrupted by the outbreak of the First World War when he joined the Artists' Rifles, receiving a commission with the 10th Scottish Rifles. After the War he settled in London and turned his attention to portraiture, exhibiting regularly at the Royal Glasgow Institute of Fine Arts and at the Royal Academy from 1923. He became an A.R.A. in 1953 and a full Academician in 1961, also serving as President of the Royal Society of Portrait Painters between 1953 and 1964. He was knighted in 1963 and received honorary degrees from the Universities of Manchester and Glagow in 1945 and 1963 respectively.

Throughout his career Gunn received a wealth of commissions from eminent field-marshals, politicians, academics, judges and bankers as well as fellow artists and writers. His sitters included Field-Marshall Lord Montgomery (Monty),[1] the Rt. Hon. Harold Macmillan M.P.[2] and W. O. Hutchinson, President of the Scottish Academy.[3] His obituary in *The Times* praised such paintings for their 'honesty', 'the precision of workmanship' and 'the pleasure in catching a likeness', describing how 'in boardrooms and college halls the visitor is often stopped by one of Gunn's portraits, severe and even bitter in expression, painted with scrupulous distinction, with nothing evaded, neither the wrinkled hands nor the pinstripe suit.'[4]

Parallel to these formal portraits were paintings of his wife and children as well as a few conversation pieces and group portraits, the best known being that of the three writers, Hilaire Belloc, G. K. Chesterton and Maurice Baring, which was exhibited in 1932 (London, National Portrait Gallery) and one of George VI and his family at the Royal Lodge, Windsor, (London, National Portrait Gallery). In 1953, Gunn was commissioned to paint a state portrait of Queen Elizabeth II[6] in which he drew upon a long tradition of monumental royal portraits from Van Dyck to Sir Gerald Kelly (q.v.), depicting the rich robes with characteristic precision and detail.   E.C.W.

NOTES
1. Exh., R.A., 1945 (cat. 201).
2. Exh., R.A., 1961 (cat. 58).
3. Exh., R.A., 1952 (cat. 199).
4. *The Times*, 1 Jan 1965.
5. Exh., R.A., 1950 (cat. 245).
6. Exh., R.A., 1954 (cat. 157); repr., *Royal Academy Illustrated*, 1954, frontispiece.

*repr. in colour on p. 35*

## 27   Pauline Waiting

76 × 64 cm   30 × 25 in
Signed tl: *James Gunn*
Diploma work, accepted 10 Oct 1961 (C.M. 1961, p. 548)

This painting was submitted as a token Diploma work in 1961. Gunn may have intended to replace it with another work at a later stage.

The sitter's costume suggests that the work was executed during the 1940s. Pauline, who died in 1950, was Gunn's second wife. She was the glamorous subject of several portraits in the 1930s and 1940s, two popular examples being *Pauline in the Yellow Dress*[1] and *Pauline: A Venetian Souvenir*.[2] This stylish half-length image, posed as if waiting to meet someone in the grand room of a hotel lobby, possibly 'The Ritz' in London, is a fine example of Gunn's almost photographic realism. The relatively indistinct figures in the background are a foil for the sharply defined focus with which the sitter is depicted, her face, hands, clothes and jewellery being recorded with scrupulous attention to detail. As in most of Gunn's paintings around this time, the paint has been applied quite thinly and meticulously in order to describe the different textures with such clarity.

NOTES
1. Exh, R.A., 1944 (cat. 244).
2. Exh., R.A., 1945 (cat. 498).

EXHIBITIONS: R.A., 1962 (cat. 119); Glasgow, Royal Institute of Fine Arts, 1962 (cat. 85); Bournemouth, Russell-Cotes Art Gallery & Museum, 1965 (cat. 26); Leicestershire Museum and Art Gallery, 1982 (cat. 40); Cheltenham Art Gallery & Museums, 1985 (cat. 30), Swansea, Glynn Vivian Art Gallery & Museum, 1985 (cat. 59).

# Arthur Hacker
## 1858–1919

Arthur Hacker was born in London in 1858, the son of the line engraver Edward Hacker. In 1876 at the age of eighteen he entered the Royal Academy Schools, where his fellow students included Stanhope Forbes (q.v.) and Henry La Thangue (q.v.). Hacker's work was first accepted at the Academy in 1878, but he continued his training between 1880 and 1881 in Paris, at the *atelier* of Léon Bonnat. Whilst in Paris he shared accommodation with Stanhope Forbes, and was certainly aware of the new style of *plein-air* realism. Hacker, however, usually painted genre subjects, and became a popular society portrait painter. He toured Europe for five months with another future Academician, Solomon J. Solomon, visiting Spain and North Africa, and collecting material for the classical and religious subject pictures that he began painting soon after his return to England. Pictures such as *The Waters of Babylon*, 1888 (Rochdale Art Gallery) were favourably received, and Hacker abandoned his genre subjects in favour of a grander, more academic style.

In the 1890s Hacker continued to paint orientalist subjects such as *Vae Victis*,[1] depicting the sack of Morocco, as well as more restrained religious paintings which were also well received. *The Annunciation* (London, Tate Gallery), exhibited in 1892, was purchased for the Chantrey Bequest. In this striking composition the Virgin Mary stands looking directly at the spectator, and details such as the olive tree and the pitcher at the Virgins's feet give the picture a Moroccan flavour. In this work Hacker turned to more luminous tones than he had used in the 1880s, a change perhaps due to his travels in North Africa. Following this success, Hacker was elected an Associate of the Academy in 1894, and soon began teaching at the Academy Schools. He also became much sought after as a portrait painter, but he did not abandon subject paintings. In *The Cloister or the World?*, 1896[2] (Bradford City Art Gallery), he depicts a nun struggling with the choice of following a spiritual or secular life, the two paths represented by the apparitions of an angel and a dancing girl.

In 1909, inspired by J-F. Millet, Hacker began to paint scenes of rural life such as *The Gloaming*,[3] which depicts a girl leading her cow home across the fields at dusk. In contrast to the smooth finish used in his mythological paintings, Hacker later painted quite thickly, aiming for a 'vague but pleasant iridescence'[4] although a critic noted that there was 'never quite enough force of colour in them to justify the lack of form, and they had no great success, either artistic or popular.'[5]

Hacker was elected an Academician in 1910 and experimented further with pictures of London street scenes. However, in the last years of his life he returned to mythological and allegorical subjects such as *Siesta*.[6] In this circular painting of a sleeping figure with a bowl of fruit, both the drapery and the pose of the figure are reminiscent of Leighton's *Flaming June* (Puerto Rico, Museo de Arte Ponce). Hacker died in London in 1919. H.C.V.

NOTES
1. Repr., *Royal Academy Pictures*, 1890, p. 39.
2. Repr., ibid., 1896, p. 122.
3. Repr., ibid., 1909, p. 148.
4. *The Times*, 14 Nov 1919, p. 16.
5. ibid., p. 16.
6. Repr., *Royal Academy Illustrated*, 1917, p. 10.

## 28  A Wet Night at Piccadilly Circus

71 × 91.5 cm    28 × 36 in
Signed and dated bl: *A. Hacker 1910*
Diploma work, accepted 22 Nov 1910 (C.M. XII, p. 360)

In 1911, in contrast to his previously exhibited work, Hacker submitted four London subjects among his Royal Academy exhibits of that year, including this one. These paintings were not carefully detailed renderings of the architecture of London, but rather essays in the evocative atmospheric effects seen in London during foggy afternoons or wet evenings. Hacker sought to capture both this poetic aspect of London and the teeming life of the busy streets. The viewpoint looks across Piccadilly Circus to the London Pavilion Theatre, and the familiar landmark of *Eros*, the sculpted figure by Alfred Gilbert surmounting the Shaftesbury memorial fountain, is just visible on the left.

Critical opinion was divided over *A Wet Night at Piccadilly Circus*. *The Times* felt that Hacker, in 'imposing a violently romantic colour on an almost photographic design', caused Piccadilly Circus to appear 'as if on the stage', and that although he had made 'a bold attempt to free his subject of … prosaic triviality', nonetheless, 'as soon as the novelty passes' the triviality asserts itself again.[1] However, other critics found the work 'a vivid rendering of a scene which everybody knows, but of which few have realised its beauty.'[2] The blaze of lights in this work 'subdued by the foggy atmosphere, the shimmering reflections on the pavement, and the hurry and bustle of the crowded street' were also thought to be realised with the 'greatest verisimilitude', and happily combined into artistic unity'.[3]

NOTES
1. *The Times*, 8 May 1911, p. 10.
2. *Connoisseur*, 30 (1911), p. 142.
3. idem.

EXHIBITIONS: R.A., 1911 (cat. 28); Bournemouth, Russell-Cotes Art Gallery & Museum, 1957 (cat. 857); Bournemouth, Russell-Cotes Art Gallery & Museum, 1965 (cat. 28); R.A., Winter, 1968 (cat. 438).

28

# Oliver Hall
## 1869–1957

'The most important gift is the power of the mind to think and feel the beauty underlying all natural objects.'[1] Hall's artistic creed perfectly describes his own gifts as a landscape painter in oils and watercolour, as a draughtsman and as an etcher.

Oliver Hall was born at Tulse Hill, London on 29 March 1869, the son of a Scottish businesssman. Although his parents lacked any interest in art, as a boy Hall was encouraged by the Liverpool School painter D. A. Williamson, an uncle by marriage. Williamson became a mentor of Hall's and fostered in him a love of North Country scenery which, years later, was memorably celebrated in the purchase for the Chantrey Bequest of *Shap Moors*, 1919 (London, Tate Gallery). In addition to the encouragement of Williamson, the young Hall's talent was brought to the notice of Mr Sparkes of the South Kensington Schools. At the age of seventeen, Hall went to study with Sparkes at South Kensington and later supplemented this tuition by entering evening classes at the Lambeth and Westminster Schools of Art. His first professional success came in 1891 when he was elected an associate of the Royal Society of Painter-Etchers. During the 1890s, his work was admired abroad at the 1893 Columbia Exposition in Chicago and at the Munich International Exhibition of 1897.

Hall initially established himself as a watercolourist, etcher and lithographer. As early as 1896, he had been known as 'an etcher whom the lover of free etching must needs enjoy'[2] and was renowned also as a lithographer. Hall's friend, Rex Vicat Cole noted that his work displayed 'educated sensitiveness and discrimination in the selection and following of lines – particularly in his etchings'.[3] However, his one-man exhibitions held at the Dowdeswell Galleries in 1898, 1900 and 1902 also demonstrated his facility with oils and this medium became an increasingly important part of his output. In 1902 *Angerton Moss* was awarded a gold medal at the Budapest exhibition and was purchased for that city's collection. From 1909, Hall exhibited oil paintings annually at the Royal Academy and it was the success of these which eventually led to his election as an Associate in 1920.

From 1903, Hall began to work extensively in West Sussex on the landscape surrounding the village of Fittleworth. In 1914 he settled nearby at Sutton near Pulborough, where he became a leading figure in a community of artists which included Arthur Rackham, Charles Sims (q.v.), Philip Hugh Padwick and Rex Vicat Cole. In 1924 Hall was asked to become the first President of the Society of Sussex Painters, Sculptors and Engravers.

Hall's home at Sutton commanded a magnificent view: 'It was a classical landscape with not a house in sight, and one which Claude Lorraine might have thought worthy of his genius.'[4] Hall's work testifies to his profound knowledge of the the great landscape painters from Claude, to the Norwich and Barbizon Schools. As regards modern art he considered much of it to be 'a cancerous growth from the underworld'.[5]

During the 1920s he visited Spain frequently with his friend the artist Ernest McAndrew, and the resulting work included many powerful compositions. Official recognition of Hall's status as a painter came in 1930, when he was commissioned to produce large canvasses depicting Indian seaforts, to hang in Government House at Delhi. Oliver Hall's work fell out of fashion during the 1930s and at his one-man exhibition at The Fine Art Society in 1937 only one small canvas was sold.     T.J.B.

NOTES
1. M. Muncaster, *The Wind in the Oak*, London, 1978, p. 11.
2. F. Wedmore, 'The Revival of Lithography – II', *Art Journal*, 1896, p. 46.
3. Rex Vicat Cole, *The Artistic Anatomy of Trees*, London, 1916, p. 42.
4. M. Muncaster, op. cit., p. 12.
5. ibid., p. 51.

## 29  Spring

60 × 74 cm    23½ × 29 in
Signed br: *Oliver Hall*
Diploma work, accepted 26 July 1927 (C.M. XXV, p. 326)

As with many of Hall's exhibited paintings, this landscape does not concern us principally as a record of a particular locality, but as a pictorial arrangement of elements to be found in any English village, at a specific season and under a characteristic effect of light.

The study of trees was Hall's everyday activity: 'nothing to me is more fashionable and enjoyable than to stroll out into the byways of an old forest, ruminating on and analysing the beauty of trees, noting their characteristics of form and colour and lines of composition. The play of sunshine and shadow, swept on a day of west wind in March, is very beautiful.'[1] In these lines, Hall summarises his intentions in *Spring*. Through the constant and intensive study of tree forms which comprised his life's work, he was able to depict the skeletal trees in *Spring* with complete confidence and with a precise knowledge of their anatomy. His artist-son, Claude Muncaster, when writing a textbook on painting, recalled the cabinet containing 'hundreds of lovely pencil studies of trees and tree compositions'[2] which was a repository of Hall's experience as a painter and draughtsman. When this was destroyed by fire Hall was still able to refer to his store in visual memory: 'the study of years had become an integral part of his mind and imagination and . . . he was soon at work again and painting and drawing trees better than ever.'[3]

In his oil paintings, Hall employed a bold impasto and, in *Spring*, clearly enjoyed the textures of bark and of the fall of shadow over the track in the foreground. It is the trees, however, boldly and solidly designed, which distinguish the work.

NOTES
1. M. Muncaster, *The Wind in the Oak*, London, 1978, p. 11.
2. C. Muncaster, *Landscape and Marine Painting (in oil and water-colour)*, London, 1958, p. 69.
3. idem.

EXHIBITIONS: R.A., 1928 (cat. 247); Bournemouth, Russell-Cotes Art Gallery and Museum, 1965 (cat. 29); South London Art Gallery, 1973 (cat. 68).

29

# George Harcourt
## 1868–1947

George Harcourt, a Scottish painter of landscapes, portraits and subject pictures, was born in 1868 in Dunbartonshire. He studied for three years at Hubert Herkhomer's School of Art in Bushey, Hertfordshire where he benefitted from the artist's unconventional ideas about art education. In a book entitled *My School and My Gospel*,[1] Herkhomer described his teaching principles as a 'search for the personality of each student' as opposed to the traditional academic method which 'involved squeezing the supple mind of a young painter into a master's manner, from which he may never wholly extricate himself.'[2] It was at an exhibition of the pictures of Hubert Herkhomer and his pupils at The Fine Art Society, that Harcourt's paintings first gained public attention. Soon after, in 1893, he began exhibiting at the New English Art Club and at the Royal Academy, where his symbolic subject paintings and group portraits received much critical acclaim. Influenced by G. F. Watts, Harcourt's paintings were praised for their sentiment, colour and drawing as well as for their dramatic qualities. Some, like *At the Window* (exh. R. A., 1893) and *Psyche: Farewell*,[3] were accompanied by quotations from Victorian poets such as Keats and Tennyson. Particularly famous was his painting of *The Leper's Wife*,[4] described as 'a representation of the great ideal of self-sacrifice'.[5]

After completing his training, Harcourt taught at Herkhomer's School for a while before being appointed as governor of the Art School at Hospitalfield near Arbroath in Scotland. While teaching there he was commissioned by the Stock Exchange to paint a fresco entitled *The Founding of the Bank of England in 1694*. It was one of a series of frescos at the Royal Exchange, the first of which had been painted by Lord Leighton. In 1909, Harcourt returned to live at Bushey and in the following years exhibited many domestic scenes at the Academy featuring his home and children, such as *The Birthday*[6] and *Fairy Tales*.[7] As the years passed he painted more commissioned portraits, probably as a result of his involvement with the Royal Society of Portrait Painters of which he became a member in 1912 and was later President.

Harcourt was elected an Associate of the Royal Academy in 1919 and a full Academician in 1926. A year later, in the summer term of 1927, he acted as a temporary Director of the Royal Academy Schools before the appointment of Walter Westley Russell (q.v.) as Keeper. He also stood as a candidate for the Presidency of the Royal Academy in 1938 but was defeated by Sir Edwin Landseer Lutyens. His work was successful internationally, winning him medals at the Paris Salons of 1896, and 1923 and at the Amsterdam International Exhibition of 1912.   E.C.W.

NOTES
1. Professor Sir Hubert von Herkhomer C.V.O., *My School and My Gospel*, 1908.
2. Herkhomer, op. cit., p. 15.
3. Repr., *Royal Academy Pictures*, 1894, p. 195.
4. Repr., ibid., 1896, p. 109.
5. *Studio*, 70 (1917), p. 167.
6. Repr., *Royal Academy Pictures*, 1910, p. 39.
7. Repr., ibid., 1912, p. 62.

## 30   Miss Anne Harcourt

126 × 103 cm    49½ × 40½ in
Signed and dated br: *George Harcourt 1921*
Diploma work, accepted 2 Nov 1926 (C.M. XXV p. 243)

This is a portrait of Harcourt's daughter Anne who later became a painter herself and a regular exhibitor at the Royal Academy. Casually seated with her violin, the elegant young lady is seen in a familiar domestic setting, certain details of which are highlighted in the painting. Like other Edwardian portrait painters, such as Frank Bramley (q.v.), Philip Wilson Steer and John Singer Sargent (q.v.), Harcourt makes use of a relatively dark background to accentuate the effects of light and colour on the sitter's dress and to create a sense of drama in the painting. Its spontaneous quality probably results from Harcourt's particular technique. As the critic in the *Studio* wrote, 'he does not build up his pictures on a basis of multitudinous studies. After preparing a slight sketch of the composition and colour, he designs the picture direct on the canvas, evolving his idea as he proceeds.'[1]

NOTE
1. *Studio*, 70 (1917), p. 169.

EXHIBITIONS: R.A., 1927 (cat. 165); Bournemouth, Russell-Cotes Art Gallery & Museum, 1965 (cat. 30).

30

# George Henry
## 1858–1943

Little is known about the early life of George Henry, but it seems that he was born in 1858,[1] perhaps near Kilmarnock in Scotland, and was brought up by an uncle after the death of his parents. He began to draw while working in a patent office, although he complained that 'one learns precision from engineering drawings, but there is not exactly scope for originality.'[2]

Henry worked as a commercial artist producing posters and designs for domestic stained glass, but he was determined to become a painter, and to this end he joined James Guthrie and E. A. Walton at Brig o'Turk in 1881. The village had been colonised by artists for many years, but Henry and the other 'Glasgow Boys' (as they later became known), chose not to depict the beautiful landscape which had attracted other artists to the area, but instead painted the village, its gardens and its people.

In 1882 Henry enrolled for a summer term at the Glasgow School of Art, still giving his occupation as a 'clerk'. However, when attending further classes in 1883 he at last described himelf as an 'art student'. Henry never trained in Paris, but between 1883 and 1886 made many visits there 'to see the methods of work there and look in at Julian's studio.'[3] He continued to work with the 'Glasgow Boys', attending informal classes at W. Y. Macgregor's studio and painting with Guthrie at Cockburnspath in 1883. His paintings of this period, such as *Playmates*,[4] painted in 1884, show the influence of the French naturalist painter Bastien-Lepage (distilled through Guthrie) in its subdued tones and thick paint, applied with square brushes.

The beginning of a long and creative partnership occurred in 1885 when Henry met Edward Atkinson Hornel (1864–1933) in Cockburnspath. Both artists gradually moved away from the depiction of rustic subjects in the new realistic style, and became more interested in colour and design. A work such as *Autumn* (Glasgow Art Gallery) painted in 1888, typifies Henry's work of this period. From patches of rich colour which verge on abstraction, he builds up the image of a girl standing in a woodland glade. Barely distinguishable from the trees amongst which she stands, the girl is perhaps a personification of autumn itself. The painting's high horizon is emphasised by a perspective which deliberately avoids an illusionistic approach. The surface texture created by Henry's square brushstrokes and heavy impasto, is of primary importance.

Whilst working in Galloway with Hornel in 1889, Henry painted the extraordinary *A Galloway Landscape* (Glasgow Art Gallery), which stands comparison with Gauguin's work done at Pont-Aven. The impact of the picture is two-dimensional; cows are placed in profile on a hillside with no real effort at the illusion of reality, and the burn creates swirling patterns as it winds through the countryside. In 1890, inspired by Celtic myths, Henry and Hornel jointly painted several highly decorative canvasses, including *The Druids* (Glasgow Art Gallery) which depicts a pagan procession winding down a hill.

Encouraged by Whistler's enthusiasm for Japanese art and Alfred East's (q.v.) visit to Japan in 1889, Hornel and Henry, sponsored by the Glasgow art dealer Alexander Reid, sailed to Japan in 1893 and stayed there for eighteen months. Unfortunately many of Henry's oil paintings stuck together during the voyage home and so little of his work from the trip survives. His watercolours, however, fared better and critics noticed an 'extraordinary delicacy in his tones'[5] and paid compliment to the linear qualities in his designs. On his return from Japan, Henry worked in Glasgow, and in 1899 was commissioned, with artists such as Lavery (q.v.), to paint a mural in the Glasgow City Chambers. Lured, however, by the financial rewards of portraiture he moved to London in about 1901 and settled in Chelsea. He began to exhibit portraits, usually of women, at the Royal Academy in 1904. Elected an Associate in 1907, he became a full member in 1920. Only in the 1930s did Henry again paint and exhibit landscapes, often depicting the Sussex Downs. He died in 1943 aged eighty-five.   H.C.V.

NOTES
1. Letter from George Henry to the Secretary of the R.A., 27 May 1921, gives birth date as 14 March 1858, R.A. Archives, George Henry file.
2. Quoted G. Buchanan, 'A Galloway Landscape', *Scottish Arts Review*, VII, no. 4 (1960), pp. 13–17.
3. idem.
4. Repr., R. Billcliffe, *The Glasgow Boys*, 1985, p. 152.
5. *Studio*, 68 (1916), p. 76.

## 31   Brambles

76.2 × 76.2 cm   30 × 30 in
Signed and dated bl: *GEORGE HENRY – 1920*
Diploma work, accepted 22 March 1921 (C.M. XXIV, p. 318)

*The Times* obituary felt that Henry had always tried 'to make the best of two worlds; the world of naturalistic representation and that of intense colour with a decorative intention.'[1] *Brambles* reflects this dichotomy in that, despite the dappled light falling naturally on the figure, the painting is stylised, owing to Henry's concentration on the decorative pattern made by the tree and brambles. As a contemporary reviewer noticed, by the use of 'sumptuous colour he endeavoured to render, at once by symbol and by interpretation, the profound richness of nature.'[2] Here the very complexity of the surface decoration creates an impression of abundance.

*Brambles* recalls the style of Henry's earlier works. The figure, in profile, the high horizon and the limited depth emphasise the two-dimensional decorative aspect of the work, relating it to earlier compositions such as *Autumn* (Glasgow Art Gallery) painted in 1888 at Kirkcudbridge when he was working closely with Hornel. The dress worn by the figure indicates another influence, Henry's trip to Japan. He frequently returned in his later works to paint geisha women or Japanese gardens, perhaps inspired by photographs he had taken during his stay.

NOTES
1. *The Times*, 24 Dec 1943.
2. *Studio*, 31 (1904), p. 5.

EXHIBITIONS: R.A., 1921 (cat. 119); Bournemouth, Russell-Cotes Art Gallery & Museum, 1965 (cat. 32); Swansea, Glynn Vivian Art Gallery & Museum, 1985 (cat. 27).

31

# Sir Herbert Hughes-Stanton
1870–1937

Sir Herbert Hughes-Stanton was born in 1870 in Chelsea, the son of William Hughes, a still life painter. Early in his career he added Stanton to his surname, probably to distinguish him from the other artists in his family (his brother Talbot Hughes also became an artist as did his son, Blair Hughes-Stanton).

Herbert Hughes-Stanton never studied at an art school but 'received the whole of his art education from his father'.[1] Though initially he had not thought of pursuing an artistic career, when he was sixteen he had a work accepted at the Grosvenor Gallery in London. He painted regularly in the Sussex countryside around Arundel and in 1897 had a work accepted at the Academy.

Between 1906 and 1914 Hughes-Stanton made annual trips to France and also toured other parts of Europe. His work was widely admired in France and was collected by many major museums: in 1907 he exhibited at the Paris Salon and won a gold medal. In the following year his artistic reputation in England was consolidated by the purchase of *A Pasturage among the Dunes* (London, Tate Gallery) for the Chantrey Bequest.

Elected an Associate of the Academy in 1913, Hughes-Stanton's 'excellent eye for arrangement' and 'pleasant instinct for effect' made him a popular member of the Hanging Committee for the Academy's annual Summer Exhibitions.[2] Towards the end of the First World War, Hughes-Stanton again painted in France and in 1919 an exhibition of his paintings of the British War zones was held at The Fine Art Society.

Hughes-Stanton often worked in watercolour and *The Times* thought his work was 'saved from being topographical by close regard for atmospheric conditions and delicacy in following gradations of colour according to the direction and quality of light.'[3] In 1920 he was elected President of the Royal Watercolour Society, the year in which he also became a full Academician. Further honours followed, including a knighthood in 1923.

Around 1924 Hughes-Stanton visited Japan, and The Fine Art Society held an exhibition of his work on his return. He refrained from depicting the more obvious subjects such as 'the brilliance of our Flowers and Geishas' and concentrated instead on 'the sterner aspects of our land'.[4] *Sunrise, Mount Fuji, Japan,*[5] exhibited in 1924, is an example of his interest in depicting the effect of morning sunlight over a panoramic landscape.

Hughes-Stanton continued painting until his death in 1937; a memorial exhibition of his work held at The Fine Art Society shortly after his death included watercolours he had recently painted in Greece.   H.C.V.

NOTES
1. *Art Journal,* 1910, p. 78.
2. *The Times,* 6 Aug 1937.
3. *The Times,* 4 Aug 1937.
4. *Landscapes of Japan in water-colour by Sir H. Hughes-Stanton,* foreword by G. Komai, exhib. cat., Fine Art Society, 1925, p. 2.
5. Repr., *Royal Academy Illustrated,* 1924, p. 29.

## 32   Evening: Equihen, Pas de Calais

60 × 86 cm   23½ × 34 in
Signed and dated bl: *Hughes-Stanton 1920*
Diploma work, accepted 10 June 1920 (C.M. XXIV, p. 239)

Equihen, in the Pas de Calais was one of Hughes-Stanton's favourite sketching grounds, where he had worked regularly since 1906, interrupted only by the outbreak of the First World War. Here, as in most of his landscapes, he 'indulges his love of massive and stately design', but nonetheless preserves 'all the accidental charm and truthful look of a sketch done direct from Nature'.[1] An air of serenity is conveyed by the absence of any human incident in the picture, the only figure being that of a farmer with his load, walking along the lane. It was because of Hughes-Stanton's concentration on the broad sweep of nature rather than on its human inhabitants that the *Studio* considered his landscapes to capture 'the great solemnity, the hush, and something of the impassive dignity of nature'.[2]

NOTES
1. *Studio,* 75 (1918), p. 9.
2. *Studio,* 42 (1907), p. 270.

EXHIBITIONS: R.A., 1921 (cat. 186); Bournemouth, Russell-Cotes Art Gallery & Museum, 1965 (cat. 34).

32

# Richard Jack
## 1866–1952

Born in Sunderland in 1866, Jack first studied at the York School of Art before attending the South Kensington Schools. Here he won a Gold Medal and in 1888 a travelling scholarship to study in Paris at the Académie Julian. He returned to Paris for the following two years and exhibited at the Salon. When he was back in London in 1891, he joined the staff of *The Idler* as an illustrator. With Melton Fisher, John H. Bacon, John Collier, Solomon J. Solomon, George Henry (q.v.) and George Harcourt (q.v.) he provided the central consensus of Edwardian portraiture at the annual Royal Academy and New Gallery exhibitions. His work showed the influence of various contemporaries, Sargent (q.v.) and Lavery (q.v.), Orpen (q.v.) and John (q.v.).

Jack made his debut at the Royal Academy in 1893 and, for the following six or seven years, exhibited allegorical nudes and portraits. He was a founder member of the Royal Miniature Society and also exhibited regularly with the Society of Portrait Painters. During the first decade of the century his portraits were mostly of fashionable women, and his style and props often recalled those of Romney and Gainsborough. He became an Associate of the Royal Academy in 1914 and a full Academician in 1921. In 1912 his painting of the conductor Arthur Nikisch, *Rehearsal with Nikisch,* was purchased by the Chantrey Bequest for the Tate Gallery.

In 1916, Jack accepted a commission in the Canadian Army to go to France and paint for the Canadian War Records. There he spent two years making preparatory sketches for two vast canvasses which recorded battle scenes at Ypres and Vimy Ridge and which now hang in the National Gallery of Canada in Ottawa. Like Augustus John, Jack painted many portraits of celebrated officers and men whilst in France.

In 1926 Jack was commissioned to paint a full-length portrait of King George V for the Royal Borough of Fulham which the King later purchased himself. He subsequently painted a portrait of Queen Mary and in 1927 two large interiors of Buckingham Palace, *The Chinese Chippendale Room* and *The Blue Drawing Room*. During 1927 and 1928, Jack made two extensive tours in Canada, painting many portraits and a large number of landscapes of the Canadian Rockies. In 1938 he and his wife moved to Canada where both his son and daughter had settled, and he remained in Montreal until his death in 1952. E.C.W.

*repr. in colour on p. 33*

## 33 On the Moors

63.5 × 76 cm    25 × 30 in
Signed and dated br: *R. Jack. 1921.*
Diploma work, accepted 7 April 1921 (C.M. XXIV, pp. 323–4)

This informal portrait represents either the artist's daughter or his wife with their dog. Although the painting is naturalistic and depicts a rural, outdoor scene, both the lady and the dog appear deliberately posed, as if in a studio. The landscape is treated like a stage or platform, and the sky, occupying a large part of the picture surface, acts as a backdrop.

The fashionable outdoor clothes of the sitter give the painting a contemporary mood whilst also serving to link the figure more closely with its environment. The brown and grey colours applied in solid patches over the whole painting capture the bucolic mood of the subject. The broad handling of paint contrasts with the more highly finished society portraits which Jack was also painting at this time, although stylistically it shows similarities with other outdoor scenes and townscapes by the artist done in the early 1920s.

EXHIBITIONS: R.A., 1921 (cat. 23); Sunderland Art Gallery, 1951 (cat. 16); Bournemouth, Russell-Cotes Art Gallery & Museum, 1957 (cat. 878); Bournemouth, Russell-Cotes Art Gallery & Museum, 1965 (cat. 35).

# Augustus Edwin John
## 1878–1961

For many, Augustus John symbolised artistic independence and bohemianism. Thus, when he was finally elected an Associate of the Royal Academy in 1921, John felt that he had to defend his decision to join the establishment. He wrote, that, 'to many it seemed to be not a triumph but a surrender. Had I not been a Slade student? Was I not a member of the New English Art Club? Did I not march in the front ranks of the insurgents? The answer to these questions is "Yes". But had I cultivated the Royal Academy in any way? Had I ever submitted a single work to the Selection Committee? ... History answers "No". Without even blowing my own trumpet the walls of Jericho had fallen ... I acknowledged and returned the compliment.'[1] John became a full member of the Royal Academy in 1928 although he resigned in 1938 as a protest against the Selection Committee's rejection of Wyndham Lewis's portrait of T.S. Eliot (see cat. 19). He was, however, re-elected in 1940 and two years later received the Order of Merit. He was later honoured by a major retrospective exhibition at Burlington House in 1954.

Born in 1878 in Tenby, Wales, Augustus Edwin John was the son of a Welsh solicitor, E.W. John and younger brother of the artist Gwen John. At the age of seventeen, after a general education at Tenby and at a private school in Clifton, John entered the Slade School of Art in 1894 on a scholarship. There he soon gained a reputation for his drawing which was described by Professor Tonks as 'unequalled since Michelangelo'.[2] One of his fellow pupils and rivals at the Slade was Sir William Orpen (q.v.), with whom he organised the running of the Chelsea Art School between 1903 and 1907. In 1899 he began to exhibit at the New English Art Club and in the same year, at the age of twenty-one, he held a successful one-man show at the Carfax Gallery where most of his work continued to be shown until his election to the Royal Academy in 1921.

In 1901 he married his first wife, Ida Nettleship, and went to live in Liverpool where he taught at the art school affiliated to the University. While he was there he embarked on a series of etchings which established him as a master of the art. At about this time, he developed his lifelong interest in the Romany cult, which led him a few years later, to adopt their lifestyle by living with his family in a picturesque gypsy caravan on Dartmoor.

Throughout his career John worked in a wide range of genres including society and literary portraits, landscapes and imaginative figure paintings which often included members of his large family. Although mainly based in England, John travelled widely, making regular painting trips to Paris, Provence, Wales and Ireland. In 1923 he visited the United States for various portrait commissions and in 1937 went to Jamaica in search of new subjects. During the First World War John became an Official War Artist with the Canadian forces but failed to finish a large-scale commemorative painting intended to honour the dead. However, while the Peace Conference was on in Paris in 1919, he painted several official portraits of Field-Marshals and High Commissioners.

Despite being briefly associated with the Camden Town and Bloomsbury artists and being invited to contribute to Roger Fry and Clive Bell's Second Post-Impressionist exhibition, John remained outside artistic groups and movements. He was, however, very aware of recent developments in European art, particularly the paintings of Puvis de Chavannes, Gauguin, Picasso, Modigliani and Matisse. Much of his own work was also influenced by past European masters such as Hals, Rembrandt, Goya and El Greco. He died in October 1961, just before his eighty-fourth birthday.  E.C.W.

NOTES
1. M. Holroyd, *Augustus John*, Vol. II, 1975, pp.105–6.
2. R. Shone, *Augustus John*, 1979, p.60.

34  *repr. in colour on p. 36*

# Sir Gerald Festus Kelly
## 1879–1972

## 34  Portrait of a Young Man

61 × 46.5 cm    24 × 18¼ in
Signed tl: *John*
Diploma work, accepted 10 April 1930 (C.M. XXV, pp. 543–4)

The young man in this portrait is John's son, Robin, whose mother was the artist's first wife, Ida Nettleship. Born in October 1904 he was probably in his early twenties when this portrait was painted. Throughout his career, John drew and painted portraits of his family alongside his commissioned works of society beauties and distinguished writers. Unlike his earlier, more highly finished portraits which demonstrate John's interest in the Old Masters, this informal and apparently spontaneous study of his son reflects the artist's awareness of French art, particularly the work of the Impressionists. Most of John's well-known portraits in the 1920s, particularly those of fashionable female sitters such as *The Marchesa Casati*, 1919 (Toronto, Art Gallery of Ontario) and *Madame Suggia*, 1923 (London, Tate Gallery), are characterised by strong contours and clearly defined forms. Here, however, John is less concerned to create a monumental image by virtue of his draughtsmanship. Each part of the figure is treated in a similar, almost incidental manner with the paint loosely handled and applied quite thinly in short, swift strokes using a narrow tonal range. According to his biographer Michael Holroyd, Augustus John painted energetically, 'with intense physical concentration',[1] often going up very close to his subject and staring hard before setting to work: 'These were unorthodox methods for a painter who was presumed to be growing more conventional: the methods almost of an action painter rather than the Royal Academician he had recently become.'[2]

NOTES
1.  M. Holroyd, *Augustus John*, Vol II, 1975, pp.104–5.
2.  idem.

EXHIBITIONS: R.A., 1930 (cat. 266); R.A., Winter, 1956–57 (cat. 802); Glasgow, Royal Glasgow Institute of the Fine Arts, 1961 (cat. 226); Bournemouth, Russell-Cotes Art Gallery & Museum, 1965 (cat. 36); R.A., Winter, 1968 (cat. 4); Leicestershire Museum and Art Gallery, 1982 (cat. 47); Folkestone, Arts Centre, 1974 (cat. 22); South London Art Gallery, 1973 (cat. 14); Cheltenham Art Gallery and Museums, 1985 (cat. 3).

Apart from his success as a portrait painter, Kelly is probably best remembered as the President of the Royal Academy between 1949–54. Kelly succeeded Sir Alfred Munnings (q.v.) in the post, and his first concern was to try and negotiate a *rapprochement* between the Academy and the rest of the art world. He increased the number of loan exhibitions and his lively and enthusiastic commentaries on television helped to re-vitalise the Academy's public image. It was through his initiative that Sir Stanley Spencer (q.v.) was re-elected to the Academy in 1950 and that an exhibition of the Ecole de Paris 1900–1950 was held at the Royal Academy in 1951 in an effort to encourage the modern movement. In addition it was Kelly who was responsible for organising major retrospectives of Royal Academicians (such as Augustus John (q.v.), Sir Alfred Munnings (q.v.) and Frank Brangwyn (q.v.)) at Burlington House while the artists were still alive and able to contribute to the selection and hanging of their work. At first, Kelly refused his own retrospective in 1957 on the grounds that he was not good enough: 'I thought the Academy had invited me because I had been a useful President rather than because I was a good Painter.'[1]

Born in London in 1879, the son of a vicar, Kelly had a conventional education at Eton and then Cambridge, where he read English. On deciding to become a painter, Kelly went to Paris to study. He had not had any serious training to date and did not enter any of the Paris studios. Rather he preferred to work independently. His first two exhibited pictures were hung 'on the line' in the Salon of 1902. Whilst in Paris, Kelly was introduced to Renoir, Monet, Degas and Rodin by the art-dealer Paul Durand-Ruel, and he also met Sickert (q.v.), Sargent (q.v.), Clive Bell and Somerset Maugham. It was Maugham who encouraged Kelly to go to Burma in 1908; the pictures he painted there of temple dancers are among his best-known work. On his return to England in 1909 Kelly became a regular exhibitor at the International Society, the National Portrait Society, the Modern Portrait Painters Society and the Royal Academy, of which he became an Associate in 1922 and a full member in 1930. Until the outbreak of the Second World War when he joined the Intelligence Department of the Admiralty, Kelly alternated between long stays in Spain and portrait paint-ing in London. Although his fame rests chiefly on his portraits, Kelly executed spontaneous landscapes and seascapes on small panels throughout the 1900s, largely influenced by the Impressionists and Whistler.

Throughout his career, Kelly was much in demand for com-memorative portraits whose sitters included members of the royal family, Winston Churchill, Ralph Vaughan Williams and other celebrities. In 1938 he was appointed a member of the Royal Fine Art Commission and was commissioned to paint two state portraits of King George VI and Queen Elizabeth. On completion of the portraits in 1945 he was rewarded with a knighthood. He died in 1972 at the age of ninety-two.    E.C.W.

NOTE
1.  *Art and Antiques Weekly*, 2 Feb 1972.

## 35 Jane XXX

75 × 63.5 cm    29½ × 25 in
Diploma work, accepted 24 April 1930 (C.M. XXV, p. 548)

In 1920 Kelly married Lilian Ryan, a young artist's model who first sat for him in 1916 on the recommendation of Clausen (q.v.). Kelly re-christened his wife Jane and painted her no fewer than fifty times in varying guises and poses throughout his career, exhibiting a portrait of her nearly every year at the Royal Academy. When asked why, he replied, 'I paint her because I think nobody has a prettier wife than I.'[1] Year after year a portrait of her would appear with the simple title 'Jane', and roman numerals which referred to the year in which the painting was first exhibited at the Academy. Hence the title of this Diploma work on being elected Academician in 1930. When Kelly's wife was introduced to Queen Mary, Her Majesty exclaimed, 'Jane of many Janes'.[2] Kelly was very particular both about dress in a portrait and about the pose, which often took him days to find. According to Jane, the robes she wore for this portrait so meticulously painted by Kelly, generated much interest: 'Everyone said how wealthy the Kellys must be – look at the gorgeous clothes she is wearing.'[3] However, a friend of the Kellys reported: 'Actually, Jane had bought 3 or 4 yards of velvet and attached it to a fur collar belonging to a friend. G. K. wished to paint moiré; she had no moiré dress and so bought a yard of it which she made into a strap that appears over the cloak.'[4]

Kelly's portraits were so popular largely because they captured such a good likeness of the sitter and because of their high degree of realism. The obituary in *The Guardian* said that 'if it be true, as many maintain, that the test of a portrait painter is whether he can delineate character by combining truthful representation of the facts with good draughtsmanship, then Kelly was one of the most accomplished portraitists of his generation.'[5] He was a perfectionist in technique, every brushstroke was carefully judged and every detail was delicately expressed. In order to ensure a high level of realism, Kelly often worked from enlarged photographs which he subsequently squared up like a graph before transferring the image to the canvas.

Jane was not the only subject to be painted several times in different poses. His lifelong friend, W. Somerset Maugham, for example, sat for him half-a-dozen times at different periods of his life, the most well-known portrait being an intimate study

35    *repr. in colour on p. 34*

of the writer as a young man, sitting against an Oriental screen, surrounded by 'objets d'art' and dressed for a walk. Executed in 1911 this painting was given the title, *The Jester*, and was later bought for the Chantrey Bequest.

NOTES
1.  *Art and Antiques Weekly*, 2 Feb 1972.
2.  D. Hudson, *For Love of Painting*, p. 41.
3.  ibid., p. 50.
4.  From the diary of Mr Hilles, 19 Dec 1930, quoted D. Hudson, op. cit., p. 50.
5.  *The Guardian*, 6 Jan 1972.

EXHIBITIONS: R.A., 1930 (cat. 14); Bournemouth, Russell-Cotes Art Gallery & Museum, 1965 (cat. 37); Leicestershire Museum and Art Gallery, 1982 (cat. 48); Cheltenham Art Gallery and Museums, 1985 (cat. 5).

# Harold Knight
## 1874–1961

Harold Knight was born in Nottingham in 1874, the son of William Knight, an architect and amateur painter. He trained at the Nottingham School of Art where he met a fellow student, Laura Johnson, whom he married in 1903. Dame Laura Knight went on to become a highly successful painter in her own right and the couple became the first husband and wife Academicians in the history of the Royal Academy. In 1893, whilst at Nottingham School of Art, Harold won a travelling scholarship which took him to Paris for a year where he studied at the Académie Julian under Jean-Paul Laurens and Benjamin Constant. He first exhibited at the Royal Academy in 1896 and in 1906 had his first joint exhibition with his wife at the Leicester Galleries.

In 1894, on his return from Paris, Harold settled in Staithes, a picturesque fishing village on the coast of Yorkshire where he began painting landscapes, seascapes and interior scenes showing members of the local community. Until around 1907 the Knights lived mainly in Staithes, although they made several visits to Holland where, in Amsterdam, they spent some time studying the work of Vermeer, Rembrandt and Hals. While staying in the artist's colony of Laren, Harold painted simple interior scenes with peasants and farm subjects in the manner of the nineteenth-century artists of the Hague School.

After their return to England, Harold and Laura went to live in the artists' colony of Newlyn, Cornwall which included Alfred Munnings (q.v.), Dod Proctor (1892–1972), Ernest Proctor (1886–1935) and Stanhope Forbes (q.v.). Initially, Harold continued painting the same genre subjects as he had in Holland and Staithes, using local inhabitants and landscapes executed 'en plein air', although like his wife he began to work in brighter colours partly in response to the Cornish light. Around 1909 he embarked upon a more sophisticated series of paintings of women in well-furnished interiors. These were subjects which he worked on until the end of his life; later examples bear close comparison with the work of his contemporary, Leonard Campbell Taylor (q.v.) and show the artist's interest in the seventeenth-century Dutch paintings of Vermeer and Pieter de Hooch.

During the First World War Harold Knight was a conscientious objector and worked on the land instead of joining the army. After the War the Knights moved to London where Harold received a steady flow of commissions for portraits from clients who were well known in public or social life. He exhibited regularly at the Royal Academy and at the Royal Society of Portrait Painters. He was elected A.R.A. in 1928 and R.A. in 1937, in each case one year after his wife. He died in Gloucestershire in 1961. E.C.W.

## 36 Ethel Bartlett

61 × 49.5 cm   24 × 19½ in
Signed tr: *Harold Knight*
Diploma work, accepted 17 March 1937 (C.M. XXVII, p. 6)

Ethel Bartlett was a pianist whom Knight painted on more than one occasion. A formal, full-length portrait of the sitter was exhibited at the Royal Academy in 1935. Although this work is a more intimate study of her, she is shown in both paintings with her head turned away and tilted upwards, a pose intended to emphasise her artistic sensibility. Like his contemporary, Gerald Kelly (q.v.), Knight possessed the necessary technical skill to capture a likeness with apparent ease. He admired seventeenth-century Dutch genre paintings, particularly the work of Vermeer and Pieter de Hooch. Here he is clearly influenced by Vermeer's attention to detail, carefully recording the sensation of light across the woman's figure and picking out the silky folds in her dress which are repeated on the pillow behind her. The subtle gradation of tone enhances the quiet mood of the painting whilst not detracting from the freshness and brilliance of the image. The space in the painting is ambiguous and the relationship between the figure and the pillow unclear. It is difficult to tell whether Ethel Bartlett is sitting, lying or standing, on account of the enclosed nature of the painting.

EXHIBITIONS: R.A., 1930 (cat. 119); R.A., 1937 (cat. 162); Nottingham Castle Museum, 1951 (cat. 248); Bournemouth, Russell-Cotes Art Gallery & Museum, 1965 (cat. 38); R. A., Winter, 1968 (cat. 464); Leicestershire Museum and Art Gallery, 1982 (cat. 51); Cheltenham Art Gallery and Museums, 1985 (cat. 12); Swansea, Glynn Vivian Art Gallery & Museum, 1985 (cat. 41).

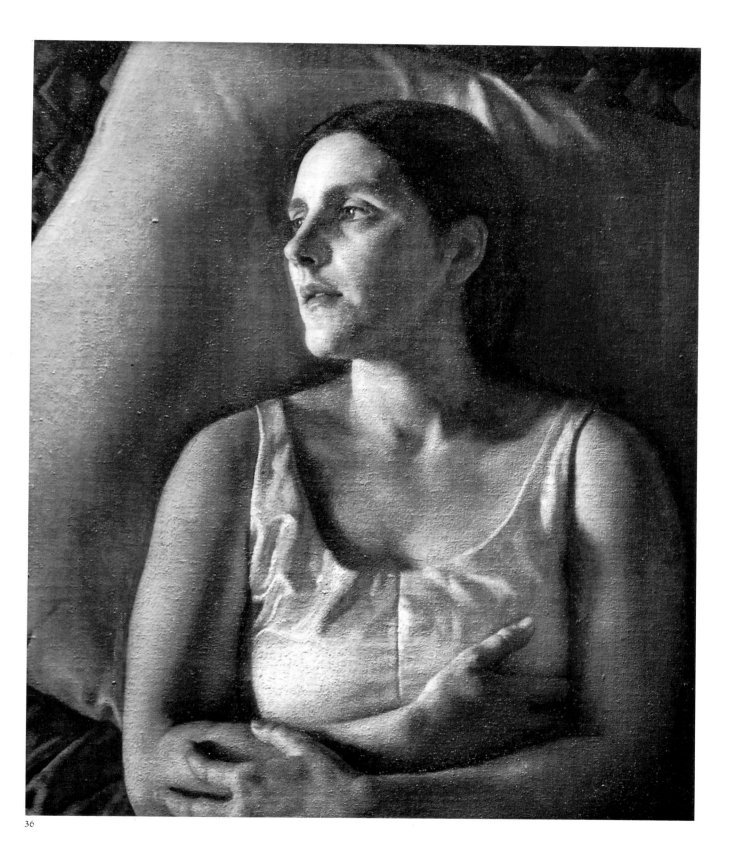

36

# Henry Herbert La Thangue
## 1859–1929

'Sunlight was the thing that attracted him: this and some simple motive of rural occupation, enhanced by a picturesque surround.'[1] Writing in 1931, Clausen (q.v.) felt these were the main preoccupations of La Thangue's work.

Born in Croydon in 1859, he attended Dulwich College, where one of his fellow pupils was Stanhope Forbes (q.v.), the Newlyn School painter. La Thangue studied briefly at the South Kensington Schools, which he found to be 'at a low ebb'.[2] In 1875 he entered the Royal Academy Schools, winning a gold medal there in 1879. Armed with a letter of introduction from Lord Leighton, La Thangue gained a place to complete his training at Gérôme's *atelier* in Paris. Although he gained much technical expertise in the three years spent there, it was *plein-air* painting which really absorbed him. The tradition of *plein-air* painting, from the Barbizon School painters to Bastien-Lepage, inspired La Thangue to spend his summer holidays during the early 1880s sketching with Forbes at Cancale and Quimperlé on the Brittany coast. Square brushstrokes and a lighter palette were soon adopted on these sketching trips and the historical subject pictures which he had exhibited at the Academy up until 1880 were abandoned.

La Thangue was a central figure in the circle of painters who, dissatisfied with the art establishment in England, had grouped together to found the New English Art Club in 1886 as an alternative venue for exhibitions. La Thangue, however, proposed even more fundamental reforms. Attacking the Royal Academy as 'the diseased root from which other evils grow',[3] because it elected its own members for life, he published his ideas for 'A National Art Exhibition'[4] in 1887. Drawing his inspiration from the recently established Salon des Indépendants in Paris, he suggested that all artists should be able to vote for a jury to be responsible for the selection of each exhibition. Despite support from eminent artists such as Clausen (q.v.) and Holman Hunt, his proposal was ignored, marking the end of his active involvement in the politics of the art world.

Preferring to live in the countryside, he moved to the Norfolk Broads and then to Rye before settling at Bosham in Sussex in 1891. *The Return of the Reapers* (London, Tate Gallery), with its high horizon, is typical of this period, reflecting the influence of Bastien-Lepage. He hoped to achieve a naturalistic effect within the confines of good taste and had a 'horror of emphasising the story by cheap and vulgar means, thereby violating the sentiment of nature'.[5]

In 1891 La Thangue exhibited at the Royal Academy for the first time in over a decade, perhaps hoping to effect reforms from the inside. His election as an Associate in 1898 was prompted by the success of *The Man with the Scythe* (London,

Tate Gallery), a Chantrey Bequest purchase. In this work La Thangue combines elements of the Victorian narrative tradition with a symbolist intensity wholly French in its origins. The figure of Death suggested by an old reaper with a scythe, is integrated into the rustic naturalist genre which La Thangue had developed.

In 1898, after moving to Graffham in Sussex, La Thangue abandoned such heavily loaded narrative subjects and began a series of canvasses illustrating such scenes as fruit-gathering and bracken-cutting. In treating the subject of rural labour his intentions were pictorial rather than political: his interest was not to provide social comment but to explore the artistic potential of his subjects for light and colour. The *Graphic* described these works as 'tender idylls and delightful pastorals that quite reconcile us to the joys of country life.'[6] In the 1890s he became particularly attracted by the strong light of Provence and Liguria, where he regularly stayed. In his many exhibited paintings of orchard and vineyard subjects, La Thangue gained a new freedom in the vigour of his brushwork — each stroke visible and confidently applied — and in the vivid use of his colour. Initially these pictures were favourably received but in 1905 one critic wrote that, 'every touch appears to have been put on with a heavily loaded spatula and jumps at your eye' creating a 'bewildering' effect.[7]

Nevertheless success followed, with his election as R.A. in 1912 and a one-man exhibition at the Leicester Galleries in 1914. Increasingly, though, La Thangue found it difficult to find the rural types who had peopled his early works. The countryside familiar from his years as a rustic naturalist in the 1890s had all but disappeared by the First World War, and yet there was no commensurate change in La Thangue's art during his later years. He became nostalgic, as Munnings (q.v.) recalled, searching for a 'quiet old world village where he could live and find real country models'.[8] Though his virtuosity in depicting sunlight, a feature of many of his works, remained undiminished, his late work continued to refer to a rural way of life which had become little more than a memory.   H.C.V.

NOTES
1. *Pictures by the late H. H. La Thangue*, exhib. cat., Fine Art Society, 1931, p. 4.
2. *Studio*, 9 (1896), p. 163.
3. *Magazine of Art*, 10 (1887), p. 30.
4. ibid., pp. 30–2.
5. *Art Journal*, 1893, p. 172.
6. *Graphic*, 12 May 1900, p. 698.
7. *The Academy*, 1905, pp. 498–9; quoted K. McConkey, *A Painter's Harvest: Works by Henry Herbert La Thangue, R.A.*, exhib. cat., Oldham Art Gallery, 1978, p. 13.
8. A. Munnings, *An Artist's Life*, 1950, pp. 97–8; quoted K. McConkey, op. cit., pp. 13–14.

37

## 37 Violets for Perfume

109 × 95 cm    43 × 37½ in
Signed bl: *H. H. LA THANGUE.*
Diploma work, accepted 27 May 1913 (C.M. XXIII, p. 42)

*The Times* obituary remembered La Thangue for his 'vigorous representations of Mediterranean subjects' painted 'generally in dappled light and a strongly personal note in the colour, bronze and violet predominating'.[1] As a work from La Thangue's later period, *Violets for Perfume* well illustrates this description. The *Magazine of Art* noted in 1904: 'Subjects such as goat herding, orange growing, the culture of the violet have employed his energies and inspired his art', but also saw La Thangue's recording of 'the local industries of the country' as supplying 'material for the historian'.[2] La Thangue himself seemed conscious that the kind of rural life he depicted was fast disappearing; he idealised the lot of his farm labourers, whom he saw as living simple, idyllic lives.

La Thangue made little use of the studio, and occupied one for only a short time when he lived in Chelsea. Otherwise, as Clausen described, 'he would never paint except with the object before him: holding this to be the only way and that its limitations were balanced by the general truth obtained. This practise he kept to throughout his life.'[3] Clausen also worked in the open air, making many sketches before starting a canvas, but he wrote admiringly that La Thangue, 'so far as I know ... never made studies or sketches for his pictures, but planned them out on the actual canvas ... This is very unusual and means a lot of preliminary thinking.'[4]

Despite La Thangue's insistence on *plein-air* painting, he frequently resorted to certain favourite compositional motifs. For instance, *The Man with the Scythe* and *Violets for Perfume* show his regular use of a strong diagonal leading the eye sharply to some further activity in the middle distance. However, in contrast to his often stiffly posed workers, such as those depicted in *Cutting Bracken* (Newcastle-upon-Tyne, Laing Art Gallery), the movement of the principal figure appears fluent.

His distinctive technique, with broad brushstrokes and heavy impasto, was the subject of much debate. A critic of 1889, discussing the execution of La Thangue's work and others of the 'Square Brush School', thought that because they 'leave the brush marks and do not smooth away the evidence of method' they were 'insisting on the way the picture is painted perhaps at the sacrifice of subtleties in the subject.'[5] However, Sickert upheld the merits of this technique, considering that in using 'an opaque mosaic for recording objective sensations about visible nature, [La Thangue] is using it in a personal manner ... the fact that La Thangue does not give us, ready-made, and over again, the gamut of Monet ... is just what gives La Thangue his reason for existence.'[6] In *Violets for Perfume*, La Thangue's characteristic devices are, as always, employed to serve the subject, on which he most loved to dwell; for 'it was primarily, the beauty of things in sunlight that excited him.'[7]

NOTES
1. *The Times*, 23 Dec 1929, p. 12.
2. *Magazine of Art*, 2 (1904), p. 1.
3. *Pictures by the late H. H. La Thangue, R.A.*, exhib. cat., Fine Art Society, 1931, p. 4.
4. ibid., p. 5.
5. M. Roberts, 'A Colony of Artists', *Scottish Arts Review*, August 1889, p. 73; quoted K. McConkey, *A Painter's Harvest: works by Henry Herbert La Thangue, RA*, exhib. cat., Oldham Art Gallery, 1978, p. 10.
6. *New Age*, 7 May 1914; quoted W. R. Sickert, *A Free House!*, ed. O. Sitwell, 1947, p. 271.
7. *Pictures by the late H. H. La Thangue, R.A.*, op. cit., p. 6.

EXHIBITIONS: R.A., 1914 (cat. 400); R.A., Winter, 1933, (cat. 190); Oldham Art Gallery, 1978 (cat. 31); Swansea, Glynn Vivian Art Gallery & Museum, 1985 (cat. 25).

# Sir John Lavery
## 1856–1941

Sir John Lavery was born in Belfast. After moving to Glasgow, he initially worked for a firm of photographers. From about 1875, he attended classes at the Haldane Academy before enrolling for six months at Heatherley's School of Art in London. On his return to Glasgow he began painting costume pieces, but in 1881 left for Paris to complete his training at the Académie Julian.

Like so many of his contemporaries, Lavery was influenced by artists outside the *atelier* system, and in particular by Jules Bastien-Lepage. Whilst spending the summer of 1883 at the artists' colony of Grès-sur-Loing, he practised *plein-air* painting under the influence of Bastien-Lepage's distinctive naturalist style. Lavery returned to Glasgow in 1885 and embarked upon the large canvas, *The Tennis Party* (Aberdeen Art Gallery) which was exhibited at the Royal Academy in 1886. The carefully observed tennis players reflect the instructions given to him on his sole meeting with Bastien-Lepage in Paris: 'Always carry a sketchbook. Select a person – watch him – then put down as much as you remember. Never look twice.'[1]

The Glasgow International Exhibition of 1888 provided Lavery with the important commission to record Queen Victoria's State Visit. Lavery made countless sketches for many of the two hundred and fifty portraits which had to be included in the picture.

After exhibiting at the Grosvenor Gallery in 1890, Lavery and other artists from Glasgow, including Sir James Guthrie and E. A. Walton, were invited to show in Munich. The 'Glasgow Boys', as they became known, were highly acclaimed by the critics in Germany and a series of important articles in England subsequently established the reputation of the Glasgow School as a whole, and singled out Lavery in particular for special mention. A work such as *The Tennis Party*, while being praised for its 'exquisite delicacy' and 'fine harmony'[2] of tone, was seen to epitomise the School's commitment to modern-life subjects and open-air settings.

In 1890 Lavery visited Morocco – the first of many visits – and in about 1903 he bought a house outside Tangiers where he often wintered. The Moroccan subjects he exhibited on his return were praised for their masterly brushwork and rich tones.

Lavery toured Europe with Roche and Guthrie in the summer of 1892, probably visiting Whistler in Paris and continuing on to Spain to study Velazquez. Copying the work of Velazquez strengthened Lavery's concern for 'scale in portraiture'. He thought this to be 'among the most subtle difficulties that a painter has to contend against'[3] and one that he knew Whistler

had taken trouble over. The results of these studies are apparent in Lavery's portrait of *R. B. Cunninghame Graham* (Glasgow Art Gallery and Museum) which he painted 'frankly in the manner of Velazquez'[4] as a harmony in brown.

Moving to London in 1896 Lavery borrowed a studio from Alfred East (q.v.). He became involved in the foundation of the International Society, acting as vice-president during Whistler's presidency. The Society aimed to foster exhibitions of international modern art in London and its first exhibition, held in 1898, included the work of Manet and Degas. Lavery had not lost touch, however, with his Glasgow contemporaries, and in 1899 was commissioned to paint a triptych for Glasgow City Chambers celebrating the achievements of the modern shipbuilding industry.

By 1910, in spite of not having exhibited at the Royal Academy since 1896, Lavery had won himself a glittering international reputation. With successful exhibitions in America and Europe, and over fifty works exhibited at the Venice Biennale in 1910, his work was soon being collected by leading institutions all over the world. In 1911, the year in which Walter Shaw-Sparrow's biography appeared, Lavery was elected an Associate of the Academy and from this date the Academy became his principal exhibition venue.

During the First World War Lavery became an Official War Artist, recording subjects ranging from the cemetery at Etaples to the signing of the surrender by the German Navy (*The End*, London, Imperial War Museum). Lavery was rewarded with a knighthood in 1918, and election to full membership of the Academy in 1921.

Though in the 1920s Lavery was still occasionally commissioned to paint large, formal group portraits such as *The Opening of the Modern Foreign and Sargent Galleries* (London, Tate Gallery), he also painted a contrasting series of dramatic and freely sketched portraits of his wife Hazel. In the late 1920s he returned to Ireland where he worked on pictures such as *St Patrick's Purgatory* (Dublin, Hugh Lane Municipal Gallery of Modern Art), a representation of the ancient Irish Pilgrimage at Lough Derg. Lavery published his memoirs in 1940, the year before his death.    H.C.V.

NOTES
1. J. Lavery, *The Life of a Painter*, 1940, p. 57.
2. *Weekly News*, 20 Sept 1890; quoted K. McConkey, *Sir John Lavery*, exhib. cat., Belfast, Ulster Museum and London, Fine Art Society, 1984–5, p. 29.
3. W. Shaw-Sparrow, *John Lavery and His Work*, 1911, p. 96; quoted K. McConkey, op. cit., p. 26.
4. J. Lavery, op. cit., p. 89.

*repr. in colour on p. 31*

## 38   The Van Dyck Room, Wilton

63.5 × 76 cm    25 × 30 in
Signed br: *J. Lavery*
Diploma work, accepted 19 July 1921 (C.M. XXIV, p. 364)

Lavery initially deposited a portrait of his wife, *Lady Lavery*, as his diploma work in April 1921,[1] but in July requested to exchange this for *The Van Dyck Room, Wilton*, because he had not taken 'into consideration the possibility of this work deteriorating owing to frequent repainting'. The replacement, he explained, 'was painted direct and at once, and is more likely to stand the test of time.'[2] The picture depicts the west end of the Double Cube Room at Wilton House in Wiltshire. Van Dyck's portraits of the royal family and of the Herberts, Earls of Pembroke and Montgomery, dominate the room, these paintings having provided the basis for its re-design by Inigo Jones and John Webb in 1649. The formality of Van Dyck's sitters is contrasted with the relaxed attitudes of their descendants.

In his earliest work, Lavery had occasionally painted interiors, such as *A Quiet Day in the Studio*, 1883 (Glasgow Art Gallery and Museum), which shows a girl reading before a fire in a sparsely furnished room. However, when he returned to this theme in the 1920s the results were very different. *The Van Dyck Room, Wilton* was the first in a series of portrait interiors which the *Apollo* noted were 'records of our time and significant commentaries upon that reckless changing thing called "good taste"'.[3] The work was favourably reviewed, critics finding it an 'attractive and accomplished' painting, rich in tone and 'yet sparkling',[4] the artist having 'made good use of the crimson upholstery of the furniture'.[5] The sketch-like quality of the work was seen in some ways as underlining the brilliance of the aristocratic world that he was depicting. Lavery had presumably seen Sargent's *Interior in Venice* (see cat. 54) and there are obvious parallels in both subject and scale; the two works portray similarly opulent interiors and are painted on canvasses of roughly the same size. Both are pervaded by a curiously languid atmosphere, but in Lavery's work the room itself takes on a far greater importance, its occupants being treated quite literally as part of the furniture, scarcely distinguishable from the portraits of their ancestors hanging on the walls. This of course serves to express the family's sense of continuity and ease in such surroundings and is in sharp contrast to the transitory quality of Sargent's image. Lavery appears to have prepared the canvas himself by laying in the ground with a large brush. The paint has then been applied so thinly, and with hardly any alterations, that the brushmarks from the preparation of the ground are still clearly visible, confirming the sure and delicate touch of the artist's hand, and confirming his statement concerning its speed of execution.

NOTES
1.   C.M. XXIV, p. 324, 7 April 1921.
2.   Letter from Sir John Lavery to the Secretary of the R.A., 14 July 1921, R.A. Archives, RAC/1/LA 12.
3.   *Apollo*, 2 (1925), pp. 267–8.
4.   *The Scotsman*, 24 June 1921; quoted K. McConkey, *Sir John Lavery*, exhib. cat., Belfast, Ulster Museum, and London, Fine Art Society, 1984–5, p. 93.
5.   *Connoisseur*, 60 (1921), p. 115.

EXHIBITIONS: R.A., 1921 (cat. 27); Bournemouth, Russell-Cotes Art Gallery & Museum, 1957 (cat. 847); Bournemouth, Russell-Cotes Art Gallery & Museum, 1965 (cat. 40); R.A., Winter, 1968 (cat. 411); Leicestershire Museum and Art Gallery, 1982 (cat. 55); Belfast, Ulster Museum, and London, Fine Art Society and touring 1984–5 (cat. 93); Swansea, Glynn Vivian Art Gallery and Museum, 1985 (cat. 28).

# Sydney Lee
## 1866–1949

Throughout a long, creative life, Sydney Lee proved himself to be among the most versatile of artists associated with the Royal Academy. Malcolm C. Salaman, himself an etcher, wrote of Lee: 'A painter first and foremost, he skillfully handles the etching needle and the mezzotint scraper, while he has been one of the most prominent and effective members of the society of Graver-Painters in Colour.'[1]

Sydney Lee was born in Manchester on 27 August 1866 and studied at the Manchester School of Art. He subsequently worked at the *atelier* Colorossi in Paris and gradually developed a characteristic, careful oil technique ideal for the topographical landscapes and architectural subjects for which he became known.

From early in his career, Lee was fascinated by the potential of a number of printmaking techniques. In 1937, an exhibition at Colnaghi's provided a retrospective of work including, as Lee noted, 'all the processes of engraving at which I have worked at various times during a period of many years ..., etchings, drypoints, aquatints, mezzotints, lithographs, wood-engravings and woodcuts (printed in black or in colours).'[2] As early as 1914, the engraving *Limestone Rock* had been described as 'distinguished among the best original wood engravings of our time by not only its pictorial qualities, its design, its well-balanced masses of tone, but by the expressive manner in which the material has been used, the absolute eloquence of the wood itself.'[3] Lee could be described as an architect of the revival in the art of wood engraving, a distinguished exponent in a tradition which stretches back to Thomas Bewick (1753–1828). In 1937 Lee wrote: 'it is particularly gratifying to me, remembering my own attempts to revive an interest in this attractive medium, to witness the great interest now taken in wood engravings.'[4]

Oil painting was, however, Lee's principle medium and he began exhibiting oils at the New English Art Club in 1903. The N.E.A.C. had already lost much of the radicalism and opposition to the Royal Academy which had been the cause of its foundation in 1886. Many of the founder-members had become Academicians, and Lee himself first exhibited at the Academy in 1905. A regular contributor to the Summer Exhibitions from 1909, he was elected an Associate in 1922. Lee took a keen interest in the Academy and was its Treasurer from 1932 until 1940. In the election to find Sir William Llewellyn's successor as President, which took place in December 1938, Lee polled the highest number of votes in the first ballot, but was finally defeated by Sir Edwin Lutyens by the narrow majority of twenty to eighteen votes.

In 1924 his *Amongst the Dolomites*, reflecting his somewhat architectonic attitude to landscape composition, was purchased for the Chantrey Bequest. Many of his Academy paintings were of continental subjects derived from tours of France, Switzerland and Italy, where he became particularly attracted to Venetian scenes.

A series of one-man exhibitions of his work as a printmaker and draughtsman held at Colnaghi's in 1937, 1939 and 1945 maintained Lee's early reputation in these fields. He died in London, aged eighty-four, in 1949.    T.J.B.

NOTES
1. *Studio*, 63 (1914), p. 19.
2. S. Lee, Foreword, *Exhibition of Aquatints, Etchings, Mezzotints, Wood-Engravings and Woodcuts by Sydney Lee, R.A.,R.E.,* exhib. cat., Colnaghi's, 1937.
3. *Studio*, op. cit. p. 19, repr., opp. p. 19.
4. S. Lee, op. cit.

## 39    The Red Tower

150 × 114.5 cm    59 × 45 in
Signed and dated br: *SYDNEY LEE 1928*
Diploma work, accepted 24 Feb 1930 (C.M. XXV, p. 534)

Sydney Lee's Diploma work, *The Red Tower* is a typical, and important example of his work, though it was not his original choice. The Council, when offered *The Roman Wall* 'resolved that it be suggested to him that he offer two smaller works for selection by the Council.'[1] The most likely explanation for this is that the very limited space available in the Diploma Galleries was causing concern.

*The Red Tower* probably depicts a subject in Italy, but Lee only rarely gave topographically specific titles to his works and there is no record of the precise subject. First exhibited at the Summer Exhibition of 1928, it is typical of Lee's continental town scenes. Characteristically he would build a composition around an historic building, forming a strong central motif, whose surface texture of brick or plaster would be lovingly evoked. Lee would frequently add figures, carefully observed in the locality. In *The Haunted Chateau,*[2] a single, hunched figure adds to the painting's atmosphere, but *The Red Tower* includes a horse and trap, and many distant, brightly dressed figures introduce a modest sense of animation into an otherwise monumental, solemn scene dominated by the architecture of the tower itself.

NOTES
1. C.M. XXV, p. 531, 18 Feb 1930.
2. Repr., *Royal Academy Illustrated*, 1926, p. 39.

EXHIBITIONS: R.A., 1928 (cat. 378); R.A., 1930 (cat. 638); Bournemouth, Russell-Cotes Art Gallery & Museum, 1957 (cat. 841).

*(Illustrated overleaf)*

39 Sydney Lee *The Red Tower*

# Sir Walter Thomas Monnington
## 1902–1976

40  *repr. in colour on p. 50*

## 40  The House with the Closed Shutters

95 × 84 cm    37½ × 33 in
Signed br: *SYDNEY LEE*
Purchased by the Royal Academy in 1963 (Stott Fund)

EXHIBITIONS: R.A., 1926 (cat. 229); R.A., 1943 (cat. 183); R.N.V.R. Club, 1947–57, long term loan; London, Arts Club, 1957–64, long term loan.

Monnington was born in London in 1902, the son of a barrister. After a general education in Sussex, he went to the Slade School of Art in 1918 where he studied until 1923 under Professor Henry Tonks. From here he won a scholarship in mural painting which enabled him to work at the British School in Rome for three years from 1923 to 1926, developing a keen interest in perspective under the influence of the Italian primitives and the artists of the Quattrocento, notably Piero della Francesca. On his return to England, Monnington maintained his association with the Slade, becoming a member of the Faculty of Painting of which he was chairman from 1949 to 1967. He was also appointed part-time teacher in the Painting School at the Royal College of Art and, in 1927, received his first public commission for a mural at St Stephen's Hall, Westminster. In 1931 he was given another major commission, this time for a mural at the Bank of England entitled *Announcing a New Bank Rate*.

Monnington first exhibited at the Royal Academy in 1931 when he was represented by three drawings, including a study for his tempera altarpiece in St Mary's Church, Bolton of the *Supper at Emmaus*. In the same year he was elected an A.R.A. and began teaching at the Academy Schools where he stayed until 1939. Apart from drawings and landscape paintings, Monnington also executed several portraits during the 1930s which were noted for their attention to detail, particularly one of *Lord Baldwin* as Chancellor of Cambridge University. He was elected a full Academician in 1938 at the age of thirty-six.

At the outbreak of the Second World War, Monnington joined the Directorate of Camouflage, later becoming an Official War Artist on active service with the R.A.F., going on raids to Germany and making a number of drawings. After the War, he returned to teaching, joining the staff at Camberwell School of Arts where he taught until 1949, the year in which he accepted the post at the Slade. Among his public works of the post-War period, the most important was his vast mural for the ceiling of the Conference Room in the new Council House at Bristol in 1956. The commission coincided with his growing interest in Abstract painting and despite the demand for a historical theme, the mural was one of the first works he did in this style. It was followed by another in 1957 for the staircase at the University of London Union building.

Monnington was elected President of the Royal Academy in 1966 and while in office was responsible for introducing more contemporary and twentieth-century themes into the exhibition programme and for making the Summer Exhibition more accessible to artists who were not members of the Institution. He is quoted as saying: 'I do not believe that the Academy's function is to maintain a status quo or to further the acceptance of the acceptable ... any development in art derives from perception free from preconception.'[1] Monnington was knighted in 1967 and died in 1976, aged seventy-three.    E.C.W.

NOTE
1.  *The Times*, 8 Jan 1976.

## 41  Piediluco

Oil on panel
42.5 × 60.5 cm    16¾ × 23¾ in
Diploma work, accepted 1 Nov 1938 (C.M. XXVII, p. 147)

This atmospheric painting of the Italian lake, Piediluco, was probably executed when the artist was in Rome, between 1923–6. It was around this time that Monnington developed his interest in landscape painting, inspired by the work of Italian Quattrocento artists. As in the landscapes of Piero della Francesca there is a strong sense of space, and a fascination with form and pattern. The calm lake and undulating hills stretch right across the painting, uninterrupted by any dominant vertical elements, and the artist's sensitivity as a draughtsman is expressed through the careful delineation of the vegetation and houses in the middle distance. The tightly handled paint on a panel surface and the use of cool tones give the painting an austere quality that is normally associated with tempera.

EXHIBITIONS: R.A., 1939 (cat. 57); Lyons, Salon, 1955; Bournemouth, Russell-Cotes Art Gallery & Museum, 1965 (cat. 46); R.A., Winter, 1968 (cat. D.62); Nottingham University Art Gallery, 1973 (cat. 41); Leicestershire Museum and Art Gallery, 1982 (cat. 64); Cheltenham Art Gallery & Museums, 1985, (cat. 13).

# Sir Alfred James Munnings
## 1878–1959

Although best known for his grand, commissioned paintings of horses and their owners executed between 1920 and 1940, Munnings was primarily interested in, 'painting the English scene'.[1] Smaller works from the beginning and the end of his career show his fascination with recording the English landscape and its inhabitants. Typical subject matter included gypsies and farmers, country fairs, hunting scenes and racecourses, usually painted outdoors in a spontaneous manner. The immediacy of his brushstrokes enabled him to express the sensation of movement and to capture the changing effects of light and weather on the landscape. Stylistically his paintings can be likened to the work of the English Impressionists such as Sargent (q.v.), La Thangue (q.v.) and Clausen (q.v.).

Munnings was born in 1878 at Mendham in Suffolk, the son of a miller. Between 1893 and 1898, he was apprenticed to a lithographic firm in Norwich where he worked on designs for decorative chocolate boxes and posters. In the evenings he attended Norwich School of Art where he learnt to draw from the Antique and the life model and began working in oil and watercolour. He continued his education at the Académie Julian in Paris between 1903–4 before settling at Swainsthorpe near Norwich where he lived and worked until 1911. From 1911 until 1916, Munnings lived at Lamorna in Cornwall where he was connected with the Newlyn School of painters, particularly Laura and Harold Knight (q.v.). He exhibited at the Royal Academy Summer Exhibition from 1899 onwards and his first one-man show was held at the Leicester Galleries in 1913.

After a period in the army horse supply service, Munnings was sent to France in 1918 as a War Artist attached to the Canadian Cavalry Brigade. This attachment proved particularly appropriate for the artist because he was able to pursue his interest in recording men and horses on the move in over fifty works. As a result of these paintings he was elected an Associate of the Royal Academy in 1919 and from then on found no shortage of commissioned work. Except for the years 1941–6 when he settled on Exmoor, Munnings lived at Dedham in Essex (he also had a studio in Chelsea). His growing popularity was marked by official honours: Royal Academician in 1925, Associate of the Royal Watercolour Society in 1921 and member in 1929. In 1944 he was elected President of the Royal Academy and was knighted in the same year. Whilst in office Munnings was well known for his reactionary statements about modern art, particularly his attack on Picasso and Matisse at the Royal Academy Annual Dinner of 1949. He resigned as President in 1949 and for the remaining ten years of his life worked on capturing the drama of horse racing. He also published a three-volume autobiography, *An Artist's Life*, 1950, *The Second Burst*, 1951 and *The Finish*, 1952.    E.C.W.

NOTE
1.  *Alfred Munnings 1878–1959*, exhib. cat., Manchester City Art Galleries, 1987, p. 6.

## 42  Kilkenny Horse Fair

62.2 × 74.9 cm    24½ × 29½ in
Signed bl: *A. J. Munnings*
Diploma work, accepted 28 July 1925 (C.M. XXV, p. 153)

This busy scene at Kilkenny Horse Fair was painted on a visit
to Ireland in 1922 where Munnings had gone to complete a
commissioned painting of Isaac Bel, Master of the Kilkenny
Hounds. Although the grey horse is central to the picture, the
scene is evocative of mood and incident rather than being
straightforward portraiture. Each element of the painting contributes to the overall sensation of movement, from the gath-
ering clouds to the randomly arranged figures and horses. The
handling of paint is less rigid than in the larger, more formal
compositions which often came between Munnings and his real
interest in capturing the transience of nature.

EXHIBITIONS: R.A., 1923 (cat. 387); R.A., 1926 (cat. 431); Lyons, Salon, 1955; Bournemouth, Russell-Cotes Art Gallery & Museum, 1965 (cat. 47); R.A., Winter, 1968 (cat.
491); Folkestone, Arts Centre, 1974 (cat. 34); Leicestershire Museum and Art Gallery, 1982
(cat. 66); Cheltenham Art Gallery and Museums, 1985 (cat. 1); Swansea, Glynn Vivian Art
Gallery & Museum, 1985 (cat. 36).

# Sir David Murray
## 1849–1933

*repr. in colour on p. 44*

On his eighty-second birthday David Murray announced that a 'landscape painter should be the happiest man alive' as he works 'in the open air ... and his job is the most fascinating in the world.'[1] Murray lived until the age of eighty-four and became known as the 'grand old man of British art', having exhibited at the Royal Academy regularly for nearly sixty years.

Murray was born in Glasgow, the son of a boot and shoe maker. Before embarking upon an artistic career he worked for almost twelve years with a firm of merchants in Glasgow, but spent his spare time sketching in the countryside around Glasgow. His early work was meticulously detailed, and passages of minute, almost Pre-Raphaelite observation appear in some of his later landscapes. Murray trained at the Glasgow School of Art under Robert Greenlees, and had his first work accepted at the Royal Academy in 1875.

As a young man Murray went to live in Skye, where, in a little hut that he built himself, he had to fight 'the dozens of rats which used to make a meal off his blankets.'[2] He travelled to London in about 1883 and, already prosperous, moved into the Pre-Raphaelite painter Millais's old studio in Langham Chambers, Portland Place, where he remained for the rest of his life. He soon achieved recognition with the purchase of *My love has gone a-sailing* (London, Tate Gallery) for the Chantrey Bequest in 1884. Before 1886, Murray painted mainly Scottish landscapes, but in this year he travelled to Picardie, in France, and on his return exhibited his work in a one-man exhibition at The Fine Art Society. Thereafter his subjects were taken mainly from the southern counties of England, and from his occasional visits to the Lake District.

In 1891 Murray was elected an A.R.A. *Mangolds,*[3] exhibited that year, was typical of his work. The picture, according to critics, was 'really a study in atmosphere and light' and 'a record of his observations of subtleties of aerial perspective, expressed with infinite delicacy'.[4]

In 1903 a second work of Murray's, *In the Country of Constable* (London, Tate Gallery), was bought for the Chantrey Bequest; depicting the Suffolk countryside, this was Murray's tribute to his great predecessor, John Constable. Paintings such as this were admired for 'the charm of rhythmic lines in stems and branches'[5] arranged delicately against the sky. He was elected a full member of the Academy in 1905.

Murray was an Honorary Visitor at King's College for Women in the 1890s and 'endeared himself to students' by his encouraging visits each year. His advice for students was summed up in his motto: 'Worship Nature and Study Art'.[6] He was also an Honorary Visitor from 1910 at the newly opened Byam Shaw and Vicat Cole Art School. In 1909, after a visit to Venice, Murray exhibited many views of that city in the Academy that year, and in the following seven years. He was elected President of the Royal Institute of Painters in Watercolour in 1917 and was knighted in the following year. Murray died in 1933 and in his will bequeathed a large sum to the Royal Academy to be used for grants to encourage students of the Schools to study landscape painting.   H. C. V.

NOTES
1. Obituary, 13 Nov 1933, R.A. Archives, D. Murray file.
2. ibid.
3. Repr., *Royal Academy Pictures*, 1891, p. 34.
4. *Art Journal*, 1897, p. 328.
5. R. Vicat Cole, *The Artistic Anatomy of Trees*, 1916, p. 42.
6. R. Vicat Cole, *The Art and Life of Byam Shaw*, 1932, p. 135.

## 43   Swedes

119.4 × 182.9 cm   47 × 72 in
Signed and dated br: *David Murray. 1905*
Diploma work, accepted 3 April 1905 (C.M. XXI, p. 417)

Murray's Diploma work falls recognisably into that category of his work which treats as its subject the broad skies of the English lowlands. Although of Scottish Highland extraction, Murray was never more assured in his painting than when depicting the flat landscapes of East Anglia, employing a daringly low horizon and filling almost two thirds of his canvas with sky. As in the earlier *Mangolds,*[1] dating from 1891, Murray uses here a sharply defined perspective, emphasised by receding furrows and a track leading from the right foreground to the church tower in the far distance. In both paintings the viewer seems to be standing at the edge of a great field and the overwhelming impression is of the blending of the various colours seen amongst the crops. The late Victorian public enjoyed the use of details in large landscapes. Murray here includes partridges in the foreground and, in the middle distance, a farmer with his dog gives chase to two horses, carrying the eye across the painting to the windmill, the most prominent landmark in the countryside. The essence of Murray's vision, as conveyed in *Swedes*, was to discover beauty in the most ordinary of English landscapes. Yet, unlike Constable's landscape paintings, the inclusion of narrative incidents tends to convert the celebration of man in harmony with nature into a rural tale.

NOTE
1. Repr., *Royal Academy Pictures*, 1891, p. 34.

EXHIBITION: R.A., 1905 (cat. 257).

# John Northcote Nash
## 1893–1977

Like his friend and contemporary, Gilbert Spencer (q.v.), John Nash drew his inspiration from the English landscape, although unlike Spencer he was interested in exploring the abstract qualities of a landscape rather than the 'genius loci'.

Born in London in 1893, John Nash was the younger brother of the artist Paul Nash. It was partly through the encouragement of his brother that John became an artist rather than a journalist, and in the early years their work was quite similar. In 1913 they had their first public exhibition together in the Dorien Leigh Gallery in South Kensington. Here, John's work attracted the attention of Harold Gilman who invited him to become a founder member of the London Group in 1914. It was only around this time that he began to paint seriously in oils. Until then most of his work was in pencil or watercolour.

Nash never underwent any official art training. Well acquainted with such English modernists as Wadsworth and Rothenstein through his brother Paul, who attended the Slade School of Art, he developed a personal style with a strong sense of design and drawing which was based on the inspiration he received from nature. After serving in the trenches in the Artist's Rifles during the War, he was commissioned as an Official War Artist early in 1918, the year of his marriage to Christine Kuhlentharl.

In 1920 Nash was elected a member of the New English Art Club and had his first one-man show at the Goupil Gallery in 1921. He was also involved in book illustration during these years as a result of which he was elected to the Society of Wood Engravers in 1921. In between painting and engraving there were brief periods of teaching, at the Ruskin School of Drawing in Oxford from 1922–7 and in the Department of Design at the Royal College of Art between 1934–40. After showing at the Royal Academy for the first time in 1940 Nash was elected an Associate of the Royal Academy, becoming a full member in 1951. Soon after the outbreak of the Second World War, Nash was chosen as Official War Artist to the Admiralty, making records of the ports and dockyards; later in the War he decided to play a more active role in the fighting, and served first as a Captain and then as a Major in the Royal Marines. After the War Nash settled permanently in Essex at Wormingford near Colchester where, apart from painting trips to Cornwall, Wales, the Derbyshire Dales and Skye, he lived until the end of his life. At Wormingford, Nash also pursued his interests in gardening and botanical illustration. He was awarded a C.B.E. in 1964 and an honorary doctorate from the University of Essex in 1967. He died in 1977. E. C. W.

44   *repr. in colour on p. 52*

45   *repr. in colour on p. 52*

## 44   The Barn, Wormingford

66 × 82.5 cm   26 × 32½ in
Signed bl: *John Nash*
Diploma work, accepted 15 June 1954 (C.M., 1954, p. 103)

After the Second World War, Nash settled at Bottengoms Farm at Wormingford in Essex, a secluded cottage in the Stour valley with two acres of land. Although opposed to the idea of a 'genius loci', Nash appreciated the particular light and atmosphere of the area around Wormingford, making many painting expeditions into the local countryside. Situated just upstream from 'Constable Country', the area is characterised by modest uplands and dense hollows.

Nash rarely attempted to paint directly from nature, preferring to work in the constant light of his studio from sketches and watercolours made on the spot. Judging by the artist's viewpoint in *The Barn, Wormingford*, this was one of the scenes from his studio on the top floor of his cottage, looking down over his garden to the farmland beyond. The painting exemplifies Nash's analytical approach to landscape. Although the

46

imagery is representational, the evenness of the artist's gaze expresses his interest in the shapes and patterns running through nature, rather than depicting the details of a rural scene for its own sake. His use of colour is naturalistic yet subordinate to his fascination with design and drawing.

EXHIBITIONS: R.A., 1955 (cat. 74); Bournemouth, Russell-Cotes Art Gallery & Museum, 1965 (cat. 48); R.A., Winter, 1967 (cat. 253); Colchester, The Minories, 1967 (cat. 47); South London Art Gallery, 1974 (cat. 88); Nottingham University Art Gallery, 1973 (cat. 42); London, New Grafton Gallery, 1978 (cat. 16); Leicestershire Museum and Art Gallery, 1982 (cat. 67); Cheltenham Art Gallery and Museums, 1985 (cat. 22).

## 45  The Fallen Tree

68 × 90 cm    26¾ × 35½ in
Signed bl: *John Nash*
Diploma work, accepted 31 July 1951 (C.M. XXVIII, p. 495), but replaced by *The Barn, Wormingford* in 1954

In both *The Fallen Tree* and *The Lake, Little Horkesley Hall* (cat. 46), Nash is preoccupied with the lyrical qualities of line. These landscapes set a poetic mood rather than being naturalistic, and there is a strong sense of pattern which is emphasised by the twisting, almost abstracted rhythms of the trees. Unlike the more domestic landscapes of his contemporary, Gilbert Spencer (q.v.), Nash's scenes appear isolated, remote and devoid of human presence. His interest in strongly delineated forms often led him to paint wintry scenes in which the bare branches of the trees provided suitably simplified subject matter.

EXHIBITION: R.A., 1955 (cat. 715).

## 46  The Lake, Little Horkesley Hall

61 × 76 cm    24 × 30 in
Signed bl: *John Nash*
Purchased by the Royal Academy (Stott Fund) 29 July 1958 (C.M., p. 249)

See entry for *The Fallen Tree* (cat. 45)

EXHIBITIONS: R.A., 1958 (cat. 7); Arts Club, 1960–64, long term loan; R.A., Winter, 1967 (cat. 241); Colchester, The Minories, 1967 (cat. 40); London, Royal Institute Gallery, 1969 (cat. 67).

# Julius Olsson
## 1864–1942

Julius Olsson was born in London in 1864 of a Swedish father and an English mother. Inheriting his father's physical characteristics, he was described as a 'Nordic type, blue-eyed and powerful in frame'.[1]

It appears Olsson left employment with a commercial firm to pursue a career as an artist, but opinions differ as to whether he received any formal artistic training or not. His work was first accepted at the Royal Academy in 1890 and he joined the New English Art Club in 1891. He moved to St Ives in Cornwall, probably in 1896, and soon became involved in the local community, later being created a Justice of the Peace. He began to establish a reputation as a painter of seascapes, although he occasionally experimented with mythological subjects such as The Coasts of the Sirens,[2] exhibited in 1899. Despite an ability to paint the sea 'throughout the whole gamut of its phenomena – from the furl of the storm to the sensuous beauty of the calm,'[3] it was, however, studies of the moon reflected on the sea 'that Mr Olsson ... made peculiarly his own'.[4] These made quite an impact in the 1890s and in 1911 The Moonlit Shore (London, Tate Gallery) was bought for the Chantrey Bequest.

In about 1911 Olsson moved to London. He continued to make regular visits to Cornwall and, in his yacht, came to know 'the coast from the Scillies to the Isle of Wight as well as most men know their way to the nearest railway station.'[5] He must have visited the Pyrenees at some time, since a Studio article of 1910 reproduces a work painted there, and in 1916 he exhibited Morning in the Pyrenees. The Studio thought 'a great sea painter' could also be 'a great snow painter' and that 'Mr Olsson's pictures of the higher Pyrenees prove him to be no exception to this rule.'[6]

In 1914 Olsson was elected an A.R.A. and full membership followed in 1920. During the First World War he served as a lieutenant in the Royal Naval Volunteer Reserve, which gave him the opportunity of painting naval ships in action in such works as A lame duck in the Channel,[7] which depicts a damaged vessel being towed through a rough sea.

After the Great War Olsson painted in London, Ireland and Sweden, always taking rivers, streams, canals or the sea as his principal subjects. Occasionally he painted imaginary scenes such as Deep Sea Phantasy,[8] depicting mermaids swimming underwater, but his real strength lay in his ability to capture the effects of the fall of light on the sea, whether it was the sun or the moon. After his home in England was damaged during an air raid in the Second World War, Olsson moved to Dalkey in Ireland, and died there in 1942.   H. C. V.

NOTES
1. The Times, Sept 1942, press cutting R.A. Archives, J. Olsson file.
2. Repr., Royal Academy Pictures, 1899, p. 70.
3. Studio, 48 (1910), p. 274.
4. ibid., p. 282.
5. ibid., p. 283.
6. ibid., pp. 282–3.
7. Repr., Royal Academy Illustrated, 1919, p. 82.
8. Repr., ibid., 1939, p. 68.

## 47   Sunset: Cornish Coast

63.5 × 79 cm   25 × 31 in
Signed bl: Julius Olsson
Diploma work, accepted 4 Nov 1920 (C.M. XXIV, p. 268)

The painter of a seascape requires a different approach to that of a landscapist, as his subject is never still, and the artist has therefore to retain in his memory the images of its various moods. Olsson was always praised for his 'ability for noting and remembering the thousands of forms which the ever-moving water is constantly assuming', an ability which enabled him to depict the 'majestic onward sweep of the waves more thoroughly ... than any other English painter'.[1] In Sunset: Cornish Coast, 'broadly seen and broadly painted',[2] Olsson has effortlessly captured the motion of the waves breaking on the shore. A reviewer of his pictures in the 1921 Academy exhibition felt that although he gave 'less definition to his wave forms than formerly' he had now succeeded 'in conveying the movement and tumble of the foaming water with a degree of illusion that few, if any, of his predecessors have equalled.'[3] The Times, however, thought that the 'perpetual iridescence of Mr. Olsson's seas becomes a little wearisome'[4] although other critics found it revealing that Olsson 'saw in the waves and their foaming crests all the colours of the opal', as they learnt that 'while foam may be all the colours of the rainbow, it is rarely, if ever, white.'[5]

NOTES
1. Studio, 48 (1910), p. 278.
2. ibid., p. 274.
3. Connoisseur, 60 (1921), p. 115.
4. The Times, 13 May 1920, p. 20.
5. Studio, 48 (1910), p. 280.

EXHIBITIONS: R.A., 1921 (cat. 296); Bournemouth, Russell-Cotes Art Gallery & Museum, 1965 (cat. 49).

## 48   Light Airs off the Needles

61 × 76 cm   24 × 30 in
Signed bl: Julius Olsson
Purchased by the Royal Academy (Stott Fund) 7 May 1938 (C.M. XXVII, p. 119)

The Needles are a string of pointed rocks off the Isle of Wight, and Olsson presumably painted them from on board his yacht. Although he depicts three sailing boats – possibly taking part in a race – the real subject of the picture is the effect of the sun filtering through the clouds onto the becalmed sea. By rendering the scene in 'those subtle colours which ... the sea reveals to those who are in sympathy with her',[1] Olsson has here captured the conditions of light and atmosphere characteristic of a hazy summer's day.

NOTE
1. Studio, 48 (1910), p. 278.

EXHIBITIONS: R.A., 1938 (cat. 199); London, R.N.V.R. Club 1947–57, long term loan; London, Arts Club 1957–9, long term loan.

47

48

# Sir William Orpen
## 1878–1931

William Orpen was an Irishman of ancient family and the fourth son of Arthur Herbert Orpen, a lawyer from County Dublin. Born in Ireland on the 27 November 1878, he entered the Metropolitan School of Art in Dublin at the age of eleven and remained there for seven years before enrolling at the Slade School of Art in 1897. Whilst at the Slade he became an accomplished draughtsman, winning prizes for head painting and figure drawing and making an earnest study of such old masters as Rembrandt, Goya, Hogarth, Chardin and Watteau. Along with Augustus John (q.v.) he was one of the most outstanding students at the School. After he left the Slade in the summer of 1899 his career was largely dictated by his association with the Carfax Gallery and the New English Art Club where in 1900 he exhibited one of his best-known figure paintings, *The Mirror* (London, Tate Gallery).

After his marriage in 1901 to Grace Knewstub, Orpen settled down to a career as a portrait painter, working in England and Ireland. From 1902 to 1914 he taught part-time at the Metropolitan School of Art in Dublin and exhibited regularly at the Royal Hibernian Academy, becoming an Associate in 1904 and a full member in 1909. Whilst in Ireland he also became involved in the Irish cultural renascence, with the poet W. B. Yeats and the novelist and critic George Moore.

Orpen first exhibited at the Royal Academy in 1908, becoming A.R.A. in 1910 and R.A. in 1919. From that date he became established as a popular society portrait painter and his best works were hung at Burlington House every year with one exception from 1910 until his death in 1931. He became the natural successor to Sargent (q.v.) and was patronised by the dealer Charles Wertheimer whose brother had been responsible for promoting the older artist. Whilst he was financially successful as a portrait painter, Orpen continued to explore other subject matter, exhibiting nudes, *plein-air* landscapes and conversation pieces at the New English Art Club. In addition, between 1913 and 1916, he produced three large-scale allegorical works in which he expressed his feelings and attitudes towards his Irish heritage and explored a more two-dimensional style and a new tempera-like medium.

Orpen joined the army in 1916 and in 1917 was sent to France as an Official War Artist where he painted formal portraits of military officers and desolate, battle-scarred landscapes. Orpen was knighted in 1918, and after the Armistice moved to Paris where he was commissioned to record the Peace Conference. As a result of his first-hand experiences during the War he later wrote a witty account of events, *An Onlooker in France 1917–19*. During the 1920s he kept homes and studios in both London and Paris. One of the most fashionable and wealthy portrait painters of the day, his earnings seldom dropped below £45,000 p.a. and his sitters included the Prince of Wales, Lloyd George and Neville Chamberlain. In 1928 he stood for election as President of the Royal Academy but was beaten by Sir William Llewellyn. Two years after his death in 1931 the Royal Academy held a retrospective exhibition of his work.  E. C. W.

## 49  Le Chef de l'Hôtel Chatham, Paris

127 × 101.5 cm  50 × 41 in
Signed br: *ORPEN*
Diploma work, accepted 24 May 1921 (C.M. XXIV, p. 345)

Orpen originally sent this portrait to the Royal Academy in 1921 for purchase under the terms of the Chantrey Bequest, and was informed that the painting had been selected for the nation at the price of £735.00. However, since the terms of the Bequest stated that the money could only be used to purchase work that had been 'entirely executed within the shores of Great Britain', questions were soon raised as to the eligibility of the painting. The sitter was apparently in Paris, the city where Orpen had been working, and therefore the press challenged the fact that it had been entirely executed in Great Britain. In the end the work was accepted as Orpen's Diploma work rather than being acquired for the Chantrey Bequest.

The painting received much critical acclaim at the Summer Exhibition of that year and was widely reproduced, appearing in colour in *The Outline of Art* where the caption talked about the 'human appeal of its democratic subject'.[1] The critic from the *Connoisseur* called it a ' "tour de force" which has soared into popularity less by reason of its undoubted merits than because of the unconventionality of the subject.'[2]

This portrait demonstrates Orpen's considerable technical facility and his interest in past masters such as Goya, Velasquez and Manet. Orpen has chosen to paint the chef as if he were executing a society commission. The chef is seen in full costume, arrogantly posed with the tools of his trade in front of him. The figure is given added stature by virtue of the contrast between the brilliant costume and the dark background. Although regarded as being highly skilled, Orpen was often criticised by contemporary critics for relying on illustration instead of being expressive in his use of form.

NOTES
1. *The Outline of Art*; quoted in B. Arnold, *Orpen, Mirror to an Age*, 1981, p. 396.
2. *Connoisseur*, June 1921, p. 11.

EXHIBITIONS: R.A., 1921 (cat. 115); R.A., Winter, 1933 (cat. 134); Rye, 1968 (cat. 38); R.A., Winter, 1968 (cat. 458); Camden Arts Centre, 1969 (cat. 122); Columbus Gallery of Fine Arts, 1971 (cat. 73); Folkestone, Arts Centre, 1974 (cat. 38); South London Art Gallery, 1973 (cat. 29); Swansea, Glynn Vivian Art Gallery & Museum, 1985 (cat. 29).

49

# Alfred Parsons
1847–1920

The novelist Henry James wrote that: 'it would be strange if the words "Happy England" should not rise to the lips of the observer of Mr Alfred Parsons's numerous and delightful studies of the gardens great and small of his country.'[1] Parsons became known for his many paintings of gardens, informed by an extensive botanical knowledge.

Alfred Parsons was born in Beckingham in Somerset in 1847, the son of a doctor who was an expert on perennial and rock plants. He worked as a post office clerk from 1865 whilst studying at the South Kensington Schools in the evenings. Apart from this training he owed 'little to any of the formal systems of art teaching', his real experience being gained from 'studying always directly from nature'.[2] Parsons's work was first accepted at the Royal Academy in 1871, and from 1874 he exhibited there every year until his death. His subjects were either panoramic landscapes or studies of particular flowers or gardens. However, in the 1880s and 1890s he worked widely as an illustrator, contributing charming pastoral scenes to *Harper's Monthly Magazine* (1891–2) and delicate drawings to books such as the *Poetry of Robert Herrick* (1882) and *The Warwickshire Avon* (1892). He also illustrated books such as *Old Songs* (1889) with E. A. Abbey.

In about 1885 Parsons visited the village of Broadway in Worcestershire. Laurence Hutton, a New Yorker and editor of *Harper's Monthly Magazine* spent the summer there, and was joined by the Anglo-American artists E. A. Abbey and Frank Millet who both contributed to his magazine. Literary figures such as Henry James and Edmund Gosse were delighted by the atmosphere of the village and spent many subsequent summers there, and John Singer Sargent (q.v.) painted *Carnation, Lily, Lily, Rose* (London, Tate Gallery) there. Parsons became part of this group, sharing a house with the Millets in London and a studio with E. A. Abbey.

Parsons had his first notable success with the purchase in 1887 of *When Nature Painted all Things Gay* (London, Tate Gallery) for the Chantrey Bequest. The painting depicts a shepherd in an orchard to create a landscape scene that is quintessentially English. Parsons, as usual, favoured an even light for this painting, so that details far in the distance are clearly defined.

After a nine-month stay in Japan, Parsons held an exhibition of paintings at The Fine Art Society in 1893. Japan had attracted him both for its landscapes and for its flowers, in particular the lotus blossom which he thought to be 'the finest flower in Japan, and ... certainly one of the most difficult to paint [being] only in perfection for a few hours in the early morning.'[3]

Parsons was elected an Associate of the Academy in 1897 and became a full Academician in 1911. He worked in watercolour as assiduously as in oils, becoming President of the Royal Society of Painters in Watercolour in 1913. He also executed more than

50   *repr. in colour on p. 41*

one hundred and fifty watercolours for an Edwardian botanist, Ellen Ann Willmott, who had magnificent collections of roses in her gardens at Great Warley in Essex and on the Franco-Italian Riviera. He was commissioned 'to paint the roses as they blossom and reach perfection,'[4] so work progressed slowly. The project began in the 1890s and the complete series entitled *The Genus Rosa* was eventually published in book form between 1910 and 1914. Parsons occasionally returned to painting Japanese subjects in the 1910s, but his pictures most often depicted gardens and various English flowers. He died at Broadway in 1920.

NOTES
1. *Drawings by Alfred Parsons*, exhib. cat., intro. by Henry James, London, Fine Art Society, 1891, p. 3.
2. *Studio*, 16 (1899), p. 153.
3. *Water-colour drawings by Alfred Parsons illustrating landscapes and flowers in Japan*, exhib. cat., London, Fine Art Society, 1893.
4. G. S. Thomas, *A Garden of Roses*, 1987, p. 17.

# Glyn Warren Philpot
## 1884–1937

## 50  Orange Lilies, Broadway

92 × 66 cm   36¼ × 26 in
Signed and dated br: *ALFRED PARSONS*
Diploma work, accepted 7 Nov 1911 (C.M. XXII, p. 451)

An expert gardener, Parsons was a sometime judge at the Chelsea Flower Show and also advised on the laying out of the garden at Wightwick Manor, near Wolverhampton. This painting probably depicts Parsons's own garden and, although carefully tended, it reflects the revival of the cottage garden which the landscape gardener, Gertrude Jekyll, working in partnership with the architect Sir Edwin Lutyens, developed at the turn of the century. Here the plants in the herbaceous border are allowed to grow naturally together, rather than being laid out formally.

Parsons was dedicated to painting studies of individual flowers and his friends remember 'the simple narcissus on which he was engaged, off and on, for years, trying it in all lights and from every angle.'[1] However, although Parsons's detailed knowledge of flowers is used to good effect here, he does not let this detract from the overall effect of the composition. The *Connoisseur* pointed out that 'minute expression of nature does not preclude the use of fluent and sentient brushwork' in Parsons's work, 'or the realization of beautiful colour'.[2] Despite working up his finished paintings in the studio from the many studies and sketches made out of doors, he nonetheless 'gained a peculiar freshness of interpretation.'[3] In this painting the white doves on the lawn of this idyllic garden evoke the languid atmosphere of a perfect English summer's day.

NOTES
1.  *The Times*, 21 Jan 1920, p. 15.
2.  *Connoisseur*, 38 (1914), p. 66.
3.  *Studio*, 16 (1899), p. 154.

EXHIBITION: R.A., 1912 (cat. 128).

For most of his career, Glyn Philpot received great critical acclaim for his stylish society portraits in the manner of Sargent (q.v.) and Shannon (q.v.), although his later years were characterised by a rejection of the academic style. He also painted genre scenes and religious, mythological and allegorical subjects, and was a competent sculptor.

Born in London in 1884, Philpot received his initial training under Philip Connard (q.v.) at the Lambeth School of Art where he enrolled in 1900. In 1905 he attended the Académie Julian in Paris under J.P. Laurens. He first exhibited at the Royal Academy in 1904 and was elected an Associate member in 1915 and a full member in 1923. By his late twenties, Philpot was well established and exhibiting regularly at the International Society, the Royal Institute of Oil Painters, the Modern Society of Portrait Painters and the National Portrait Society. He had his first one-man show at the Baillie Gallery in 1910 and won a gold medal at the Carnegie Institute, Pittsburg, U.S.A. in 1913. During these years his work showed the influence of Titian, Goya, Velazquez and Manet, his interest being strengthened by trips to Spain in 1906 and 1910. When war broke out in 1914 he enlisted in the Fusiliers. He was invalided out in 1917 but continued his service by painting portraits of four admirals for the Imperial War Museum in 1918.

The 1920s brought Philpot even more success with the establishment. A one-man show at the Grosvenor Gallery in 1923 received considerable critical approval and at the end of that year he was given a commission to paint King Faoud I of Egypt. This was followed in 1925 by commissions for the portrait of the Prime Minister Stanley Baldwin and for a mural for the final phase of the decoration of St Stephen's Hall, Westminster. His appointment as Trustee of the Tate Gallery in 1927 and his election as President of the Guild of Catholic Artists in 1929 added to his honours.

It was around this time, however, that Philpot began to show signs of dissatisfaction with his success and to look for a new direction in his art. With this in mind he took a studio in Paris in 1931 where he stayed for nearly a year working in seclusion on experimental work inspired by contemporaries such as Picasso and Matisse. A trip to Berlin renewed his acquaintance with the work of Beckmann, Grosz and Dix. The paintings exhibited on his return to England showed a preoccupation with decorative cubist forms, surrealist ideas and a lighter and brighter palette. His simpler style and modern outlook caused uproar in the press and nearly led to financial ruin although he did acquire a new and more progressive circle of admirers. He died suddenly in 1937 at the age of fifty-three.   E. C. W.

51

## 51 A Young Man

51 × 41 cm   20 × 16 in
Diploma work, accepted 18 March 1924 (C.M. XXV, p. 41)

Philpot's sitters were drawn from high society, politics and the worlds of literature, theatre and ballet. Many, like Brian Farrell, the subject of this portrait, were personal friends of the artist. Farrell died young and in 1922, Philpot painted as a memorial to him, a large-scale religious painting entitled, *The Altarpiece of the Sacred Heart* which was intended to hang in the Catholic Church of St Peter, Morningside, Edinburgh. It has been suggested[1] that the portrait shows close similarities with Philpot's sensuous bronze mask, *The Dead Faun c.* 1920 (private collection), which he had created as a timeless elegy to the passing of youth. The main similarity between the sculpture and the painting resides in the flat, mask-like features of the face which in the painting are realistically represented against a plain, dark background. Unlike many of the grand and stylish portraits which Philpot painted in the 1920s this portrait only shows the head and shoulders of the sitter. Accordingly, it has a psychological intensity which distinguishes it from Philpot's more self-consciously elegant paintings. Its melancholic mood is emphasised by the use of deep, sombre colours for the sitter's clothes and the background of the painting, enlivened only by a stroke of cream at the bottom of the canvas.

Although submitted as a Diploma work in 1924, it is likely that it was painted as early as 1921, closer to the date of the sculpture *The Dead Faun*, and before the death of the sitter.

NOTES
1. *Glyn Philpot 1884–1937*, exhib. cat., London, National Portrait Gallery, 1984, cat. 120, p. 119.

EXHIBITIONS: R.A., 1924 (cat. 66); Bournemouth, Russell-Cotes Art Gallery & Museum, 1957 (cat. 858); Bournemouth, Russell-Cotes Art Gallery & Museum, 1965 (cat. 50); Leicestershire Museum and Art Gallery, 1982 (cat. 70); Swansea, Glynn Vivian Art Gallery & Museum, 1985 (cat. 34).

# Bertram Priestman
## 1868–1951

Bertram Priestman was born in Bradford in 1868 into a family of Quaker industrialists with a strong artistic background. His father was a well-known Bradford collector and his uncle, Arnold Priestman, became a successful landscape painter, taking his schoolboy nephew on sketching holidays.

Bertram Priestman's early artistic training was provided by Edwin Moore (eldest brother of the distinguished painters Albert and Henry Moore) and after leaving school in 1886, he toured Italy, Egypt and Palestine, sketching extensively. Perhaps under family pressure, Priestman made a brief attempt at training for a conventional career, by attending a course in engineering at Bradford Technical College, but he soon abandoned this and enrolled at the Slade School of Art in 1888. The following year he joined the studio of Sir William Llewellyn, later President of the Royal Academy. Priestman's work was first accepted for exhibition at the Academy in 1890 although, as he later ruefully noted, he had 'nothing more accepted during the next six years'.[1] In 1892 Priestman took a studio in Chiswick, where he met Charles E. Holloway (1838–97), a painter whose east coast seascapes were noted for their 'robust method and sturdy directness'.[2] An article in the *Studio* suggested that his influence on Priestman was 'perhaps, seen in the force of brushwork and fearless use of rich colour which is now a characteristic of Mr Priestman's pictures.'[3] During the 1890s Priestman painted extensively on the coast near Great Yarmouth, favouring marine subjects. A visit to Holland in 1895, however, brought him into contact with William Maris (1844–1910), the Hague School painter whose favourite subject matter of rural scenes, often with cattle, was taken up by Priestman. Many studies of cattle resulted in his Academy picture of 1900, *The Watering Place*,[4] which was favourably received, combining a Dutch composition with a sketch-like freshness of effect.

Priestman always felt that 'the most important thing to remember ... is to paint, so to speak, in "hot blood" ',[5] and the critics agreed that it was 'better to be rough in execution than tame and Spiritless.'[6] His bold brushwork and free use of paint, which shocked the conservative critics of the early 1900s, allowed Priestman a considerable range of expression.

The search for new subject matter took him to Montreuil-sur-Mer in France in 1903 and 1905, and 1911 saw the first of Priestman's large-scale treatments of his native industrial landscape of West Yorkshire, *Outskirts of a Northern City*.[7] The combination of the grandeur of the moorland and valley landscape of Airedale with the grimly impressive industrial architecture of its cities inspired Priestman's memorable 1916 Academy painting, *The Heart of the West Riding* (Bradford Art Galleries and Museums). The *Art Journal* had commented that 'beauty, broadly understood, is not invariably destroyed by the presence of tall chimneys and the association of modern labour with ancient country peace.'[8] Priestman's imagination responded powerfully to the smoking factory chimneys, viaducts, and mill buildings of his home town of Bradford. *The Heart of the West Riding* was already hanging in the Summer Exhibition by the time of the Academy elections in 1916, and probably con- tributed to Priestman's success in being elected an Associate.

During the First World War Priestman lived with his family in Wharfedale and exhibited a series of paintings of Yorkshire Dales scenery. By 1920 he was back in Suffolk and once again painting the flat landscapes of eastern England. In 1923, at the age of fifty-five, he was elected an Academician and in the following year moved to Chiswick. He established a reputation as a portraitist and five of his 1926 Academy exhibits were portraits.

Priestman's palette lightened in 1925, perhaps as a result of his taking up watercolour painting for the first time in the 1920s, partly at The Fine Art Society's request. In 1933, as a senior landscape Academician, he wrote a series of articles for *The Artist* in which he described his methods of painting in some detail. Always interested in teaching, he began an annual summer school on the Isle of Wight from 1913 and also taught in Suffolk and Essex in later years. In 1940, Priestman moved to Crowborough in Sussex, and remained there for the rest of his life. Returning in his old age to rural subjects such as cattle in the meadows, Priestman continued to produce broad landscapes which captured 'in natural objects, massiveness, and not multiplicity of detail.'[9]    H. C. V.

NOTES
1. Quoted *Bertram Priestman*, exhib. cat., Bradford Art Galleries and Museums and Hull, Ferens Art Gallery, 1981, p. 6.
2. *Studio*, 14 (1898), p. 85.
3. idem.
4. Exh., R.A., 1900 (cat. 332) entitled *The river meadow*.
5. *The Artist*, March 1933 p. 5.
6. Quoted *Bertram Priestman*, op. cit., p. 8.
7. Exh., R.A., 1911 (cat. 8).
8. Quoted *Bertram Priestman*, op. cit., p. 18.
9. *Art Journal*, 1907, p. 184.

## 52  Near Wareham, Dorset

64.5 × 77.5 cm    25½ × 30½ in
Signed and dated br: *B. Priestman 23*
Diploma work, accepted 8 Jan 1924 (C.M. XXV, p. 19)

As early as 1895 Priestman had been attracted by the low, flat countryside of Holland, but it was while painting at Walberswick in Suffolk and Wareham in Dorset that he began to devote particular attention to the painting of sky.

Executed in 1923, *Near Wareham, Dorset* is a work typical of this period. The landscape is dominated by the sky, and as *The Yorkshire Post* noted, Priestman 'delights in skies half veiled by dense masses of moving clouds'.[1] Indeed, to Priestman 'skies may fairly be described as the keynote of landscape painting.'[2] The sky here is of the type that Priestman described as 'a warm evening sky' with 'the sun behind the clouds illuminating their edges'.[3] The watery countryside provides an ideal vehicle for reflecting the warm evening glow, and with the bright highlights, particularly on the sea in the distance, presents the results of keen observation. Priestman could only obtain these

effects by working out of doors, and was aware that landscapes produced in a studio 'gradually tend to possess that indoor appearance'.[4] His aim was to record nature as he saw it; he wrote that 'nature is more surprising and more beautiful than anything the mind of man can conceive.'[5] This did not mean that Priestman painted minute detail, but, in works such as *Near Wareham, Dorset* he used bold brushstrokes to create an impression of breadth, despite the small size of the canvas. He advised other artists 'to paint with a full brush' in order to 'give a richer and probably more translucent effect'.[6]

To paint trees which 'seem capable of movement in the wind, with the possibility of rain dripping through them' Priestman proposed that a 'tone rather darker than the sky and slightly lighter than the trees should be placed between them.'[7] The centrally placed tree here demonstrates this method exactly.

The effect of the edge of the foliage breaking into this intermediary tone 'keeps the freshness whilst it appears to surround the trees with atmosphere.'[8]

NOTES
1. Quoted *Bertram Priestman*, exhib. cat., Bradford Art Galleries and Museums and Hull, Ferens Art Gallery, 1981, p. 31.
2. *The Artist*, April 1933, p. 39.
3. *The Artist*, May 1933, p. 73.
4. *The Artist*, April 1933, p. 39.
5. *The Artist*, May 1933, p. 74.
6. *The Artist*, March 1933, p. 5.
7. *The Artist*, June 1933, p. 103.
8. idem.

EXHIBITIONS: R.A., 1924 (cat. 115); Bournemouth, Russell-Cotes Art Gallery & Museum, 1957 (cat. 876); Leicestershire Museum and Art Gallery, 1982 (cat. 72).

# Sir Walter Westley Russell
## 1867–1949

According to his obituary in *The Times*, the 'outstanding characteristic of the late Sir Walter Westley Russell, R.A. was his extreme quietness, in his art, as in his life.... As a painter he was remarkable for sensibility rather than force and for evenness of quality ... he found himself equally in landscape and figure subjects, in oil and in watercolour.'[1]

Born in 1867 in Essex, Russell was the son of a bookbinder. In his early twenties he studied at the Westminster School of Art under Professor Frederick Brown where Henry Tonks was a fellow pupil. Like Tonks he was recognised early on for his ability as a draughtsman so that when Tonks and Brown left Westminster two years later in order to take up posts at the Slade School of Art, Russell followed, becoming assistant teacher of drawing there in 1895 at the age of twenty-seven. Among his pupils were Augustus John (q.v.), William Orpen (q.v.) and Ambrose McEvoy. He taught continuously at the Slade until 1927 apart from a period of War service from 1916 to 1919 when, as a lieutenant in the Royal Engineers, he was involved in camouflage work.

Russell's early work consisted of illustrations and etchings reminiscent of the work of the illustrators of the 1860s and portraits and interiors which he exhibited at the New English Art Club (of which he became a member in 1895). His first one-man show was at the Goupil Gallery in 1910 although he had been exhibiting at the Royal Academy since 1898. Russell was elected an Associate member in 1920 and a full member in 1926, becoming Keeper of the Royal Academy Schools in 1927. Noted for his abilities both as a teacher and as a practising artist, Russell took up this post at a time when teaching at the Academy was undergoing major reforms, involving the replacement of the two- or three-month visitor system with a permanent teaching staff. He retired from the Keepership in 1942 on becoming a Senior Academician. A member of the International Society, the National Portrait Society and the Royal Watercolour Society, Russell was appointed as a Trustee of the Tate Gallery between 1927 and 1934, and between 1938 and 1944. He was knighted in 1935.

For most of his life Russell lived in Chelsea although he often worked in Yorkshire, Norfolk and Sussex where he painted impressionistic landscapes and seascapes which show the influence of Philip Wilson Steer. In 1926 he painted a series of Venetian scenes as a prelude to an increasing interest in the atmospheric effects of light and colour. He also worked on 'low-life' interior scenes in the manner of Sickert (q.v.) and in later years he was usually represented in the first room of the Royal Academy exhibitions by small paintings of female figures and portraits in domestic settings. His slightly humorous and informal portraits which showed the sitter *chez lui* surrounded by objects which best illustrated his character were very popular with the public who attended the Summer Exhibition, a particular favourite being the portrait of *Mr Minney* (London, Tate Gallery) exhibited in 1920.   E. C. W.

NOTES
1.   *The Times*, 22 April 1949.

*repr. in colour on p. 48*

## 53   Studland Beach

45.7 × 64 cm    18 × 24 in
Signed bl: *W. Russell*
Purchased by the Royal Academy (Stott Fund) 5 Jan 1943 (C.M. XXVII, p. 450)

This small landscape admirably demonstrates Russell's interest in the effects of light falling on objects. The less rigid handling of the paint, the light tones and the sketch-like figures all contribute towards a freshness and spontaneity which is reminiscent of the painters of the Barbizon School and the Impressionists. Although the composition is carefully structured, the spectator's eye is not encouraged to rest on any specific detail, thus accentuating the sensation of movement and activity at this busy seaside location. The size of the painting and its immediacy suggest that it was probably painted out of doors in front of the subject.

In spite of his achievements as a landscape painter, Russell deposited a portrait, *Alice*, as his Diploma work.

EXHIBITIONS: London, R.A., 1943 (cat. 848); Arts Club, 1957–1964, long term loan.

# John Singer Sargent
## 1856–1925

Born in Florence on 12 January 1856 of American parents, John Singer Sargent spent his childhood travelling through Europe, Dr FitzWilliam Sargent being of the rather optimistic opinion that he could cultivate his son's 'memory and his observing and discriminating faculties without his being bothered with the disagreeable notion that he is actually studying.'[1] Encouraged by his mother it seems that Sargent decided as early as 1868 to pursue a career as a painter. Lessons were taken from Carl Welsch in Rome and classes attended at the Accademia di Belle Arti in Florence in the early 1870s. But it was soon apparent that he would have to train in Paris or London if he was seriously to fulfil his aim. He entered the *atelier* of the fashionable portrait painter Carolus-Duran in 1874 and supplemented what he learned there with tuition at the Ecole des Beaux-Arts and sketching holidays in the summer to practise *plein-air* painting. Carolus-Duran encouraged his pupils to paint in a realistic manner, working directly onto the canvas. To achieve this he advised them to 'search for the half-tones, place your accents, and then the lights' and 'ceaselessly study Velazquez'.[2] Sargent's talents were recognised by Carolus-Duran when he asked him to assist with his large ceiling decoration for the Louvre in 1877. Further recognition followed in the form of favourable reviews for a large subject painting exhibited in the Salon of 1878, *Oyster Gatherers of Cancale* (Washington D.C., Corcoran Art Gallery), worked up from *plein-air* sketches done in Brittany.

A winter spent in southern Spain in 1879–80, proved to be the watershed in his artistic development. Impressed by the dignified grandeur of Velazquez's paintings, his own work — and particularly his portraits – became more refined and formal. He also visited Haarlem in 1880 to study Frans Hals, an artist to whom he was attracted not so much for his subjects as for his exuberant, stylish brushwork.

Ambitious for success, Sargent exhibited what he considered to be a major work at the 1884 Salon, *Madame Pierre Gautreau* (New York, Metropolitan Museum of Art). Unfortunately, a minor scandal ensued because of the provocative air of the sitter and her questionable reputation, and Sargent retreated to England for the remainder of that summer. His close friend, Henry James, urged him to stay, 'there being such a field in London for a real painter of women'.[3] With few portrait commissions in Paris, perhaps because of the Gautreau scandal, Sargent returned to England in 1885. By chance he was invited to stay at Broadway in Worcestershire, the retreat of a group of English and American artists and writers, including E. A. Abbey, Edmund Gosse, Frank Millet and Alfred Parsons (q.v.). He found the company and place so congenial that he finally decided to settle in England in 1886. Sargent's work at Broadway in this and subsequent years represents his most impressionistic period, being particularly concerned with cap-

turing the momentary effects of light. He certainly knew, and was influenced by Monet, visiting him at Giverney in 1887. *Carnation, Lily, Lily, Rose* (London, Tate Gallery), painted at Broadway, was very favourably received when exhibited at the Academy in 1887, and was bought for the Chantrey Bequest.

A visit to America in 1887 was a great success, with portrait commissions coming from the highest ranks of American society. He returned to England in 1889 and the following year he received a major commission to decorate Boston Public Library. His ambitious scheme to represent on a monumental scale the development of religious thought involved trips to Egypt, Sicily, and Ravenna, and took over twenty-five years to complete. He was traditional enough to consider this the most important work of his career.

In the 1890s Sargent's reputation was at its height: elected an Associate member in 1894, by 1897 he was a full Academician and the most sought-after society portraitist. His unashamedly extravagant images, particularly of women, influenced a whole generation of portrait painters and now seem to epitomise their era.

In the late 1890s he began to paint his sitters full length, often in idealised landscapes, consciously echoing the portraits of eighteenth-century painters such as Reynolds, Gainsborough and Lawrence. By the 1900s, however, Sargent was heartily sick of painting portraits. Completing nearly sixteen commissions a year it is little wonder that he exclaimed: 'I abhor and adjure them and hope never to do another especially of the Upper Classes.'[4] By 1907 he had almost abandoned portraiture altogether, although he occasionally undertook charcoal sketches to satisfy his more persistent patrons. Freedom from portrait commissions, and financial security gave him the opportunity to take long sketching holidays in Europe. Working mostly in watercolour he broadened his subject matter to include architectural themes, formal gardens and figures in landscapes.

Sargent spent most of his time in America during the First World War, but returned to England in 1918 to undertake a commission for the Ministry of Information, which resulted in the forceful and realistic *Gassed* (London, Imperial War Museum). In the last years of his life he became increasingly involved with mural work in Boston, having undertaken further commissions for the Museum of Fine Art in 1916. After his death in 1925 the full measure of his international reputation became apparent with important memorial exhibitions held in New York, Boston and at the Royal Academy.   H. C. V.

NOTES
1.  E. Charteris, *John Sargent*, 1927, p. 5.
2.  ibid., p. 28
3.  L. Edel, *Henry James: The Middle Years, 1884–94*, 1963, p. 47.
4.  E. Charteris, op. cit., p. 155.

*repr. in colour on p. 30*

## 54   An Interior in Venice

66 × 83.5 cm    26 × 33 in
Signed and dated bl: *John S. Sargent 1899*
Diploma work, accepted 1900 (A.R., p. 54)

'Dark shapeless smudges reveal themselves at the right distance as cherubs and festoons in the decoration of the ceiling ... In what limpid, brilliant air this picture lives'.[1] This contemporary critic responded, as many did, both to this picture's painterly qualities and to its mood, which evoked fashionable society at its most elegant.

The setting is the salon of the Palazzo Barbaro in Venice, and in the sumptuously decorated room sit Mr and Mrs Daniel Curtis (on the right) and their son Ralph, a close friend of Sargent, and his wife (on the left). This expatriate American family were the leading social lights of the Anglo-Venetian community, and often entertained artists and writers, amongst them Henry James who used the Palazzo as a setting for *Wings of a Dove* (1902). Sargent stayed there for the summer of 1899, and clearly appreciated his surroundings. In a letter thanking Mrs Curtis for a previous visit he wrote that the 'Barbaro is a sort of Fontaine de Jouvence, for it sends one back twenty years, besides making the present seem remarkably right.'[2]

The picture, intended for Mrs Curtis (nicknamed 'the Doga-ressa' by Sargent), was rejected because 'the portrait of herself was said to anticipate advancing years, and her son seated on a table in an attitude of nonchalance was inconsistent with the deportment observed by Mrs & Mr Charles P. Curtis [sic].'[3] The raking light certainly does not flatter Mrs Curtis, but the

strength of the painting lies very much in its informality, and it is partly this which makes it seem to capture so convincingly the spirit of the age.

Mrs Curtis's loss was the Academy's gain as the picture was subsequently given as Sargent's Diploma work. The *Art Journal* perceptively noted in 1900 that this work 'will henceforth rank as one of the most precious possessions of the Royal Academy.' It replaced a portrait of the violinist *Johannes Wolff* (Massachusetts, Fogg Art Museum) temporarily deposited by Sargent in 1897.[4]

His previous Venetian interiors, painted from 1880, were essentially genre pieces, sombre in tone and mood. This picture, however, seems to belong more in the British tradition of the conversation piece. Comparing *An Interior in Venice* with seventeenth-century Dutch interiors, Whistler dismissed Sargent's 'little picture' as 'smudge everywhere. Think of the finish, the delicacy, the elegance, the repose of a little Terborgh or Metsu.'[5] However, Sargent was not aiming for such an exquisite composition, but rather to capture the mood of the moment and set the scene down as realistically as possible, with his models caught in the act of turning the page of a book or pouring a cup of tea. Sargent's debt to Velazquez is apparent in the richness of tone and in the figures emerging from the dark interior, revealed by sunlight streaming in through the window.

Most critics were unanimous in their praise of the picture, finding it 'quite astounding in its superb command of craftsmanship and its acute observation of subtle gradations of tone and colour'[6] and that despite its small size it 'has breadth and dignity of an almost monumental kind'.[7] Perhaps it was Evan Charteris, however, who best perceived that *An Interior in Venice* possessed a 'quality of charm, indefinable, but to as great a degree, perhaps, as any picture by Sargent'.[8]

NOTES
1. W. H. Downes, *John S. Sargent*, 1926, p. 190.
2. Letter, 27 May 1898; quoted in R. Ormond, *John Singer Sargent*, 1970, p. 251.
3. E. Charteris, *John Sargent*, 1927, p. 163.
4. C.M. XX, p. 319, 27 July 1897.
5. *The Whistler Journal*, eds, E. R. and J. Pennell, Philadelphia, 1921, p. 39.
6. *Magazine of Art*, 1900, p. 385.
7. idem.
8. E. Charteris, op. cit., p. 163.

EXHIBITIONS: R.A., 1900 (cat. 729); R.A., Winter, 1926 (cat. 14); Bournemouth, Russell-Cotes Art Gallery & Museum, 1957 (cat. 840); London, Royal Society of Portrait Painters, 1960 (cat. 22); Washington, Corcoran Gallery of Art, 1964 (cat. 63); R.A., Winter, 1968 (cat. 414); Columbus Gallery of Fine Arts, 1971 (cat. 91); London, Wildenstein & Co., 1972 (cat. 37); South London Art Gallery, 1973 (cat. 90); Liverpool, Walker Art Gallery, 1976 (cat. 62); Royal Scottish Academy, 1976 (cat. 16); Milton Keynes, Great Linford Art Centre, 1982; U.S.A., R.A., Touring exhibition, 1983–4 (cat. 41); Swansea, Glynn Vivian Art Gallery & Museum, 1985 (cat. 19); The Fine Art Museums of San Francisco, 1985 (cat. 60); New York, Whitney Museum, 1987 (cat. 44).

# Sir James Jebusa Shannon
## 1862–1923

Sir James Jebusa Shannon was born in Auburn, New York in 1862. His parents were of Irish descent, but the name Jebusa was chosen in honour of an Indian his father had met on his travels as a railway contractor.

Shannon had demonstrated an early interest in painting whilst still in America by copying pictures by artists such as Landseer. He came to London in 1878 and enrolled with the South Kensington Schools, where he studied until 1881, winning a gold medal for figure painting in 1880. Success came early to Shannon in the form of a commission to paint one of the Queen's Ladies-in-Waiting, the Hon. Horatia Stopford. The portrait was exhibited in the 1881 Academy exhibition by command of the Queen, and signalled the beginning of Shannon's long and successful career as a portraitist.

Although Shannon never studied in Paris he was nevertheless influenced by artists who had trained at the Paris *ateliers*. Adopting a square-brush technique for his early portraits, Shannon's style broadened in the 1890s when he came under the influence of the painterly technique of John Singer Sargent (q.v.).

Shannon was a founding member of the New English Art Club, which was established in 1886 by artists seeking an alternative exhibition venue to the Royal Academy. Six years later he resigned, when two of his portraits were rejected by the N.E.A.C. His harsher critics felt that he was too ready to flatter his sitters, and that 'through Mr Shannon our duchesses realise all their aspirations, present and posthumous.'[1] Whistler, however, admired his paintings and Shannon's work was included in the exhibitions of the International Society of Sculptors, Painters and Gravers.

At the turn of the century Shannon's reputation was consolidated with his first one-man show at The Fine Art Society in 1896, his election as Associate of the Academy in 1897, and the purchase of *Flower Girl* (London, Tate Gallery) for the Chantrey Bequest in 1901. This work, painted in the open air, vividly captures the effects of dappled sunlight on the figure of a young woman nursing her child.

Shannon's patrons were often drawn from the highest ranks of English society. Violet, Duchess of Rutland and Marchioness of Granby frequently commissioned portraits of herself from the 1880s onwards: a memorable example from 1913 depicts the Duchess in an enormous exotic headdress which complements her striking, but refined features.[2] In the 1910s, under the influence of Sargent (q.v.), Shannon began to paint full-length portraits in a manner derived from eighteenth-century painters such as Gainsborough or Reynolds. In *Mrs Frederic Montagu*,[3] for example, exhibited in 1910, the sitter is shown in an idealised landscape, standing against an enormous plinth surmounted by a classical sculpture.

Shannon was made a full Academician in 1909 and in the following year was elected President of the Royal Society of Portrait Painters. Although he spent his last years in a wheelchair (as a result of a horse-riding injury), illness did not prevent him from continuing to paint and in 1922, the year before he died, he received a knighthood.   H. C. V.

*repr. in colour on p. 32*

NOTES
1.  G. Moore, *Modern Painting*, 1893, p. 191.
2.  Repr., *Royal Academy Pictures*, 1913, p. 111.
3.  Repr., ibid., 1910, p. 126.

## 55   Black and Silver

85.1 × 101 cm    $33\frac{1}{2}$ × $39\frac{3}{4}$ in
Signed bl: *J. J. Shannon*
Diploma work, accepted 6 Dec 1909 (C.M. XXII, p. 275)

Contemporary critics were unanimous in finding *Black and Silver* 'a most satisfactory portrait ... which is worthily his Diploma work.'[1] Unlike so much of his work, this was not a commissioned portrait, but rather 'a charming fancy picture of his daughter'.[2] Nonetheless, the picture is highly evocative of the Edwardian era. The sitter's leisurely lifestyle is suggested by her relaxed pose, as she reclines on a chaise-longue with a pet dog at her side.

Although Shannon requested permission to remove his Diploma work from the Academy in order to do some further work on it,[3] much of the background is very freely painted, suggesting heavy brocaded drapery behind the figure. Parts of the figure and the arm of the chaise-longue, however, are painted in thick impasto with great virtuosity. Critics found Shannon's technique 'fascinating in its frank and expressive vivacity of style and in its delightful freshness of colour.'[4]

NOTES
1.  *Art Journal*, 1910, p. 169.
2.  *The Times*, 30 April 1910, p. 10.
3.  C.M. XXII, p. 275, 6 Dec 1909.
4.  *Studio*, 48 (1910) p. 10.

EXHIBITIONS: R.A., 1910 (cat. 3); R.A., Winter, 1928 (cat. 2); Bournemouth, Russell-Cotes Art Gallery & Museum, 1965 (cat. 55); Swansea, Glynn Vivian Art Gallery & Museum, 1985 (cat. 23).

# Walter Richard Sickert
## 1860–1942

Walter Richard Sickert was born in Munich in 1860, the son of Oswald Adalbert Sickert, a painter and illustrator of Danish descent. After a brief period living in Dieppe, the family moved to London in 1868. Discouraged by his father from pursuing an artistic career, Sickert became an actor and worked with repertory companies from 1878 for about three years. His love for the theatre remained with him and he painted subjects from the music halls throughout his life. In 1881 he enrolled at the Slade School of Art for two years before becoming the pupil and assistant of Whistler, from whom he learnt the technique of etching. In his painting, Sickert followed Whistler in concentrating above all on tonal values.

In 1883 Sickert visited Paris, and from 1885 began making regular visits to Dieppe. Whilst in France, he met leading Impressionists such as Monet, Pissarro, Gauguin and, significantly for his development as a draughtsman, Degas. By 1888 Sickert was exhibiting with the recently-formed New English Art Club. The following year, wishing to hold an exhibition which departed even further from establishment precepts he organised, with Wilson Steer, a show of 'The London Impressionists' at the Goupil Gallery. Sickert's subjects at this time were urban scenes in Dieppe and the music halls of London.

In 1893 he opened in Chelsea the first of his seven private art schools. Although each school lasted only a short time, and all owed their birth partly to financial need, Sickert was nonetheless a committed and stimulating teacher, and was much appreciated during his brief spell teaching at the Royal Academy Schools in 1926.

Between 1898 and 1905 Sickert lived mainly in Dieppe, although he spent several long periods in Venice. Through painting street scenes in Dieppe and architectural subjects in Venice, Sickert developed his characteristic style, using subdued tones, strong outlines and paint which was often rubbed right down to the canvas or applied leaving areas of the canvas quite bare. On a visit to Venice in 1903 he began painting figures in interiors, and continued developing this theme both in Dieppe and London. Spencer Gore had persuaded Sickert to return to London in 1905, and the two painters formed the nucleus of a group of artists that included Harold Gilman and Malcolm Drummond. In 1907 this became known as the Fitzroy Street Group, taking its name from the street in which Sickert's studio stood. Committed to painting urban scenes, these artists recorded their subjects in a direct and unglamorous manner.

*Mornington Crescent Nude,* c. 1907 (private collection), represents a typical Sickert subject, a nude in a decrepit bedsit. Influenced by Gore and by Lucien Pissarro, Sickert used thick touches of púre colour to capture the effects of light on the figure. In a series of paintings from 1908 to 1910 Sickert depicted an actual murder which had taken place in Camden Town. In these works his colours became darker, but richer, and only lightened again in 1911 when Sickert led the more advanced nucleus of the Fitzroy Street Group to form the Camden Town Group.

During the First World War, Sickert took a studio in Red Lion Square, London, but his principal subjects at this time were vaudeville scenes observed at Brighton. He lived in Bath between 1916 and 1917, where he took once again to architectural subjects. Sickert returned to Dieppe in 1919, and painted a series depicting people playing Baccarat, using flat areas of colour and clear outlines.

In 1926 Sickert settled permanently in England and from about 1927 he increasingly based his work on photographs from newspapers, magazines and on Victorian engravings. By using a camera in preparation for a work such as *High Steppers,* c. 1938–9 (Edinburgh, Scottish National Gallery of Art), Sickert was able to freeze the action of a chorus line in full swing. In the finished work, broadly painted on a deliberately rough-textured surface, he succeeded in capturing the energy of the high-kicking dancers.

Sickert had been elected an Associate of the Academy in 1924, and full membership followed in 1934. However, he resigned in 1935 as a protest against the Academy's refusal to support the fight to save Jacob Epstein's sculptures on the British Medical Association's headquarters on the Strand. Sickert felt 'if the Royal Academy cannot throw its shield over a great sculptor, what is the Royal Academy for?'[1] He retired from painting in 1940. He died at Bathampton, Somerset in 1942 at the age of eighty-one and his collected art criticism, *A Free House!,* was published in 1945.  H. C. V.

NOTE
1. Letter from W. R. Sickert to Sir William Llewellyn, President of the Royal Academy, 19 May 1935, R.A. Archives, RAC/1/SI 7.

56 *repr. in colour on p. 51*

## 56 Santa Maria della Salute, Venice

56 × 46 cm  22 × 18 in
Signed bl: *Sickert*
Diploma work, accepted 3 August 1934 (C.M. XXVI, p. 341)

Sickert initially offered *Fabia Drake as 'Lady Macbeth'* as his Diploma work, but this was rejected and the Council requested that he 'submit some more representative work.'[1] Sickert therefore presented *Santa Maria della Salute*, which was accepted. The picture had previously belonged to a former pupil and close friend of Sickert's, Sylvia Gosse, the daughter of the poet and writer, Sir Edmund Gosse.

*Santa Maria della Salute* was probably painted in 1901 during Sickert's third stay in Venice.[2] He first visited the city in 1895, when his subjects included the panoramic views of the city as treated by Canaletto and Turner. In an earlier picture entitled *The Dogana and Santa Maria della Salute*, 1896 (private collection), the church is seen across a wide stretch of lagoon, a principal feature of the Venetian skyline. Here, however, he takes a low view-point, representing the church rising up out of the lagoon, with only a narrow strip of water visible. By concentrating on this single building, Sickert gives a surprisingly monumental feel to a relatively small canvas. Sickert's intention was obviously to convey the sculptural presence of this baroque church with its richly ornate decorations, and for this purpose he adopted a heavier manner than previously, roughly defining the ornamentation with a thick impasto of rich deep colours. The tonal range is limited and sombre, but dramatic effects are achieved by the juxtaposition of light greys and dark greens.

Just visible are the vermillion squaring-up lines, revealing that the composition of *Santa Maria della Salute* was carefully transferred from a drawing, belying its freely painted appearance. Apparently it was not Sickert's intention that these lines should be seen, as he once refused payment for a picture, on the grounds that 'there are certain alterations to be made, those cursed lines in paint of the squaring up . . . [are] . . . showing too much.'[3]

Contemporary reviewers were enthusiastic about Sickert's work, stating that without it (and that of Augustus John, q.v., and Stanley Spencer, q.v.) 'any distinction which the Academy of 1935 can claim to possess would disappear.'[4] *The Times* described *Santa Maria della Salute* as 'a lovely piece of low-toned colour on a small scale, firm and judicious in every touch.'[5]

NOTES
1.  C.M. XXVI, p. 304, 20 March 1934.
2.  W. Baron, *Sickert*, 1973, p. 326.
3.  Letter from W. R. Sickert to Jacques-Emile Blanche, *c.* 1903; quoted W. Baron, op. cit., 1973, p. 67.
4.  *Studio*, 110 (1935), p. 16.
5.  *The Times*, 14 May 1935, p. 15.

EXHIBITIONS: New Zealand & Australia, Empire Arts Loan Exhibition 1934–5; R.A., 1935 (cat. 532); Bournemouth, Russell-Cotes Art Gallery & Museum, 1957 (cat. 821); Arts Council Midlands Touring Exhibition, 1964 (cat. 5); R.A., Winter, 1968 (cat. 448); Northampton Central Museum & Art Gallery, 1972 (cat. 86); London, Wildenstein Gallery, 1972 (cat. 47); Leicestershire Museum & Art Gallery, 1982 (cat. 78); Cheltenham Art Gallery & Museums, 1985 (cat. 8); Swansea, Glynn Vivian Art Gallery & Museum, 1985 (cat. 39).

# Charles Sims
## 1873–1928

Harold Speed, in his tribute to Charles Sims published in 1928, remembered a man who, like his pictures, was 'full of strange conceits and whimsicalities'.[1] Sims's son ascribed this 'determination to escape from the actual confines of physical life into a region of his own fancy,'[2] to the painful experience of being lame when young. Certainly Sims's imagination was fertile and although his decorative compositions sometimes appear deliberately obscure, his originality and technical virtuosity surpass the work of many of his contemporaries at the Royal Academy.

Charles Sims was born in 1873 in Islington, the son of a draper. He was sent to Paris at the age of fourteen to learn the family trade, but it was not to his taste and on his return to England, Sims entered a firm of engravers. In 1890 he enrolled with the South Kensington Schools before leaving for Paris in 1891 to join the Académie Julian under Jules Lefebvre and Benjamin Constant. Sims completed his studies at the Royal Academy Schools from 1893 to 1895 winning the Landseer scholarship, before being expelled for a trivial offence. Sims's early work was exhibited at the Academy and included subjects such as *The Kingdom of Heaven*,[3] shown in 1899. The work is pure fantasy, depicting a procession of children winding across an imaginary landscape painted in light silvery tones. In about 1900 Sims took a cottage at St Lawrence in Essex. Around 1902, he returned to lessons learnt while in Paris and began with a series of paintings executed in the open air on the theme of the mother and child. These are typified by *The Kite*,[4] which captures the freshness of a windy day, as the mother watches her child fly a kite.

Sims briefly returned to Paris in 1904 to study under Baschet. By now his own reputation was growing, and his one-man exhibition at the Leicester Galleries in 1906 proved a great success. Sims settled around this time in Fittleworth, West Sussex and continued to paint figures out of doors as well as imaginary compositions such as *An Island Festival* (Sydney, National Gallery of New South Wales). The subject of this work had no specific literary source but was rather a celebration 'of the most agreeable aspect of the furnishings of life. Children, dewy morning, the playful side of love, the coming of spring, a basket of flowers, butterflies, and the pagan creatures of the woodland and stream.'[5] The popularity of this picture when exhibited at the Academy in 1907 must have influenced his election as Associate the following year.

Always interested in experimenting with different techniques, Sims gradually perfected a distinctive method of painting in tempera with an oil finish. He used this mixed medium in works such as *The Wood beyond the World* (London, Tate Gallery), purchased for the Chantrey Bequest in 1913. The subject is still purely imaginative but the treatment draws on the iconography of the Italian Renaissance. Sims concentrated on the linear qualities of the figures weaving between the trees, rather than creating his usual sparkling atmospheric effects. He refined this style further in a group of paintings representing the Seven Sacraments, which was exhibited at the Dowdeswell Galleries

in 1918. Executed solely in tempera, the figures are shown in profile against simple backgrounds or landscapes. Sims felt that for an artist 'to express the same ideas as early painters, his best hope lies in adopting something of their manner along with the symbols they used.'[6]

During the First World War, Sims visited France in 1916 to collect material for a commission for a Canadian War Memorial Panel for the Parliament House in Ottawa. He visited France again in 1918 as an Official War Artist, and painted *The Old German Front Line, Arras, 1916* (London, Imperial War Museum), a detailed study of the shattering effects of war on the landscape.

Sims had been elected an Academician in 1916, and four years later he took up his post as Keeper of the Royal Academy Schools. He turned to portraiture and achieved great success with *The Countess of Rocksavage and her son* (private collection) in 1922. Sims combined his historicist manner – placing the figures in front of an arched parapet like a Madonna and Child – with all his old virtuosity in painting the effects of shimmering light. A portrait of George V,[7] commissioned on the advice of the Royal Academy and exhibited in 1924, was less successful, perhaps because Sims with 'his disposition to dwell in fairyland' turned the monarch 'into a fairy king'.[8] The king refused the painting, and although a superb example of Sims's technical expertise, it was later destroyed. Sims travelled to America in 1925, where he achieved great success with his portraits, and held an exhibition at the Knoedler Galleries in New York in 1926. It was perhaps his new prospects in America that led Sims to resign as Keeper in 1926.

Feeling, however, that as a portraitist he was not true to his own imagination, he returned to London, and from 1927 began painting a series of six 'spirituals'. These paintings represented mystical ideas, intending to 'put lovely thoughts into being' and 'appeal to tender souls'.[9] Abandoning the Edwardian wonderland of his earlier imaginative compositions, in these pictures he aspired to an altogether more challenging mode of expression. Exhibited after his death, they seemed jarringly modern and unfamiliar to the conservative audiences of the Royal Academy. In *My Pain Beneath your Sheltering Hand*,[10] a jagged space opens to reveal a monumental Christ surrounded by vivid streaks of red and yellow, sheltering the nude figure of a man.

Sims never fully recovered from the traumatic loss of his son in the First World War and, dogged by ill health and psychologically exhausted after the creation of his 'spirituals', he took his own life in 1928.    H. C. V.

NOTES
1.  *The Old Water-Colour Society's Club*, VI (1928–9), p. 45.
2.  C. Sims, *Picture Making: Technique and Inspiration*, 1934, p. 87.
3.  Repr., *Royal Academy Pictures*, 1899, p. 194.
4.  Repr., ibid., 1905, p. 22.
5.  C. Sims, op. cit., p. 112.
6.  ibid., p. 122.
7.  Repr., *Royal Academy Illustrated*, 1924, p. 1.
8.  F. Rutter, *The little book of the Royal Academy*, 1924.
9.  C. Sims, op. cit., p. 129.
10. Repr., C. Sims, op. cit., pl. VI.

## 57　Clio and the Children

114.3 × 182.9 cm　45 × 72 in
Diploma work, accepted 23 May 1916 (C.M. XXIII, p. 390)

Sims initially submitted a painting entitled *The House of Sleep* as his Diploma work, but the Academy's Council, with whom Sims often found himself at odds, considered this to be an unsatisfactory example of his work.[1] He therefore offered *Clio and the Children*, which was accepted in 1916.

In about 1906 Sims had settled at Fittleworth in West Sussex where 'some of his loveliest work was done; he was supremely happy, living a very simple life with his wife and chubby children.'[2] He habitually used members of his family as models, and perhaps did so for this work. Sims enjoyed painting unorthodox combinations of the mythological and the everyday; figures from pagan and classical mythology would appear in his work set either in the Sussex countryside or in a domestic interior. In *The Little Faun*, 1908 (Truro County Museum and Art Gallery) Sims places a faun amidst a family eating breakfast. In *Clio and the Children*, the group in a Sussex meadow are boys and girls of Sims's time, but they are listening to the robed figure of Clio, the muse of history. The work was painted in 1913 but was altered in 1915 after Sims's eldest son had been killed in the First World War. As for so many artists, the Great War dealt a blow to Sims from which he never fully recovered. History could no longer be personified as a beautiful goddess reading from a scroll, passing on the wisdom of the ages to her young audience. Sims saw the lessons of modern history as more violent: 'Clio read no more to the children. Before sending the picture to the Diploma Gallery, he blotted out her scroll with blood',[3] his symbol of the defilement of history by the blood of those, including his son, killed in the Great War.

The critical reception of *Clio and the Children* was varied. The

*Studio* thought that it was 'a wonderful pictorial exercise in which exacting difficulties have been met and triumphantly overcome.'[4] Another critic found 'the charming group of children ... perfectly, though slightly finished [and] the stretching English landscape [to be] in perfect unison'.[5] The figure of Clio, central to Sims's whole concept of the picture, was considered by other commentators to be 'merely irrelevant'[6] and, seeming to lack anatomical accuracy in the modelling of the shoulder, it was described as a 'blemish to an otherwise fine picture'.[7]

In *Clio and the Children* Sims was not referring so consciously to a Renaissance idiom as he had in earlier works such as *The Wood Beyond the World* (London, Tate Gallery). However, its use of a classical subject, with some figures in modern dress against a distant landscape depicting the area of the artist's home, recall Renaissance practice. The separation of the narrative content and the landscape setting is created by the empty space in the middle distance. A quiet but expectant atmosphere pervades this picture, caused by the tension between the two unequal masses of Clio on the right and the children on the left; the rapt attention and gestures of the children, however, bind the two sides together. Sims's subsequent alteration of the work in no way devalues it, but rather adds a harsh, extra dimension which accords with the original composition and its treatment.

NOTES
1.　C.M. XXII, p. 385, 9 May 1916.
2.　*The Old Water-Colour Society's Club*, VI (1928–9), p. 49.
3.　C. Sims, *Picture Making: Technique and Inspiration*, 1934, p. 119.
4.　*Studio*, 68 (1916), p. 38.
5.　*Connoisseur*, 45 (1916), p. 123.
6.　*The Times*, 29 April 1916, p. 6.
7.　*Connoisseur*, 45 (1916), p. 123.

EXHIBITIONS: R.A., 1916 (cat. 490); R.A., Winter, 1933 (cat. 434); Bournemouth, Russell-Cotes Art Gallery & Museum, 1957 (cat. 861); R.A., Winter, 1968 (cat. 483); South London Art Gallery, 1973 (cat. 75).

# Gilbert Spencer
## 1892–1979

During his lifetime, Gilbert Spencer's work was often described as being quintessentially English. The artist himself was proud of this quality: 'Much as I have loved the French impressionists I have never felt it was my business to uproot my essentially native characteristics ... I like Cézanne for saying, "Why should I leave my own doorstep?".'[1] Once referred to as the 'John Constable of the twentieth century',[2] Spencer was primarily a painter of the domesticated English landscape, many of which captured the working atmosphere of the farms during the period. Most of his paintings were inspired by familiar countryside near his home or seen on holiday in Berkshire, Oxfordshire, Dorset, Suffolk and the Lake District. Like his older brother Stanley (q.v.), he was also well-known for his mural decorations and portraits. Although in the early days their work was quite similar, they later developed distinct styles and separate interests.

Born in Cookham, Berkshire in 1892, Gilbert was the youngest of twelve children. After attending Camberwell School of Arts, then the Royal College of Art from 1911 to 1912, where he studied wood carving, he went to the Slade School of Art in 1913, to study with Henry Tonks. Whilst there he won prizes for life drawing and landscape painting. His studies were interrupted by the outbreak of war; he joined the Royal Army Medical Corps and served mainly in Macedonia and on a hospital ship before returning to the Slade in 1919. Although he had some opportunity to draw and paint when abroad he was not inspired by foreign parts, believing, even at this stage that his art was too English. He was later given a commission for an Official War painting and began work on a hospital scene.

Elected a member of the New English Art Club in 1919, he had his first one-man show at the Goupil Gallery in 1923 and was well-received by the public. One of his main commissions in the 1930s was for a set of murals at Balliol College, Oxford which showed the story of the founding of the College. He had a distinguished teaching career as Professor of Painting at the Royal College of Art from 1932–48, and as Head of Department at Glasgow School of Art from 1948–50 and at Camberwell School of Arts from 1950–57. Gilbert was elected A.R.A. in 1950 and R.A. in 1959. He resigned ten years later, but was re-elected in 1971. In 1961, after Stanley's death, he published a biography of his brother before writing his own, *Memoirs of a Painter*, in 1974. A major retrospective of his work was held at Reading Art Gallery in 1964 and he died in Suffolk in 1979. E. C. W.

NOTES
1. G. Spencer, *Memoirs of a Painter*, 1974, p. 189.
2. *The Guardian*, 16 Jan 1979 [Tribute by Sidney Hutchison, Secretary of the Royal Academy of Arts].

*repr. in colour on p. 53*

## 58 From My Studio

100.3 × 102.9 cm    39½ × 40½ in
Signed bl: *Gilbert Spencer*
Diploma work, accepted 26 May 1959 (C.M. XXIX, p. 275)

Gilbert Spencer lived at Tree Cottage, near Pangbourne, Essex from 1936 until 1970. He normally worked out of doors, although in the winter he painted and drew from his cottage windows or from his 'little Colt studio'[1] in the garden. In *Memoirs of a Painter*, Spencer described his feelings about working in this studio: 'When I entered it for the first time I hated it so much that I knocked it about, and messed it up to get it more in sympathy with my feelings for painting in odd corners, or bedrooms, indoors. The fact is I am no "studio" artist and never have been, a hang-over from Cookham days.'[2]

Like many of his paintings, this wintry view demonstrates the artist's primary interest in cultivated landscape marked by human habitation and use. Characteristically, the scene has been carefully observed and drawn, with a well-ordered composition which makes use of apparently accidental elements to draw the spectator into the scene: 'Mostly Gilbert Spencer paints the unexceptional scene ... yet he nearly always lifts the ordinary, and to him, well known, out of any banal or conventional interpretation, translation, presentation. He shares his vision, to sharpen our own.'[3] The contrast between the intimacy of the garden and the more rural landscape beyond the hedge is heightened by the stillness of these familiar objects against the windswept trees in the background of the painting. Like Constable, Spencer shows an interest in recording weather conditions and their effects on the landscape. The naturalistic style and use of muted, earthy colours are typical of Spencer's work.

NOTES
1. G. Spencer, *Memoirs of a Painter*, 1974, p. 124.
2. idem.
3. *Gilbert Spencer Retrospective*, exhib. cat., London, Fine Art Society, 1974.

EXHIBITIONS: R.A., 1960 (cat. 540); Reading, Museum and Art Gallery 1964 (cat. 79); Bournemouth, Russell-Cotes Art Gallery & Museum, 1965 (cat. 58); Nottingham University Art Gallery, 1973 (cat. 55); Leicestershire Museum and Art Gallery, 1982 (cat. 82); Cheltenham Art Gallery and Museums, 1985 (cat. 28).

## 59 Activity at Tree Cottage No. 2

61 × 46 cm    24 × 18 in
Signed and dated br: *Gilbert Spencer 1967*
Purchased by the Royal Academy (Harrison Weir Fund) 27 April 1967 (C.M. XXIX, p. 675)

This intimate self-portrait of the artist in his outdoor studio at Tree Cottage (see cat. 58) records the conditions in which he worked. Unlike his landscape paintings, this picture is more immediate and spontaneous. Although the head is closely observed, the lower half of the picture is more sketchy and the forms consequently less carefully defined. This contradiction within the painting possibly reflects Spencer's admitted need for working in an untidy, artistic environment.[1] Indeed, by contrast with his carefully composed landscapes, this painting has an awkward, even restless quality which is emphasised by the swift delineation of the subject.

NOTE
1.   G. Spencer, *Memoirs of a Painter*, 1974, p. 124.

EXHIBITIONS: R.A., 1967 (cat. 7); London, Fine Art Society, 1974 (cat. 49).

# Sir Stanley Spencer
## 1891–1959

In his eccentric, imaginative paintings, Stanley Spencer sought to express his own beliefs and experiences through a fusion of secular and religious imagery. Many of Spencer's visionary paintings and landscapes were inspired by life in his native town of Cookham-on-Thames in Berkshire where he was born, the older brother of Gilbert Spencer (q.v.), in 1891. After an initial training at the Maidenhead Technical Institute, Spencer attended the Slade School of Art from 1908 to 1912, where his contemporaries included Mark Gertler, David Bomberg, Paul Nash and Edward Wadsworth. Although he remained an independent artist and did not join any of the currently fashionable groups of artists, he did exhibit three works at the second Post-Impressionist exhibition organised by Roger Fry and Clive Bell in 1912.

During the First World War, Spencer served as an orderly in the Royal Army Medical Corps and later as an infantryman in Macedonia, experiences that provided the themes for a series of mural paintings for the specially built Burghclere Memorial Chapel which were completed in 1932. Spencer was a member of the New English Art Club from 1919 to 1927 and in that latter year had his first one-man show at the Goupil Gallery, which included his enormous canvas *Resurrection* (London, Tate Gallery) set in the churchyard at Cookham.

In the 1930s Spencer began a series of paintings intended to decorate The Church House at Cookham in which he explored his feelings about love and marriage through appropriate Biblical and domestic narratives. The three main schemes (*The Pentecost, The Marriage at Cana* and *The Baptism of Christ*) were united in the concept of *The Last Day* (*Judgement*), and by Spencer's own belief that sexual and religious ecstacy were synonymous. Each painting in the series was designed so that it could be sold as an independent work of art. The mannered, almost grotesque figure style of these paintings was probably the cause of the rejection of two, *St Francis and the Birds* (London, Tate Gallery) and *The Dustman or the Lovers* (Newcastle-upon-Tyne, Laing Art Gallery) by the Hanging Committee of the Royal Academy in 1935. Spencer, having been elected an Associate Academician in 1932, promptly submitted his resignation. Early in the Second World War, Spencer was commissioned by the War Artists Advisory Committee to paint shipyards in Glasgow; he produced a cycle glorifying the workers entitled *Shipbuilding on the Clyde*, and a subsequent 'Resurrection' series drawing upon the same subject. After the War Spencer returned to Cookham and to his religious paintings. He was re-elected as a full member of the Royal Academy in 1950 and was knighted in 1958. He died in Cookham in 1959.    E.C.W.

*repr. in colour on p. 55*

## 60   The Farm Gate

91.5 × 58.5 cm   36 × 23 in
Diploma work, accepted 21 November 1950 (C.M. 1944, p. 430)

In this painting, Spencer and his first wife Hilda open the gate of Ovey's farm in Cookham which is opposite 'Fernlea', the artist's childhood home to which he returned before his death in 1959. Like many of his Cookham paintings, this domestic scene was created from memory. The peculiar angle from which the scene is observed demonstrates Spencer's lifelong fascination with walls and fences. Here they are used as a device both to separate areas within the painting and to express the artist's intimate involvement with the farm and the event. The figures are almost caricatured, and their over-rounded forms illustrate the childlike nature of Spencer's imagination. There is a detailed preparatory drawing dated 16 June 1946 (private collection), which is squared up and ready for transfer to the canvas.

EXHIBITIONS: R.A., 1951 (cat. 479); London, Tate Gallery, 1955 (cat. 8); Worthing, 1961 (cat. 39); Plymouth, 1963 (cat. 39); Bournemouth, Russell-Cotes Art Gallery & Museum, 1965 (cat. 59); R.A., Winter, 1968 (cat. 470); Cookham, Stanley Spencer Gallery, 1974 (cat. 1); South London Art Gallery, 1974 (cat. III); Cambridge, Arts Council, Fitzwilliam Museum, 1976 (cat. 48); R.A., Sept–Dec 1980 (cat. 255); New Haven, Yale Centre for British Art, 1981 (cat. 60); Leicestershire Museum and Art Gallery, 1982 (cat. 83); Cookham, Stanley Spencer Gallery, 1985.

61 *repr. in colour on p. 54*

## 61 The Dustbin, Cookham

76.2 × 50.9 cm   30 × 20 in
Purchased by the Royal Academy (Harrison Weir Fund) 31 July 1956 (C.M. XXIX, p. 177)

This painting was based on one of the twenty-four designs which Spencer was commissioned to make for an Almanac published in 1927 by Chatto and Windus. In the Almanac, Spencer chose to illustrate the changing seasons with domestic scenes from his childhood, life with his friends in London and his marriage to Hilda. Seven of these plates were subsequently adapted into paintings. *The Dustbin*, which was copied almost exactly from the design for *September*, was the last to be used and was painted twenty-nine years after the original drawings were made. In preparation for the painting Spencer squared up the minute illustrations in the Almanac itself before transferring the image onto the canvas.

Dustbins and rubbish had played a significant part in Spencer's imagination since his childhood, and it is probable that this painting is a recollection of early experiences. In a letter written on 12 October 1918, to his sister Florence from the War front in Macedonia, Spencer explained that his thoughts, 'just seem like a row of dustbins, but one can find interesting and very nice things in dustbins and incinerators ... I honestly think that looking for treasure on dust heaps where there is not too unpleasant a smell is a distinctly entertaining and elevating pastime. I used to love scurrying about on Farmer Hatchy's rubbish heap [at Ovey's Farm opposite Fernlea]. There I would find beads, pieces of broken china with all sorts of painted flowers on them, old books with engravings. I was almost sure to find something that really satisfied my highest thoughts.'[1]

For Spencer, these cast-off details of everyday life clearly represented the same 'homely' characteristics of people's personal lives as did the way in which they dressed, or the simple, even trivial objects with which they surrounded themselves.[2] Here, Spencer's dustbin appears to be full of discarded plants and flowers, their different shapes and colours contributing to the decorative effect of the painting.

NOTES
1. Tate Gallery Archives 756.45.; quoted in A. Causey, *Stanley Spencer R.A.*, exhib. cat., Royal Academy, 1980, p. 222.
2. A. Causey, op. cit., p. 222.

EXHIBITIONS: R.A., 1956 (cat. 56); London, Arts Club, 1960–1, long term loan; Arts Council, 1961 (cat. 40); Cookham, Stanley Spencer Gallery, 1962–3 (cat. 10); West Surrey College of Art and Design, 1977 (cat. 23); Cambridge, Arts Council, Fitzwilliam Museum, 1977 (cat. 51); R.A., Sept–Dec 1980 (cat. 271); Cookham, Stanley Spencer Gallery, 1985; Cheltenham Art Gallery and Museums, 1985 (cat. 21); Swansea, Glynn Vivian Art Gallery & Museum, 1985 (cat. 49).

# Adrian Stokes
## 1854–1935

Adrian Stokes was born in Southport in 1854. His father was a Government Inspector of Schools and his brother, Leonard, became a successful architect, later elected President of the Royal Institute of British Architects. Stokes's father planned for him to go into the Navy; however, owing to a change in government, he lost his nomination, and instead entered a firm of cotton brokers in Liverpool. It soon became apparent to the young Stokes that this trade did not suit him. On the advice of John Herbert R.A. he submitted his drawings to the Royal Academy, and was accepted into the Schools in 1872. He remained there for three years, but complained in later life that he had never received any real instruction in landscape painting, the subject which formed his principal interest throughout his career.

Stokes's work was first exhibited at the Academy in 1876 and included an historical subject-painting illustrating a scene from Shakespeare's *Richard III*. However, in this same year he left for France where, whilst working in the country near Pont-Aven, and later in the Forest of Fontainebleau, he became completely committed to landscape painting. He continued his studies in Paris under Dagnan-Bouveret in 1885. After a short trip around Denmark he returned to England and in 1886 settled at St Ives, which had become something of an artists' colony, and included among its residents artists who were similarly committed to landscape or seascape painting, such as John Arnesby Brown (q.v.) and Julius Olsson (q.v.). Stokes soon achieved recognition with the purchase for the Chantrey Bequest in 1888 of a landscape painted near St Ives entitled *Uplands and Sky*.[1]

In 1884 he married the Austrian painter Marianna Preindlsberger (1885–1927), and together they travelled widely around Europe. In 1900 they held a joint exhibition at The Fine Art Society of works painted in Holland.

One of Stokes's favourite sketching grounds was the Austrian Tyrol. In 1903 a second picture was bought for the Chantrey Bequest, *Autumn in the Mountains*,[2] which depicted a landscape in South Tyrol. The picture was painted in tempera, a technique which Stokes had perfected and for which he prepared the colours himself. Stokes's early work had been concerned with capturing atmospheric effects such as moonlight on a landscape or the freshness of a breezy day. However, as his style matured he painted decorative landscapes such as *Autumn in the Mountains*, in which he delighted in the pattern of silver birch trees against a background of snowy mountains.

In 1909 Stokes published a book entitled *Hungary*, and illustrated *Tyrol and its People* by C. Holland. The following year he was elected an Associate of the Academy. He and his wife continued travelling and painting around Europe, usually in France, Italy or Austria, and at the outbreak of the First World War were stranded in Austria, where they had been sketching with John Singer Sargent (q.v.).

Stokes was elected a full Academician in 1919. His book, *Landscape Painting*, was published in 1925, which as well as discussing techniques of landscape painting, included an analysis

62    *repr. in colour on p. 46*

of earlier landscapists. His work in watercolour was much admired, and in 1933 he was elected Vice-President of the Royal Watercolour Society. Stokes continued painting into his seventies, when his style became broader and incorporated rougher textures. He died in 1935 at the age of eighty.    H.C.V.

NOTES
1.  Repr., *Academy Notes*, 1888, p. 103 (line engraving).
2.  Repr., *Royal Academy Pictures*, 1903, p. 24.

## 62   Lago Maggiore

60.5 × 92 cm    23 × 36 in
Signed br: *Adrian Stokes*
Diploma work, accepted 20 April 1920 (C.M. XXIV, p. 218)

Painted in Italy, *Lago Maggiore* represents Stokes's mature style which had developed 'from careful naturalism to decorative abstraction, mainly through colour.'[1] Stokes had admired Japanese prints in Whistler's studio, and felt that a Japanese artist 'with the least possible means, endeavours to convey his message.'[2] This painting's delicate design, simple composition and high horizon reflect this interest. Contemporary reviewers, however, thought that Stokes was 'inclined to be a little flimsy in his Italian scenes, light and sparkling though they are.'[3]

Stokes particularly enjoyed painting autumnal landscapes and delighted in the juxtaposition of reddish-gold shades against the blue of lakes and mountains. He was more interested in poetical intimation than in representing the structure and natural details of the landscape and here, in his Diploma work, Stokes conveys the serenity of a lakeside scene.

NOTES
1.  *The Times*, 2 Dec 1935.
2.  A. Stokes, *Landscape Painting*, 1925, p. 56.
3.  *Connoisseur*, 57 (1920), p. 114.

EXHIBITIONS: R.A., 1920 (cat. 110); Bournemouth, Russell-Cotes Art Gallery & Museum, 1957 (cat. 860); Bournemouth, Russell-Cotes Art Gallery & Museum, 1965 (cat. 61); R.A., Winter, 1968 (cat. 479).

# Annie Louisa Swynnerton
## 1844–1933

Annie Swynnerton's obituary stated that 'vitality' was the word which best summed up her work. In her depictions of children, especially those painted in the open air, she could most easily express her 'youngness of heart, joy in life, and reckless abandonment to the appeal of light and colour.'[1]

Swynnerton was born in Kersal, near Manchester, one of seven daughters of Francis Robinson, a solicitor. From an early age she painted watercolours to supplement the family's reduced income, but began her serious training as an artist at Manchester School of Art, before leaving to enrol at the Académie Julian in Paris. Her work was first exhibited at the Royal Academy in 1879, and the following year she exhibited a portrait of her friend *Isabel Dacre* (Manchester City Art Gallery), with whom she later formed the Manchester Society of Women Painters. Swynnerton completed her studies by travelling for two years in Italy. During a stay in Rome she met the Manx sculptor Joseph Swynnerton, whom she married in 1883; until his death in 1910, they lived mainly in Rome. Whilst in Italy, Swynnerton painted works such as *An Italian Mother and Child* (Manchester City Art Gallery) in a style clearly reminiscent of Renaissance painting, and panoramic landscapes such as *The Olive Gatherers* (Manchester City Art Gallery).

In 1902, after a gap of sixteen years, Swynnerton exhibited again at the Royal Academy. Always greatly admired by other painters, her work was bought by prominent figures in the art world. In 1906 Sir George Clausen (q.v.) purchased *New-Risen Hope*, depicting the figure of a naked child, and later presented it to the National Gallery of Victoria in Melbourne. John Singer Sargent (q.v.) bought *The Oreads* in 1907, a sculpturesque group of sea nymphs, giving the painting to the Tate Gallery, London, in 1922.

In addition to her allegorical paintings, Swynnerton exhibited many portraits at the Academy in the 1910s. In 1922, backed by Clausen and Sargent, Swynnerton was the first woman to be elected an Associate of the Academy. The only previous women to rank as Academicians were Angelica Kauffmann and Mary Moser, who were signatories to the Instrument of Foundation in 1768 and thus were made members without being elected. The year after her election there was an exhibition of her work at Manchester City Art Gallery and another version of *New-Risen Hope* (London, Tate Gallery) was purchased for the Chantrey Bequest in 1924. In 1929 and 1930 two more works were purchased for the nation in this way.

Swynnerton's sight began to deteriorate towards the end of her life, but she continued to exhibit pictures at the Academy, although they were often works she had painted years earlier. She died at the age of eighty-eight at her home on Hayling Island, near Portsmouth.    H.C.V.

NOTE
1.  Press cutting, R.A. Archives, Swynnerton file.

## 63   The Letter

101.6 × 48.2 cm    40 × 19 in
Signed br: *ALS* (monogram)
Purchased by the Royal Academy (Stott Fund) 10 July 1934 (C.M. XXVI, p. 335)

In 1918 a critic wrote that Swynnerton's work was 'always carefully studied, and bears the impression of thought as well as feeling.'[1] In *The Letter*, the concentration of the girl reading is beautifully observed, although the significance of the letter is not apparent.

Changes were obviously made in the composition, as in the lower left-hand corner, where faint outlines of two flowers are still visible. The effect of the painting, however, is claustrophobic; the figure is hemmed in on both sides, and with no view through the window. The girl's head has a seriousness belying her years, and we are invited to speculate on the perhaps trapped life of this sad, but obviously wealthy girl, reminiscent of characters from Dickens or George Eliot.

Influences absorbed during Swynnerton's time in Italy are apparent in her sculptural grasp of form and incisive drawing, which recalls Italian Renaissance painters. The source of Swynnerton's manifest enjoyment in this work, though, lay in capturing the effect of light falling on the girl's face and golden hair. The artist also delighted in the decorative details of her dress.

NOTE
1.  *Connoisseur*, 50 (1918), p. 51.

EXHIBITIONS: R.A., 1934 (cat. 644); Liverpool, Walker Art Gallery, 1934 (cat. 945); Sheffield, Graves Art Gallery, 1953 (cat. 93); London, Arts Club, 1957–64, long term loan; R.A., Winter, 1968 (cat. 428).

# Leonard Campbell Taylor
## 1874—1969

63

Although he also painted landscapes, Leonard Campbell Taylor was best known for his subject pictures, portraits and interior scenes. During his lifetime he was described as, 'the greatest living exponent [of] a minor but lovable domestic school,'[1] and was placed within the 'great tradition of small-scale "interior" painting of which Vermeer of Delft was the supreme examplar.'[2]

Born in Oxford in 1874, Leonard Campbell Taylor was the son of James Taylor, the organist of New College, Oxford. He went to the Ruskin School of Drawing at Oxford and St John's Wood Art School, before entering the Royal Academy Schools in 1905. He first exhibited at the Royal Academy in 1899 and was elected A.R.A. in 1923 and R.A. in 1931.

When asked why he found painting interiors preferable to landscapes, Campbell Taylor replied that he liked 'the kind of effect interior lighting offers' and that he had a 'subconscious distrust of that which is not already part of a human order'.[3] Principles of arrangement, balance and composition were crucial to his art, and all his paintings were carefully designed and constructed. In this respect he admired Oriental art and Whistler's harmonious paintings which combined atmosphere, tone and colour with a decorative flatness.

Describing Campbell Taylor's style and way of working, Viscount Lee of Fareham wrote: 'He is a slow, even laborious worker and certainly possesses that form of genius which is defined as an infinite capacity for taking pains. This accounts for the high and meticulous finish of his domestic "interiors", which, even if anathema to the impressionists, makes a steady appeal to the ever widening circle of his admirers.'[4]     E.C.W.

NOTES
1. H. Furst, *Leonard Campbell Taylor R.A. His Place in Art*, p. 17.
2. idem.
3. H. Furst, op. cit., p. 42.
4. ibid., p. 18.

## 64  Arabella

62 × 49.5 cm    $24\frac{3}{8} \times 19\frac{1}{2}$ in
Signed br: *L. Campbell Taylor*
Diploma work, accepted 4 Dec 1931 (C.M. XXVI, p. 114)

This quiet, melancholy picture demonstrates Campbell Taylor's preference for painting figures in interiors and reflects his admiration for the work of Vermeer and Whistler. Rather than expressing pictorial drama, he conveys a calm, ordered vision in which the evenness of lighting allows him to develop his interest in form and pattern. Although there is a variety of textures and objects in the painting, an overall harmony is achieved through unity of tone and shape. The gentle curves of the seated figure are echoed in the still-life arrangement in the foreground whilst the opulent colours of Arabella's clothes are repeated elsewhere in the composition.

EXHIBITIONS: R.A., 1931 (cat. 382); Bournemouth, Russell-Cotes Art Gallery & Museum, 1962 (cat. 86); Cheltenham Art Gallery and Museums, 1985 (cat. 6).

*(Illustrated overleaf)*

64   Leonard Campbell Taylor   *Arabella*

# Henry Scott Tuke
## 1858–1929

By 1895 Henry Scott Tuke had no doubt that his main concern was 'to paint the nude in the open air.'[1] Having moved to Falmouth a decade earlier he had had ample opportunity to pursue this goal on 'quiet beaches, some of them hardly accessible by boat, where one may paint from the life model undisturbed.'[2]

Tuke's early years had been spent in Falmouth, but in 1874 the family moved to London and the following year he enrolled at the Slade School of Art under E. J. Poynter. Tuke's formal artistic training was leavened, however, by frequent summer trips to the Continent, and on completion of his studies in 1880, Tuke left for Florence. There, however, he found himself rather more influenced by the example of the English genre painter Arthur Lemon (1850–1912) than by the Old Masters.[3] Sketching boys with Lemon on the beaches of Italy encouraged Tuke to develop a more naturalistic painting style. Though he went on to join the Paris *atelier* of J. P. Laurens in 1881, this seems to have had less influence on him than work of other contemporary artists.

In common with several other British artists of his generation he seems to have been particularly drawn to the work of the French *plein-air* painter Jules Bastien-Lepage, and reported seeing 'many things of surpassing beauty' in his studio.[4] Alexander Harrison's paintings of nudes posed in rural surroundings also made a deep impression, seeming 'to open up fresh vistas'. It certainly, he later recalled, 'gave new interest to the study of the undraped figure, to depict it with pure daylight upon it, instead of the artificial lighting of the studio.'[5]

Although Tuke never considered himself to be part of the Newlyn School of painters, between 1883 and 1885 he spent much of his time in the Cornish town, finding it 'more bewitching than ever' and 'simply reeking with subjects'.[6] He had much in common with Newlyn School painters, striving to depict events from everyday life in the new realistic British style of *plein-air* painting. In accordance with other Newlyn painters, Tuke thought that the Hanging Committee of the Royal Academy 'consisted of men rapidly going downhill' and therefore supported the foundation of the New English Art Club as a rival exhibiting society.

Tuke returned to his native Falmouth in 1885, but continued for some time to aim at large dramatic compositions, fitting up for this purpose an old French brigantine, the *Julie*, as a floating studio in Falmouth harbour. It was here that such pictures as *All Hands to the Pumps* (London, Tate Gallery) were painted: a highly dramatic subject, the picture nonetheless lacks movement, its stiffly posed figures betraying their studio origins.

Although *All Hands to the Pumps* was purchased for the Chantrey Bequest in 1889 Tuke was clearly not satisfied, and in the early 1890s abandoned his square brush technique for more fluid brushwork, at the same time replacing his normally grey, overcast skies with bright sunshine. This opened the way for a return to the theme of the male nude, but without the mythological burdens that had cramped his earlier efforts to build a serious picture around the subject, such as in *Cupid and Sea Nymphs* (rejected, R.A., 1898; exhibited New Gallery, 1899) and the *Endymion* of 1893 (subsequently destroyed by the artist). Official recognition of Tuke's work in this new vein came in 1894 with the Chantrey Bequest's purchase of the evocatively titled *August Blue* (London, Tate Gallery), a painting of youths bathing from a dinghy that is essentially a celebration of the luminous effects of sunlight on flesh and water.

Election as an Associate of the Royal Academy came in due course in 1900 and although he did not achieve full membership until 1914, Tuke's life from this point followed a fairly regular pattern. Summers were spent in Falmouth, where he painted outdoor subjects — usually of nude boys bathing or fishing. In the autumn he moved to London, often undertaking portrait commissions, and working on his Royal Academy exhibition paintings. By the spring he would be travelling in Europe, attracted to busy ports such as Genoa by the fine spectacle of sailing ships at anchor. In 1923, however, Tuke broke this pattern by travelling to the West Indies, though ill health forced him to return the following year. A visit to North Africa in 1927 was his last trip abroad, and he died in Falmouth two years later.    H.C.V.

NOTES
1. *Studio*, 5 (1895), p. 93.
2. idem.
3. Tuke's diary, 23 Feb 1880; *Henry Scott Tuke*, exhib. cat., Falmouth Art Gallery, 1980, p. 7.
4. Quoted *Henry Scott Tuke*, p. 8
5. *Studio*, 5 (1895), p. 94.
6. Quoted C. Fox and F. Greenacre, *Artists of the Newlyn School 1880–1900*, exhib. cat., Newlyn Orion Galleries, 1979, p. 131.
7. Quoted C. Fox and F. Greenacre, op. cit., p. 134.

## 65  July Sun

54.5 × 44 cm   21½ × 17¼ in
Signed and dated bl: *H. S. TUKE–1913*
Presented by the artist, 20 March 1917 (C.M. XXIII, p. 446.)

Resolute in his commitment to *plein-air* painting, Tuke felt that 'the truth and beauty of flesh in sunlight by the sea',[1] was impossible to secure in a studio. The freshness in the observation of light effects in *July Sun* are such that it could only have been painted out of doors.

The model for the painting was an Italian named Niccolo Lucciani, who was later killed in the First World War. Tuke must have been particularly satisfied with this study for his register records that it was painted in 'practically one sitting',[2] and he felt that the study was complete enough to exhibit at the Royal Academy in 1914. Tuke presented the picture in 1917, specifying that it was 'to be hung in the Schools'.[3]

The title of *July Sun* was a typical choice for Tuke. As with other works, such as *August Blue* (London, Tate Gallery) or *Midsummer Morning*,[4] the title gives no suggestion of narrative, but instead emphasises the effect and mood of the picture. Tuke's technique of using broad strokes of the brush to follow the contours of the body is clearly visible here. The boy's shoulders are highlighted by the fall of sunlight, and spots of bright blue suggest the dancing effect of the sun reflected off the sea.

NOTES
1.  *Studio*, 5 (1895), p. 94.
2.  *The Registers of Henry Scott Tuke 1879–1928*, R766, transcribed by B. Price, 1980; typescript in R.A. Library.
3.  C.M. XXIII, p. 466, 20 March 1917.
4.  Repr., *Royal Academy Pictures*, 1908, p. 85.

EXHIBITIONS: R.A., 1914 (cat. 180); R.A., Winter, 1933 (cat. 266).

# Dame Ethel Walker
## 1861–1951

The obituary in *The Times* called Ethel Walker, 'the most important woman artist of her time in England since Berthe Morisot'.[1] Born in Edinburgh in 1861, she did not officially start her artistic career until about 1883 when she attended Putney School of Art. A visit to the Prado in Madrid in 1884 introduced Walker to the work of Velasquez, and a stay in Paris on the return journey enabled her to study that of Manet. In 1892, she resumed her studies for three months under Professor Frederick Brown at the Westminster School of Art, later following him to the Slade School of Art where she stayed for two years. After this she attended evening classes under Sickert (q.v.) who proved very influential on her work, before returning to the Slade for three periods (1912–13; 1916–19 and 1921–2) where, for part of the time, she studied sculpture under James Harvard Thomas. Throughout her career, Walker painted a wide range of subjects, portraits, figure compositions and flower pieces, landscapes, seascapes and decorative murals as well as producing some sculpture. The artists who she most admired were Whistler, Puvis de Chavannes, Gauguin and the Impressionists, study of the latter in particular producing a major transformation in her art in favour of what became her characteristically loose and decorative style. Her compositions were no longer modelled in terms of light and shade but were filled with brilliant colour.

Although based in London with a studio in Chelsea, Walker often worked from her cottage at Robin Hood's Bay in Yorkshire where she would paint seascapes outdoors, swiftly recording the effects of different weather conditions. Walker exhibited at the Royal Academy from 1898 onwards and joined the New English Art Club in 1900. Her first one-woman show was held at the Redfern Gallery in 1927. Later she exhibited regularly at the Royal Society of British Artists, the Society of Women Artists and the London Group. Elected A.R.A. in 1940, she was awarded a C.B.E. in 1938 and a D.B.E. in 1943. She died in London in 1951 aged eighty-nine.     E.C.W.

NOTE
1. *The Times*, 3 March 1951.

*repr. in colour on p. 37*

## 66   The Jade Necklace

79 × 66 cm    31 × 26 in

With their solidly modelled figures set in sombre Victorian interiors, Walker's early works reflected those of her contemporaries in the New English Art Club. By contrast, this intimate study of a woman is an example of her later understanding of the principles of Impressionism which she modified to suit her own personal ends. The paint has been applied in strokes of pure colour with an emphasis on decoration and surface pattern both on the figure and in the background. The hesitant quality of the brushwork around the head in particular, accentuates the femininity of the sitter was well as creating a sense of movement and spontaneity. Inspired by Sickert (q.v.), Walker was in the habit of working quickly, and on his advice painted across the forms rather than into them. She was well known for her portraits of young women.

# William Lionel Wyllie
## 1851–1931

William Lionel Wyllie was the most celebrated marine painter of his day. He had a detailed knowledge of the construction and handling of boats and his prolific output included subjects which ranged from historic naval battles to merchant shipping on the Thames.

Wyllie was born in London in 1851 into an artistic family: his father, brother and half-brother were all professional artists and the family regularly spent the summer months sketching around Boulogne. Wyllie began his artistic training at an early age, attending Heatherly's Art School in London at the age of twelve, and subsequently entering the Royal Academy Schools at the age of fifteen. Wyllie's first work was exhibited at the Academy in 1868, and the following year he won the Turner Gold Medal for a landscape entitled *Dawn after a Storm*. Particularly interested in capturing atmospheric effects in seascapes and coastal views, Wyllie made many free studies in oil and watercolour in the late 1860s and 1870s.

In 1873 he bought his first yacht, the *Ladybird*, which he converted into a floating studio. He began a long series of pictures of the River Thames, the most celebrated being *Toil, glitter, grime and wealth on a flowing tide* (London, Tate Gallery) which was purchased for the Chantrey Bequest in 1883. A contemporary critic felt that Wyllie's vision of the Pool of London had captured the 'Thames as it is, with all its grime and much of its wonder, all of its business and something of its pathos.'[1] Wyllie was asked by the dealer Robert Dunthorne to etch this picture and he continued to use this medium throughout his career. Producing nearly three hundred greatly varied etchings, including topographical, nautical and First World War subjects, his work became widely known.

Moving to Hoo Lodge on the Medway estuary in 1885, Wyllie's range of subjects broadened to include pictures of merchant steamships. His election as an Associate of the Royal Academy in 1889 was followed in the 1890s by commissions from steamship companies to paint 'portraits' of ships. Wyllie would often travel on board these liners for lengthy cruises, including one in 1893 to the West Indies on the *Garonne*. On these trips he made many watercolour studies which he usually exhibited on his return to England at The Fine Art Society or other London galleries. He achieved great fluency in watercolour during the 1890s, particularly when he began to adopt a 'wet' technique. By working on paper which had been soaked in water he was liberated from his tendency toward over-elaboration of detail. He published two manuals on watercolour technique: *Marine Painting in Water-Colour* in 1901 and a *Sketchbook* in 1908.

Wyllie was fascinated by naval history. He read widely to ensure accuracy in such historical subjects as the *Battle of Trafalgar*, exhibited in 1891. His achievements in this branch of his art gained recognition through the purchase in 1889 for the Chantrey Bequest of *The Battle of the Nile* (London, Tate Gallery), a picture representing the climax, in the moonlight, of Nelson's great victory of 1798.

His election as a Royal Academician coincided with his move to Portsmouth in 1907. The city was dominated by the Navy, which provided Wyllie with much of his subject matter. During the First World War he travelled with the Navy, making studies aboard H.M.S. *Revenge*. In 1918 he co-authored and illustrated *Sea Fights of the Great War*, followed the next year by *More Sea Fights of the Great War*. In 1922 Wyllie served on the committee charged with restoring Nelson's famous flagship, the *Victory*, to its original splendour, and in 1924 he began work on a great panorama of the Battle of Trafalgar. Unveiled by George V in 1930, the painting was twelve feet high and forty-two feet in diameter and hangs in the Victory Museum in Portsmouth.

Wyllie died in 1931 after exhibiting almost continuously at the Royal Academy for more than fifty years. Fittingly, his coffin was sailed up to Portsmouth harbour before finally being laid to rest.    H.C.V.

NOTE
1. *Magazine of Art*, 1884, p.314; quoted R. Quarm and J. Wyllie, *W.L. Wyllie*, 1981, p. 61.

## 67   The Portsmouth Fishing Fleet: The Breeze Falls Light

63.5 × 127.5 cm    25 × 50¼ in
Signed and dated bl: *W. L. Wyllie 1907*
Diploma work, accepted 19 Nov 1907 (C.M. XXII, p. 82)

In 1907 Wyllie moved to Tower House, which stands on the water's edge at the entrance to Portsmouth harbour. The proximity of the sea ensured that the viewpoint from the terrace of the house was similar to that from on board his yacht. *The Portsmouth Fishing Fleet: The Breeze Falls Light,* painted in the year he settled at Tower House, depicts small boats from the Portsmouth fishing fleet, presumably observed from the terrace. Though exhibited in 1908 under the title *The Breeze Falls Light* it had been accepted by Council as *The Portsmouth Fishing Fleet.* Since then these alternative titles have usually been collated.

Wyllie's paintings were built up with great attention to detail. The minutiae of boats and rigging were accurately recorded, and by the amount of sail depicted and the state of the water, even the strength and direction of the wind could be deduced. Even without considering the title it is apparent from the glassiness of the sea and the unfilled sails of the fishing boats that only a very light breeze prevails.

The perspective and construction of a picture had to be carefully worked out to accommodate all this detail. Wyllie, who frequently lectured to the students of the Royal Academy, was interested in perspective and had published *Nature's Laws and the Making of Pictures* in 1903. The placing of the boats in *The Portsmouth Fishing Fleet* leads the eye effortlessly, via various diagonals to the buoy seen far in the distance. During the years around 1905 Wyllie's brushwork became less delicate than it had been in his early work. His wife, in her biography,[1] thought that this was partly due to his use of a telescope when observing boats passing the house. Certainly the brush strokes in *The Portsmouth Fishing Fleet* are somewhat crude but Wyllie has nonetheless created a sense of the becalmed conditions on the Solent, between Portsmouth and the Isle of Wight as the fishing boats sail out to sea.

NOTE
1.   M. A. Wyllie, *We Were One,* 1935.

EXHIBITIONS: R.A., 1908 (cat. 595); R.A., Winter, 1933 (cat. 616).

# List of Artists

| | Year of election to A.R.A. | Year of election to R.A. |
|---|---|---|
| **Bell**, Robert Anning 1863–1933 (cat.1) | 1914 | 1922 |
| **Birch**, Samuel John Lamorna 1869–1955 (cat.2) | 1926 | 1934 |
| **Bramley**, Frank 1857–1915 (cat.3) | 1894 | 1911 |
| **Brangwyn**, Sir Frank 1867–1956 (cat.4) | 1904 | 1919 |
| **Brockhurst**, Gerald Leslie 1890–1978 (cat.5) | 1928 | 1937 (retired 1957) |
| **Brown**, Sir John Arnesby 1866–1955 (cat.6) | 1903 | 1915 |
| **Brundrit**, Reginald Grange 1883–1960 (cats 7, 8) | 1931 | 1938 |
| **Burn**, Rodney Joseph 1899–1984 (cat.9) | 1954 | 1962 |
| **Cameron**, Sir David Young 1865–1945 (cat.10) | 1911 | 1920 |
| **Clausen**, Sir George 1852–1944 (cats 11, 12) | 1895 | 1908 |
| **Connard**, Philip 1875–1958 (cat.13) | 1918 | 1925 |
| **Cowper**, Frank Cadogan 1877–1958 (cat.14) | 1907 | 1934 |
| **De Glehn**, Wilfred Gabriel 1870–1951 (cat.15) | 1923 | 1932 |
| **Dicksee**, Sir Frank 1853–1928 (cat.16) | 1881 | 1891 P.R.A. 1924–8 |
| **Dodd**, Francis 1874–1949 (cat.17) | 1927 | 1935 |
| **East**, Sir Alfred 1849–1913 (cat.18) | 1899 | 1913 |
| **Elwell**, Frederick William 1870–1958 (cat.19) | 1931 | 1938 |
| **Farquharson**, Joseph 1846–1935 (cat.20) | 1900 | 1915 |
| **Fisher**, Mark 1841–1923 (cat.21) | 1911 | 1919 |
| **Forbes**, Stanhope Alexander 1857–1947 (cat.22) | 1892 | 1910 |
| **Frampton**, Meredith 1894–1984 (cat.23) | 1934 | 1942 |
| **Gere**, Charles March 1869–1957 (cats 24, 25) | 1934 | 1939 |
| **Greiffenhagen**, Maurice 1862–1931 (cat.26) | 1916 | 1922 |
| **Gunn**, Sir Herbert James 1893–1964 (cat.27) | 1953 | 1961 |
| **Hacker**, Arthur 1858–1919 (cat.28) | 1894 | 1910 |
| **Hall**, Oliver 1869–1957 (cat.29) | 1920 | 1927 |
| **Harcourt**, George 1868–1947 (cat.30) | 1919 | 1926 |
| **Henry**, George 1858–1943 (cat.31) | 1907 | 1920 |
| **Hughes-Stanton**, Sir Herbert 1870–1937 (cat.32) | 1913 | 1920 |
| **Jack**, Richard 1866–1952 (cat.33) | 1914 | 1920 |
| **John**, Augustus Edwin 1878–1961 (cat.34) | 1921 | 1928 (Resigned 1938, re-elected 1940) |
| **Kelly**, Sir Gerald Festus 1879–1972 (cat.35) | 1922 | 1930 P.R.A. 1949–54 |
| **Knight**, Harold 1874–1961 (cat.36) | 1928 | 1937 |
| **La Thangue**, Henry Herbert 1859–1929 (cat.37) | 1898 | 1912 |
| **Lavery**, Sir John 1856–1941 (cat.38) | 1911 | 1921 |
| **Lee**, Sydney 1866–1949 (cats 39, 40) | 1922 | 1930 |
| **Monnington**, Sir Walter Thomas 1902–1976 (cat.41) | 1931 | 1938 P.R.A. 1966–76 |
| **Munnings**, Sir Alfred James 1878–1959 (cat.42) | 1919 | 1925 P.R.A. 1944–9 |
| **Murray**, Sir David 1849–1933 (cat.43) | 1891 | 1905 |
| **Nash**, John Northcote 1893–1977 (cats 44, 45, 46) | 1940 | 1951 |
| **Olsson**, Julius 1864–1942 (cats 47, 48) | 1914 | 1920 |
| **Orpen**, Sir William 1878–1931 (cat.49) | 1910 | 1919 |
| **Parsons**, Alfred 1847–1920 (cat.50) | 1897 | 1911 |
| **Philpot**, Glyn Warren 1884–1937 (cat.51) | 1915 | 1923 |
| **Priestman**, Bertram 1868–1951 (cat.52) | 1916 | 1923 |
| **Russell**, Sir Walter Westley 1867–1949 (cat.53) | 1920 | 1926 |
| **Sargent**, John Singer 1856–1925 (cat.54) | 1894 | 1897 |
| **Shannon**, Sir James Jebusa 1862–1923 (cat.55) | 1897 | 1909 |
| **Sickert**, Walter Richard 1860–1942 (cat.56) | 1924 | 1934 (Resigned 1935) |
| **Sims**, Charles 1873–1928 (cat.57) | 1908 | 1915 |
| **Spencer**, Gilbert 1892–1979 (cats 58, 59) | 1950 | 1959 (Resigned 1968, re-elected 1971) |
| **Spencer**, Sir Stanley 1891–1959 (cats 60, 61) | 1932 | 1950 (Resigned 1935, re-elected 1950) |
| **Stokes**, Adrian 1854–1935 (cat.62) | 1910 | 1919 |
| **Swynnerton**, Annie Louisa 1844–1933 (cat.63) | 1922 | – |
| **Taylor**, Leonard Campbell 1874–1969 (cat.64) | 1923 | 1931 |
| **Tuke**, Henry Scott 1858–1929 (cat.65) | 1900 | 1914 |
| **Walker**, Dame Ethel 1861–1951 (cat.66) | 1940 | – |
| **Wyllie**, William Lionel 1851–1931 (cat.67) | 1889 | 1907 |

# List of Exhibitions

# Select Bibliography

GENERAL

R. Billcliffe, *The Glasgow Boys*, 1985

*British Art in the Twentieth Century*, exhib. cat., Royal Academy of Arts, London, 1987

T. P. Cowdell, 'The Role of The Royal Academy in English Art 1918–1930', PhD thesis, University of London, 1980

D. Farr, *English Art 1870–1940*, Oxford, 1978

*The Glasgow Boys*, exhib. cat., Scottish Arts Council, 1968

S. C. Hutchison, *The History of The Royal Academy 1768–1986*, 2nd ed., 1986

J. Laver, *Portraits in Oil and Vinegar*, 1925

K. McConkey, *Edwardian Portraits*, 1987

*Painting in Newlyn 1880–1930*, exhib. cat., London, Barbican Art Gallery, 1985

J. Rothenstein, *Modern English Painters*, Vol. 1, 1984

F. Spalding, *British Art Since 1900*, 1986


WORKS ON INDIVIDUAL ARTISTS

**BELL, Robert Anning**
S. Erskine, 'Robert Anning Bell RA', The Old Water-Colour Society's Club, *Twelfth Annual Volume 1934–5*, ed. R. Davies, 1935, pp. 51–61

*Memorial Exhibition of the works of the late Professor Robert Anning Bell*, exhib. cat., London, Fine Art Society, 1934

T. M. Wood, 'Robert Anning Bell's work as a painter', *Studio*, 69 (1910), pp. 255–62

**BIRCH, Samuel John Lamorna**
L. Knight, 'S. J. Lamorna Birch as I knew him', The Old Water-Colour Society's Club, *Thirty Second Annual Volume*, ed. A. Bury, 1957, pp. 16–22

A. Reddie, 'Water-Colours and Oil Paintings by S. J. Lamorna Birch', *Studio*, 64 (1915), pp. 169–79

*Samuel John Lamorna Birch R.A.*, exhib. cat., London, Galerie George, 1986

J. W. Stephens, 'The Landscape Paintings of S. J. Lamorna Birch', *Studio*, 85 (1923), pp. 122–7

**BRAMLEY, Frank**
C. Hiatt, 'Mr Frank Bramley A.R.A., and his Work', *Magazine of Art*, 1902, pp. 54–9

**BRANGWYN, Sir Frank**
R. Brangwyn, *Brangwyn*, 1978

C. G. E. Bunt, *The Water-Colours of Sir Frank Brangwyn R.A.*, Leigh-on-Sea, 1958

V. Galloway, *The Oils and Murals of Sir Frank Brangwyn, R.A.*, Leigh-on-Sea, 1962

**BROCKHURST, Gerald Leslie**
*Gerald Leslie Brockhurst R.A. (1890–1978)*, exhib. cat., Sheffield City Art Gallery, 1986

J. W. Stephens, 'Gerald Leslie Brockhurst', *Apollo*, 12 (1930), pp. 113–9

**BROWN, Sir John Arnesby**
A. L. Baldry, *Studio, Modern Painting III: The Work of Arnesby Brown*, 1921

A. L. Baldry, 'Our Rising Artists: Arnesby Brown', *Magazine of Art*, 1902, pp. 97–102

C. Marriott, 'The Recent Work of Arnesby Brown R.A.' *Studio*, 71 (1917), pp. 129–37

H. Sawkins, 'J. Arnesby Brown', *The Artist*, August 1933, pp. 184–7

*Sir Arnesby Brown*, exhib. cat., Norwich Castle Museum, 1959

**BRUNDRIT, Reginald Grange**
*Reginald Brundrit*, exhib. cat., Bradford City Art Galleries and Museums, 1980

**CAMERON, Sir David Young**
A. J. Finberg, *The Paintings of D. Y. Cameron A. R. A., R. S. A.*, 1919

A. M. Hind, *The Etchings of D. Y. Cameron*, 1924

D. S. Meldrum, 'Sir David Cameron's Watercolours of the Highlands', *Apollo*, 10 (1929), pp. 220–2

*Sir D. Y. Cameron Centenary Exhibition*, exhib. cat., Glasgow Art Gallery and Museum, 1965

A. Stoddart Walker, 'The Paintings of D. Y. Cameron', *Studio*, 55 (1912), pp. 254–65

**CLAUSEN, Sir George**
*Sir George Clausen R. A.*, exhib. cat., Bradford Art Galleries and Tyne and Wear County Council Museums, 1980

**CONNARD, Philip**
M. H. Dixon, 'The Paintings of Philip Connard', *Studio*, 57 (1912), pp. 268–80

J. W. Stephens, 'The Paintings of Philip Connard A. R. A.', *Studio*, 85 (1923), pp. 303–11

**DICKSEE, Sir Frank**
E. R. Dibdin, 'The Art of Frank Dicksee R. A.', *Christmas Art Annual*, 1905, pp. 1–32

A. Kavanagh, 'Frank Dicksee and Chivalry', *The Antique Collector*, March 1987, vol. 58, no. 3, pp. 25–32

A. Kavanagh, 'A Post Pre-Raphaelite: Sir Frank Dicksee', *Country Life*, Jan 1985, pp. 240–2

**EAST, Sir Alfred**
A. East, *The Art of Landscape Painting in Oil Colour*, 1906

A. East, *Brush and Pencil Notes in Landscape*, 1914

*Sir Alfred East*, exhib. cat., Kettering, Northamptonshire, Sir Alfred East Gallery, 1949–50

F. Wedmore, 'The Work of Alfred East', *Studio*, 7 (1896), pp. 133–42

**FARQUHARSON, Joseph**
*Joseph Farquharson of Finzean*, exhib. cat., Aberdeen Art Gallery and Museums, 1985

W. M. Sinclair, 'Joseph Farquharson, A. R. A.', *Christmas Art Annual*, 1912, pp. 1–32

**FISHER, Mark**
L. Hind, 'Mark Fisher', *Art Journal*, 1910, pp. 15–20

V. Lines, *Mark Fisher & Margaret Fisher Prout*, 1966

*Memorial Exhibition of Works by Mark Fisher*, exhib. cat., London, Leicester Galleries, 1914

**FORBES, Stanhope Alexander**
L. Birch, *Stanhope A. Forbes A. R. A. & Elizabeth Stanhope Forbes A. R. W. S.*, 1906

C. L. Hind, 'Stanhope A. Forbes', *Art Journal Christmas Number*, 1911, pp. 1–32

**FRAMPTON, Meredith**
*Meredith Frampton*, exhib. cat., London, Tate Gallery, 1982

**GERE, Charles March**
*Charles March Gere R. A. Memorial Exhibition*, exhib. cat., Gloucester, Wheatstone Hall, 1963

C. Gere, Foreword in *The Earthly Paradise*, exhib. cat., London, Fine Art Society, 1969

O. Hurst, 'The Landscape Paintings of Charles M. Gere', *Studio*, 59 (1913), pp. 87–94

A. Vallance, 'The Revival in Tempera Painting', *Studio*, 23 (1901), pp. 155–64

**GREIFFENHAGEN, Maurice**
J. S. Little, 'Maurice Greiffenhagen & His Work', *Studio*, 9 (1896), pp. 234–42

W. Redworth, 'The Later Works of Maurice Greiffenhagen', *Studio*, 88 (1924), pp. 123–9

A. G. Temple, 'Maurice Greiffenhagen', *Art Journal*, 1894, pp. 225–9

**HACKER, Arthur**
A. L. Baldry, 'The Paintings of Arthur Hacker', *Studio*, 56 (1912), pp.174–83

**HALL, Oliver**
*Landscapes by Oliver Hall*, exhib. cat., London, Leicester Galleries, 1917

C. Muncaster, *Landscape and Marine Painting (in oil and watercolour)*, 1958

M. Muncaster, *The Wind in the Oak*, 1978

*Oliver Hall, R. A., R. E., Recent Oil Paintings*, exhib. cat., London, Fine Art Society, 1936

F. Rinder, 'The Art of Oliver Hall', *Art Journal*, 1904, pp. 80–4

**HARCOURT, George**
G. F. Lees, 'The Art of George Harcourt', *Studio*, 70 (1917), pp. 160–8

**HENRY, George**
P. Bate, 'The Work of George Henry R. S. A.: A review and appreciation', *Studio*, 31 (1904), pp. 3–12

G. Buchanan, 'A Galloway Landscape' *Scottish Arts Review*, VII, no. 4 (1960), pp. 73–7

*Mr. Henry and Mr. Hornel visit Japan*, exhib. cat., Scottish Arts Council, 1978–9

J. Taylor, 'Some Water-Colour Drawings by George Henry A. R. A.', *Studio*, 68 (1916), pp. 72–9

**HUGHES-STANTON, Sir Herbert**
A. L. Baldry, 'H. Hughes-Stanton A. R. W. S.', *Art Journal*, 1910, pp. 77–82

A. J. Finberg, 'The Recent Work of Mr H. Hughes-Stanton A. R. A.', *Studio*, 75 (1918), pp. 3–11

M. Hepworth-Dixon, 'The Landscape Paintings of Mr H. Hughes-Stanton', *Studio*, 42 (1908), pp. 269–79

**JOHN, Augustus Edwin**
*Augustus John*, exhib. cat., London, National Portrait Gallery, 1975

M. Easton and M. Holroyd, *The Art of Augustus John*, 1974

M. Holroyd, *Augustus John, A Biography*, Vol I, The Years of Innocence, 1974; *Augustus John, A Biography*, Vol II, The Years of Experience, 1975

R. Shone, *Augustus John*, Oxford 1979

**KELLY, Sir Gerald Festus**
D. Hudson, *For Love of Painting*, 1975

**KNIGHT, Harold**
C. Fox, *Dame Laura Knight*, Oxford, 1988

N. Garstin, 'The Art of Harold and Laura Knight', *Studio*, 57 (1912), pp. 182–200

E. G. Halton, *Modern Painting I. The Work of Harold and Laura Knight*, 1921

**LA THANGUE, Henry Herbert**
J. S. Little, 'H. H. La Thangue', *Art Journal*, 1893, pp. 169–73

*A Painter's Harvest, Works by Henry Herbert La Thangue*, exhib. cat., Oldham Art Gallery, 1978

G. Thomson, 'Henry Herbert La Thangue and his work', *Studio*, 9 (1896), pp. 163–77

**LAVERY, Sir John**
J. Lavery, *The Life of A Painter*, 1940

*Sir John Lavery*, exhib. cat., Belfast, Ulster Museum and London, Fine Art Society, 1984

**LEE, Sydney**
*Aquatints, Etchings, Mezzotints, Wood Engravings and Woodcuts by Sydney Lee R. A., R. E.*, exhib. cat., London, Colnaghi & Co., 1937

*Etchings, Aquatints and Woodcuts by Sydney Lee R. A., R. E.*, exhib. cat., London, Colnaghi & Co., 1945

M. C. Salaman, 'The Woodcuts of Mr Sydney Lee A. R. E.', *Studio*, 63 (1914), pp. 19–20

*Watercolours by Sydney Lee R. A., R. E.*, exhib. cat., London, Colnaghi & Co., 1939

**MUNNINGS, Sir Alfred James**
S. Booth, *Sir Alfred Munnings 1878–1959*, 1978

L. Lindsay, *A. J. Munnings R. A. Pictures of Horses and English Life*, 1939

*Alfred Munnings 1878–1959*, exhib. cat., Manchester City Art Gallery, 1987

A. Munnings, *An Artist's Life*, 1950

A. Munnings, *The Second Burst*, 1951

A. Munnings, *The Finish*, 1952

R. Pound, *The Englishman*, 1962

**MURRAY, Sir David**
M. Hepworth-Dixon, 'David Murray', *Art Journal*, 1892, pp. 144–8

**NASH, John Northcote**
Sir J. Rothenstein, *John Nash*, 1983

**OLSSON, Julius**
A. Stokes, 'Julius Olsson, Painter of Seascapes', *Studio*, 48 (1910), pp. 274–83

**ORPEN, Sir William**
B. Arnold, *Orpen, Mirror to an Age*, 1981

P. G. Konody & S. Dark, *Sir William Orpen: Artist and Man*, 1932

**PARSONS, Alfred**
A. L. Baldry, 'Some sketches by Alfred Parsons A. R. A.', *Studio*, 16 (1899), pp. 149–56

G. S. Thomas, *A Garden of Roses; Watercolours by Alfred Parsons R. A.*, 1987

*Water-Colour Drawings by A. Parsons illustrating Landscapes and Flowers in Japan*, exhib. cat., London, Fine Art Society, 1893

**PHILPOT, Glyn Warren**
*Glyn Philpot 1884–1937*, exhib. cat., London, National Portrait Gallery, 1984

A. C. Sewter, *Glyn Philpot 1884–1937*, 1951

**PRIESTMAN, Bertram**
*Bertram Priestman*, exhib. cat., Bradford Art Gallery and Museum, 1981

*Bertram Priestman*, exhib. cat., London, 20th Century Galleries, 1985

F. Wedmore, 'Bertram Priestman', *Art Journal*, 1907, pp. 179–84

**RUSSELL, Sir Walter Westley**
C. Baker, 'The Paintings of Walter W. Russell', *Studio*, 50 (1910), pp. 171–8

M. Salaman, 'The Art of Walter W. Russell A.R.A.', *Studio*, 83 (1922), pp. 80–8

**SARGENT, John Singer**
R. Ormond, *John Singer Sargent*, 1970

C. Ratcliff, *John Singer Sargent*, 1982

**SHANNON, Sir James Jebusa**
F. Rinder, 'James Jebusa Shannon', *Art Journal*, 1901, pp. 41–5

L. Hind, 'The Work of J.J. Shannon', *Studio*, 8 (1896), pp. 67–75

*Paintings of the Late J.J. Shannon*, exhib. cat., London, Leicester Galleries, 1923

**SICKERT, Walter Richard**
W. Baron, *Sickert*, 1973

L. Browse, *Sickert*, 1960

**SIMS, Charles**
C. Sims, *Picture Making: Technique and Inspiration*, 1934

H. Speed, 'Charles Sims', *The Old Water-Colour Society's Club*, VI (1928–9), ed. R. Davies, pp. 45–66

**SPENCER, Gilbert**
Gilbert Spencer, R.A., *Memoirs of a Painter*, 1974

*Gilbert Spencer Retrospective*, exhib. cat., London, Fine Art Society, 1974

**SPENCER, Sir Stanley**
G. Spencer, *Stanley Spencer*, 1961

*Stanley Spencer*, exhib. cat., Arts Council, 1976–7

*Stanley Spencer R.A.*, exhib. cat., London, Royal Academy of Arts, 1980

**STOKES, Adrian**
W. Meynell, 'Mr & Mrs Adrian Stokes', *Art Journal*, 1900, pp. 193–8

A. Stokes, *Landscape Painting*, 1925

**SWYNNERTON, Annie Louisa**
*Paintings by Mrs Swynnerton A.R.A.*, exhib. cat., Manchester City Art Gallery, 1923

**TAYLOR, Leonard Campbell**
C.G.E. Bunt, *Leonard Campbell Taylor R.A.*, 1949

H. Furst, *Leonard Campbell Taylor R.A. His Place in Art*, Leigh-on-Sea, 1945

**TUKE, Henry Scott**
E. Cooper, *The Life and Work of Henry Scott Tuke*, 1987

E.B. Steyne, 'Afternoons in Studios: Henry Scott Tuke at Falmouth', *Studio*, 5 (1895), pp. 90–6

*H.S. Tuke R.A., R.W.S.*, exhib. cat., Falmouth City Art Gallery, 1980

**WYLLIE, William Lionel**
R. Quarm & J. Wyllie, *W.L. Wyllie*, 1981

M.A. Wyllie, *We Were One*, 1935

# Royal Academy Trust

*The Trustees of the Royal Academy Trust wish to express their gratitude to the many companies and individuals who have already given their support to the appeal. In particular they would like to extend their thanks to:*

Sterling Guarantee PLC
Robert L. Sterling Jr
The Bernard Sunley Charitable
  Foundation
Tarmac Plc
Mr & Mrs A. Alfred Taubman
Technical Indexes Limited
Thames Television Limited
Sir Jules Thorn Charitable Trust
THORN EMI plc
Thomas Tilling plc
Trafalgar House Public Limited
  Company
Mr G. Ware Travelstead
The Triangle Trust (1949) Fund
Trident Television plc
Trustee Savings Bank (Holdings)
  Limited
TWA
Unilever PLC
Mr & Mrs Gerrit P van de
  Bovenkamp
Venice Simplon-Orient Express
Vista do Mar Hotel, The Seychelles
S. G. Warburg & Company Limited
The Wates Foundation
Mrs Keith S. Wellin
Westminster City Council
Anthony Whishaw RA
Whitbread & Company PLC
Mrs John Hay Whitney
Wilde Sapte
HDH Wills 1965 Charitable Trust
Winsor Newton (part of the Reckitt
  & Colman Group)
The Wolfson Foundation
Sir John Woolf
Mr Lawrence Wood
Mr Ian Woodner
Mr & Mrs William Wood Prince
Mr Charles Wrightsman
Dr Tomozo Yano

## Corporate Members of the Royal Academy of Arts

Arthur Andersen & Co.
BAT Industries plc
British Airways
British Alcan Aluminium plc
Chelsfield plc
Cookson Group plc
CoxMoore plc
The Daily Telegraph
Diamond Trading Company
  Limited
Ford Motor Company Limited
John Laing plc
Josef Gartner & Co (UK) Ltd
Glaxo Holdings p.l.c.
Grand Metropolitan plc
Hillier Parker

Marks and Spencer plc
MoMart Limited
Mountleigh Group plc
Nico Construction Limited
Royal Insurance plc
R J Reynolds International Inc
Shearson Lehman Hutton
  International Inc
TI Group plc
Unilever
Williams Lea Group Limited

## Corporate Associates of the Royal Academy of Arts

Allen & Overy
American Express Europe Limited
Apple Computer U.K. Limited
Arco British Limited
Arthur Young
The Arts Club
Art For Offices
Ashurst Morris Crisp
Bankers Trust
Banque Paribas
Barclays Bank Plc
Bass plc
Beecham Group plc
The BOC Group
Booker plc
Bovis Construction Limited
British & Commonwealth Holdings
  plc
British Olivetti Limited
British Telecom
Brixton Estate plc
Burmah Oil Trading Limited
H P Bulmer Holdings PLC
C & A
Cable and Wireless plc
Campbell, Johnston Associates
  Limited
Canadian Imperial Bank of
  Commerce
Carlton Beck
Charterhouse PLC
Christie's
Clifford Chance
Courage Charitable Trust
Coutts & Co
Deutsche Bank AG
Durrington Corporation
Eagle Star Insurance Company
  Limited
English China Clays plc
Gavin Martin Limited
General Accident
Global Asset Management
Gordon Yates
Granada Group
Guilford Kapwood Limited

Guinness plc
The Hammerson Group
H. J. Heinz Company Limited
IBM UK Limited
Ibstock Johnsen plc
Inchcape plc
Investors in Industry
Jaguar Cars Ltd
Johnson Wax Ltd
Joynson-Hicks
KHBB Humphreys Bull & Barker
  Ltd
Kleinwort Benson Group plc
Kodak Ltd
Laurentian Holding Company Ltd
Lewis Briggs International
John Lewis Partnership plc
Lex Service PLC
London & Edinburgh Trust plc
Marlborough Fine Art (London) Ltd
Martini & Rossi
McCann-Erickson
McCormick Publicis Limited
MEPC plc
The Worshipful Company of
  Mercers
Mercury Asset Management Group
  plc
Michael Peters Group
Morgan Guaranty Trust Co. of
  New York
Morgan, Lewis & Bockius
Nabarro Nathanson
The National Magazine Company
  Ltd
National Westminster Bank plc
NCR Limited
NEC (UK) Ltd
The Nestlé Charitable Trust
Occidental International Oil Inc
Olympia & York
Ove Arup Partnership
P & D Colnaghi & Co. Ltd
The Park Lane Hotel
Pearson plc
The Peninsular & Oriental Steam
  Navigation Company
Pentagram Design Ltd
Pentland Industries plc
Petrofina (UK) Limited
The Post Office
Renton Howard Wood Levin
  (Partnership)
Richard Ellis Services Ltd
The Royal Bank of Scotland plc
RTZ Limited
J. Rothschild Holdings plc
J Sainsbury
Sears plc
J Henry Schroder Wagg & Co
  Limited
The Sedgwick Group plc
S G Warburg & Co Ltd

W H Smith & Son Limited
Smith & Williamson
Solaglas International BV
SONY UK Limited
Sotheby's
Stanhope Properties plc
Staveley Industries plc
StoyHayward
Sun Life Assurance Society plc
Television South plc
Thames Television PLC
Thos. Agnew & Sons Ltd
United Biscuits (UK) Limited
Vogue
Waldron Allen Henry and
  Thompson Limited
The Wellcome Foundation Ltd
Wickes plc
Wolff Olins Business Ltd
Wood & Wood International Signs
  Limited
Yamaichi International (Europe) Ltd

## Corporate Friends of the Royal Academy of Arts

British Petroleum Company plc
Bryant Laing Partnership
The Clarkson Jersey Charitable
  Trust
Delta Group plc
The Guinness Mahon Group plc
Heim Gallery (London) Ltd
Imperial Chemicals industries plc
Mars Limited
Metal Box plc
Municipal Journal Limited
Norddeutsche Landesbank
  Girozentrale
Ocean Transport & Trading plc
Pilkington Glass Limited
Priest Marians Holdings plc
The Saddler's Company
Save & Prosper Educational Trust
Scott Mathieson Daines Ltd
Shell UK Limited
The Spencer Wills Trust
J. Walter Thompson Company
  Limited

# Sponsors of Past Exhibitions

*The Council of the Royal Academy thanks sponsors of past exhibitions for their support. Sponsors of major exhibitions during the last ten years have been included:*

American Express Foundation
Masters of 17th-Century Dutch
Genre Painting 1984
'Je suis le cahier': The Sketchbooks
of Picasso 1986

Arts Council of Great Britain
Robert Motherwell 1978
Rodrigo Moynihan 1978
John Flaxman 1979
Ivan Hitchens 1979
Algernon Newton 1980
New Spirit in Painting 1981
Gertrude Hermes 1981
Carel Weight 1982
Elizabeth Blackadder 1982
Allan Gwynne Jones 1983
The Hague School 1983
Peter Greenham 1985

BAT Industries plc
Murillo 1983
Paintings from the Royal Academy
US Tour 1982/4, 1984

Beck's Bier
German Art in the 20th Century
1985

Benson & Hedges
The Gold of El Dorado 1979

Boris Construction Ltd
New Architecture 1986

British Alcan Aluminium
Sir Alfred Gilbert 1986

British Gypsum Ltd
New Architecture 1986

British Petroleum plc
British Art in the 20th Century: The
Modern Movement 1987

Canary Wharf Development Co
New Architecture 1986

The Chase Manhattan Bank
Cézanne: The Early Years 1859–
1872 1988

Christie's
Treasures from Chatsworth 1980

Coutts & Co
Derby Day 200 1979

The Daily Telegraph
Treasures from Chatsworth 1980

Deutsche Bank AG
German Art in the 20th Century
1985

Electricity Council
New Architecture 1986

Esso Petroleum Company Ltd
British Art Now: An American
Perspective 1980
Summer Exhibition 1988

Financial Times
Derby Day 200 1979

First National Bank of Chicago
Chagall 1985

Friends of the Royal Academy
Elizabeth Blackadder 1982
Carel Weight 1982
Allan Gwynne Jones 1983
Peter Greenham 1985
Sir Alfred Gilbert 1986

Joseph Gartner
New Architecture 1986

J. Paul Getty Jr. Charitable Trust
Age of Chivalry 1987

Glaxo Holdings plc
From Byzantium to El Greco 1987

Calouste Gulbenkian Foundation
Portuguese Art Since 1910 1978

Dr Armand Hammer
& The Armand Hammer Foundation
Honoré Daumier 1981
Leonardo da Vinci Nature Studies
Codex Hammer 1981

Hoechst (UK) Ltd
German Art in the 20th Century
1985

IBM United Kingdom Limited
Post-Impressionism 1979
Summer Exhibition 1983

The Japan Foundation
The Great Japan Exhibtion 1981

Joannou & Paraskevaides (Overseas)
Ltd
From Byzantium to El Greco 1987

Lloyds Bank
Age of Chivalry 1987

Lufthansa
German Art in the 20th Century
1985

Martini & Rossi Ltd
Painting in Naples from Caravaggio
to Giordano 1982

Melitta
German Art in the 20th Century
1985

Mellon Foundation
Rowlandson Drawings 1978

Mercedes-Benz
German Art in the 20th Century
1985

Midland Bank plc
The Great Japan Exhibition 1981

Mobil
Treasures from Ancient Nigeria
1982
Modern Masters from the Thyssen-
Bornemisza Collection 1984
From Byzantium to El Greco 1987

Möet & Chandon
Derby Day 200 1979

National Westminster Bank
Reynolds 1986

The Observer
Stanley Spencer 1980
The Great Japan Exhibition 1981

Olivetti
Horses of San Marco 1979
The Cimabue Crucifix 1983

Otis Elevators
New Architecture 1986

Overseas Containers Limited
The Great Japan Exhibition 1981

Pearson plc
Eduardo Paolozzi Underground
1986

Pilkington Glass
New Architecture 1986

Pringle of Scotland
The Great Japan Exhibition 1981

Reed International plc
Toulouse-Lautrec: The
Graphic Works

Republic New York Corporation
Andrew Wyeth 1980

Robert Bosch Limited
German Art in the 20th Century
1985

Arthur M. Sackler Foundation
Jewels of the Ancients 1987

Salomon Brothers
Henry Moore 1988

Sea Containers & Venice Simplon-
Orient Express
Genius of Venice 1983

Shell (UK) Ltd
Treasures from Chatsworth 1980

The Shell Companies of Japan
The Great Japan Exhibition 1981

Siemens
German Art in the 20th Century
1985

Sotheby's
Derby Day 200 1979

Swan Hellenic
Edward Lear 1985

John Swire
The Great Japan Exhibition 1981

The Times
Old Master Paintings from the
Thyssen-Bornemisza Collection
1988

Trafalgar House
Elisabeth Frink 1985

Trusthouse Forte
Edward Lear 1985

Unilever
Lord Leverhulme 1980
The Hague School 1983

Walker Books Limited
Edward Lear 1985

Wedgewood
John Flaxman 1979

Winsor & Newton with Reckitt &
Colman
Algernon Newton 1980